In memory of
May Thrasher

Title: NEW HAMPSHIRE
THE STATE THAT
MADE US A NATION

Presented by:

Mary Varnum Platts-
Peterborough Chapter

Date: January 25, 1990

NEW HAMPSHIRE

THE STATE
THAT
MADE US A NATION

A Celebration of the Bicentennial
of the United States Constitution

NEW HAMPSHIRE

THE STATE
THAT
MADE US A NATION

A Celebration of the Bicentennial
of the United States Constitution

Editorial Board:
William M. Gardner
Frank C. Mevers
Richard F. Upton

Editorial Consultants:
Karen Bowden
John F. Page

Published for
*the New Hampshire Bicentennial Commission
on the United States Constitution*
and
the New Hampshire Humanities Council

by
Peter E. Randall, Publisher

Portsmouth, New Hampshire
1989

Production of this volume was made possible by the people of the State of New Hampshire through appropriations by the General Court to the New Hampshire Bicentennial Commission on the United States Constitution and by a grant from the New Hampshire Humanities Council to the Bicentennial Commission.

This is a publication of the State of New Hampshire.

Designed and produced by
    Peter E. Randall Publisher
    Box 4726, Portsmouth, N. H. 03801

Frontispiece: This rare 1796 map printed in Germany was one of the first glimpses Europeans had of the State of New Hampshire. The map, which was intended to be one of a series on the states of the union, bears the first known use of the name "Mt. Washington." (Copperplate engraving by Daniel Sotzman. Courtesy, State of New Hampshire.)

Color photographs in the portfolio were taken by Steve McManus, William M. Gardner, and Russell C. Chase.

Library of Congress Cataloging-in-Publication Data
New Hampshire: The State that made us a nation—a celebration of the bicentennial of
    the United States Constitution/editorial board, William M. Gardner, Frank C.
    Mevers, Richard F. Upton; editorial consultants, Karen Bowden, John F. Page.
        p.   cm.
    Includes bibliographical references.
    ISBN 0-914339-28-1
    1. United States--Constitutional history. 2. New Hampshire--Constitutional
    history I. Gardner, Willam M. II. Mevers, Frank C. III. Upton, Richard F. (Richard
    Francis),1914-
    KF4541.S69   1989
    342.73'029--dc20
    [347.30229]   89-24345
                                                             CIP

This volume is gratefully dedicated
by the people of New Hampshire
to

Russell C. Chase

who gave so unsparingly of himself to
lead New Hampshire through this bicentennial

His Excellency Judd Gregg, Governor of the State of New Hampshire.
Courtesy of the Office of the Governor.

FOREWORD

Judd Gregg, Governor
State of New Hampshire

*I*f the Constitution of the United States is the foundation of our republic, then the State of New Hampshire can proudly lay claim to a cornerstone of that foundation.

From the early days of original settlement New Hampshire has been guided by a fierce sense of freedom and independence. Our citizens today feel this commitment as keenly as did our ancestors. As a state New Hampshire pays tribute to the Constitution which has proven to be as durable and far-reaching as it is wise and farsighted.

No state in the Union provides greater access to its state and local government than New Hampshire. Our 424-member General Court assures that every point of view is properly represented in the legislative process. A vast array of state, county and local offices are filled every two years through popular election by the people. Who could attend a Town Meeting, the most direct and literal form of democracy, and not be moved by this special opportunity for each citizen to be a full participant in the governing process.

For two hundred years the leaders of New Hampshire have performed the duties of public office with measured restraint and a watchful eye toward preserving the unique way of life for which New Hampshire is known. We have weathered war, financial calamity, dramatic changes in our industrial base, crises in the availability of energy and threats to our environment posed by a surging population. In every case we have withstood the challenge and emerged stronger as a people.

With each new day New Hampshire builds a little more on its solid base of heritage and tradition. Our citizens are proud and strong, resolved to tackle any issue with the mix of imagination, determination and commitment which has proven so successful thus far in our state history. New Hampshire contributes with equal conviction and zeal to the decision-making process at the Federal level. In each case we are building on that foundation laid 200 years ago by our forefathers who crafted the United States Constitution.

In the early days of our nation we were known as a noble experiment, testing a democratic process that was then radical and unproven. In 200 years we have become one of the oldest, most stable national governments in the world, an unblinking beacon of freedom and individual liberty. And for all that we have achieved we can proudly give credit to "We the People."

CONTENTS

ILLUSTRATIONS

INTRODUCTION

The Honorable Russell C. Chase, Chairman

New Hampshire Bicentennial Commission on the
United States Constitution

O ur country—yours and mine—is two hundred years old!

That, in itself, is not outstanding. Many nations have existed in one form or another for much longer periods. Egypt, China, Rome, Greece, England and others have far outstripped this time.

The circumstance that makes our country outstanding is that the United States of America is operating under a written form of government, under a Constitution, that is two centuries old. No other country now existing can make this claim.

Two hundred years ago, fifty-five representatives of the independent states met in Philadelphia to resolve the governmental problems then existing under the "Articles of Confederation." The names of many of the delegates are popularly known because of their activities during the Revolution, or prominence gained later. Among these were George Washington, Benjamin Franklin, Alexander Hamilton, James Madison and Robert Morris.

During the summer months of 1787, the convention drafted the Constitution under which we still operate, the preamble of which is as follows:

> We the People of the United States, in order to form a more perfect Union, establish Justice, ensure Domestic Tranquility, provide for the Common Defense, promote the General Welfare, and secure the Blessings of Liberty to ourselves and our posterity do ordain and establish this Constitution for the United States of America.

The records indicate their strong differences, their difficulties in reaching compromises, their reservations held beyond the days of completion. The fundamental belief that the Constitution should not exist without a Bill of Rights caused several convention members to refuse to sign the completed document. This was corrected in 1791.

The work of the Constitutional Convention has been called "The Miracle of Philadelphia." William Gladstone, British Prime Minister in the late 1800s, wrote, "I have always regarded that Constitution as the most remarkable work known to me in modern times to have been produced by the human intellect at a single stroke (so to speak) in its application to political affairs."

It has been said that it would be difficult to find a group of men more qualified by knowledge of the history of governments, and the experience of living under the yoke of an unpopular government in which they had little participation. Further, many had taken part in the development of their State Constitutions. Paramount in their concerns were the dangers of centralized power and the arrogance of unquestioned laws emanating from an unreachable source.

Their solution, as we know, was to recognize (1) that government should originate in the people governed; (2) that, although people generally believed in a supreme being, religion should not be a part of national politics; and (3) that a three-pronged government with carefully designed checks and balances would enable the nationally elected representatives and officers to perform their duties and still protect the rights of citizens.

It has worked. Some have claimed the Constitution is not specific enough to carry out the "original intentions of its drafters." Others say it is arrogance for us, today, to claim knowledge of their intentions. Some say our decisions and changes by Supreme Court rulings go far afield of the original thoughts indicated by the historic record of the convention debates. Others claim all changes have been properly made and show that the true strength of the document lies in the flexibility that allows it to meet the requirements of a changing world.

The words of Benjamin Franklin come to mind. The anecdote is told that as Franklin was leaving the last convention meeting, a lady approached him and inquired, "Mr. Franklin, what form of government did you design?" Franklin is reported to have replied, "A Republic, Madam, if you can keep it."

No attempt to moralize is offered here. However, it seems evident that this successful form of government, based on the supremacy of the people, can only be "kept" if the people act in performing and protecting their function in the governmental design.

In the spring of 1787, New Hampshire was asked to send delegates to a convention in Philadelphia to meet on May 14, "to take into consideration the situation of the United States, to devise such further provisions as shall appear to them necessary to render the Constitution of the Federal Government adequate to the exigencies of the Union."

This invitation obviously referred to the existing Constitution then called "The Articles of Confederation." Hence, it would appear that the upcoming convention was limited to potential improvements in that document. As we now know, the convention discarded the Articles of Confederation and developed the Constitution we use today.

New Hampshire appointed John Langdon and Nicholas Gilman. Both were serving in Congress which was meeting in New York. Despite their appointment, no funds to cover expenses in attending the convention were made available. There are two theories concerning the New Hampshire legislature's failure to provide the necessary funds. One suggests that New Hampshire politicians were not too sure the convention should meet, and even if it did, that it could resolve the national problems. The other, and generally considered accurate, is that the legislature was unable to raise the money to support the delegates. In either case, the delegates from New Hampshire did not arrive in Philadelphia until July 23, by which time much of the convention's work had been completed. Even then, it was necessary for John Langdon to pay both his and Nicholas Gilman's expenses. He was later reimbursed.

Though they represented a small state, they supported the majority group which advocated an effective federal government. As a contemporary Portsmouth newspaper commented on May 19th:

We are authorized to inform our readers that the probability of the honorable delegates from this state not attending the convention in Philadelphia, causes great uneasiness in the minds of the true Whigs of New Hampshire, and will occasion a considerable inspection into the state of our finance.

New Hampshire joined the rest of the country in recognizing the official Bicentennial birthday of the Constitution on September 17, 1987. The State has taken historic pride in becoming the ninth and deciding state to approve the Constitution. On June 21, 1988, the Bicentennial of this event received special attention.

Leading to these special dates, the New Hampshire Bicentennial Commission on the United States Constitution embarked on a number of programs. In 1984 the Commission began what was to be a fruitful association with the New Hampshire Humanities Council, in "After the Revolution: New Hampshire and the New Nation, 1780–1800," a multifaceted program of research and public activities. The project produced studies of several New Hampshire towns in the early republic, eight of which appear in this volume. This research served as the basis for a traveling exhibit, "Building a Nation, Building a State: New Hampshire, 1780–1800," and for After the Revolution: A Collage for Town Voices, a readers' theater script by David Magidson which dramatizes the ratification debates at Exeter and Concord.

In 1987 the National Endowment for the Humanities recognized the scope and quality of "After the Revolution" with an Exemplary Award for "The Ninth State," a project which provided for a duplicate of the exhibit, a second tour of the play, and added a twenty-part newspaper series by Charles E. Clark and a symposium to observe the birthday of the Constitution, September 17, 1987.

The Commission struck and made available for sale a commemorative medal incorporating the Commission's logo recognizing New Hampshire's role as the ninth and deciding state to approve the new government. The original ratification document was restored by the Commission with direction from the State Archives, and a facsimilie has been made available to the public.

Other commemorative activties sponsored or supported by the Commission include the following: a traveling exhibit of Magna Carta in four locations in the state during the summer of 1987; the design and production of a commemorative postage stamp; two exhibits on New Hampshire's role in ratification; the day-long grand celebration in Concord on June 21, 1988, observing the bicentennial of ratification; and a speakers' bureau which offered talks on topics in Constitutional history and theory. In addition, the Commission has supported and endorsed programs initiated by other organizations.

Funds for these projects have come from legislative appropriations and gifts from individuals, businesses and organizations. The celebration of the Bicentennial promises to have long-term impact. Two copies of "Building a Nation, Building a State" continue to travel to schools and libraries throughout the state. A videotape of the premiere performance of "A Collage for Town Voices" by actors from the theater programs of the University System of New Hampshire is also available. In addition to this book, two others have emerged from Bicentennial activities: *After The Revolution: A Collage for Town Voices* was published for the Commission in 1987 by Peter Randall. In 1989 the New Hampshire Humanities Council published Charles Clark's newspaper series as *Printers, the People, and Politics: The New Hampshire Press and Ratification.* Finally, the Commission has established the New Hampshire Legacy, an endowment for educational programs on the Constitution which will be administered by the New Hampshire Humanities Council.

WE THE PEOPLE...

NEW HAMPSHIRE...9th and KEY STATE to
ratify the U.S. CONSTITUTION. June 1788 ·

Connecting people with ideas

Members of the New Hampshire Bicentennial Commission on the United States Constitution. Left to right: Senator Roger C. Heath; Senator Sheila Roberge; Senator John P. H. Chandler, Jr.; Representative Ednapearl F. Parr; Frank C. Mevers; Representative Beverly A. Hollingworth; Representative Russell C. Chase, Chairman; Etta M. Madden; Representative Natalie S. Flanagan; Richard F. Upton; Mary Louise Hancock; David R. Proper; Jeffrey R. Howard; Arthur J. Moody; William M. Gardner; Thomas J. Donnelly; Edna A. Flanagan.

Members of the New Hampshire Commission on
the Bicentennial of the United States Constitution

Representative Russell C. Chase, Chairman
Representative Ednapearl F. Parr, Vice Chairman
William M. Gardner, Secretary of State, Secretary
Mary Louise Hancock, Treasurer

Senator Charles D. Bond
Senator John P. H. Chandler, Jr.
Professor Jere R. Daniell
Representative Joseph M. Eaton
Representative Natalie S. Flanagan
Senator Roger C. Heath
Representative Beverly A. Hollingworth
Jeffrey R. Howard, Deputy Attorney General
Arthur J. Moody
David L. Nixon, Esquire
Senator Barbara B. Pressly
David Proper
Senator Sheila Roberge
William E. Sanborn
Richard F. Upton, Esquire

Honorary Members

Charles G. Bickford, Executive Director,
New Hampshire Humanities Council
Thomas J. Donnelly, U.S. Administrative Law Judge
Edna A. Flanagan, Chairman, The U. S.
Constitution Council of the Thirteen Original States, Inc.
Frank C. Mevers, State Archivist

Special thanks to:
Alice Vartanian King
Janet King
David Minnis
Peter E. Randall

Josiah Bartlett (1729–1795) portrait by John Trumbull, c. 1790. A Kingston physician and one of New Hampshire's three signers of the Declaration of Independence, Bartlett was elected temporary chairman of the New Hampshire convention in February 1788. Then a judge on the Superior Court, Bartlett firmly advocated the new government. Courtesy of the N. H. Historical Society. Photograph by Bill Finney

IDEOLOGY AND HARDBALL
Ratification of the Federal Constitution in New Hampshire

Jere R. Daniell

Dartmouth College

At 1:00 p.m., June 21, 1788, a convention of town delegates meeting at Concord, New Hampshire, ratified the proposed Federal Constitution by a vote of fifty-seven to forty-seven. The vote capped a lengthy and often acrimonious constitutional conflict which had divided state inhabitants for more than nine months. The opponents of ratification—initially a majority of the convention delegates—deeply distrusted the idea of voluntarily granting to any distant and unknown political authority powers recently won at such personal and collective sacrifice. Supporters of the new plan of union felt just as deeply that a strengthened national government was necessary to fulfill the promise of successful revolution and that New Hampshire citizens would gain far more from union than they would lose. These ideological lines were drawn early in the conflict; relatively few individuals subsequently changed their minds.

Hard nosed politics decided the issue. The Federalists, those supporting ratification, simply outmaneuvered the Antifederalists. They used influence in the state government to delay consideration of the plan until neighboring Massachusetts acted and to maximize their representation when ratification proceedings did begin. When the convention first met in February the Federalists arrived early, elected a committee to determine convention procedures, skillfully used those procedures to prevent a final vote—which they feared would be negative—and obtained adjournment until June. In the interim they worked long and hard for the June session. The final vote provided convincing evidence of their political skills.

Constitutionalism in Revolutionary New Hampshire

The ratification struggle took place in a state with a recent history of extended constitutional debate. Disputes over the proper structure of govern-

1

ment had erupted in the mid-1770s and continued throughout the war years. The disputes reflected both ideological disagreements and competition for power among inhabitants of New Hampshire's three major subregions, the Piscataqua, Merrimack and Connecticut River watersheds. Piscataqua residents, from Portsmouth and Exeter especially, had dominated the pre-revolutionary government and accumulated a great deal of wealth largely through external trade. Not surprisingly, their constitutional arguments indicated a desire to preserve as much of the status quo as possible. Citizens in the rapidly growing central part of the state drained by the Merrimack had been poorly represented in the colonial government and used the Revolution to assert themselves at the expense of the seacoast. Their fundamental constitutional stance emphasized local rather than state authority and control of state government by town delegates elected to a broadly representative legislature. Leaders in the Connecticut River valley communities tended to articulate beliefs which would free them from subordination to the more populated eastern parts of the state.

The first serious trouble occurred before passage of the Declaration of Independence. The only province in New England without a formal charter of incorporation, New Hampshire was left without legal government when the last royal governor, John Wentworth, fled in the summer of 1775. Town delegates from throughout New Hampshire had already created an extra-legal provincial congress which gradually took over responsibilities previously exercised by Wentworth and the General Court. The congress, which contained far broader town representation than its colonial predecessor, adopted a written constitution in January 1776. The constitution legitimized the congress by making it New Hampshire's official House of Representatives and by authorizing the new house to create an upper legislative body called the Council.

Adoption triggered a brief but dramatic protest movement. Western spokesmen criticized the new arrangement because it perpetuated eastern political domination. A few seacoast writers also complained about the specific form of government, but more argued simply that adoption of any constitution was premature. Portsmouth's delegates at the congress returned home and helped call a town meeting which voted unanimously to petition for reconsideration. Portsmouth also voted to send letters urging other towns to "remonstrate likewise." By the end of January eleven different Piscataqua communities and twelve individual provincial congress delegates had submitted formal protests. The congress as a whole compromised by asking the Continental Congress if taking up government had been a mistake. That body, however, never replied, and the formal Declaration of Independence ended conflict over adoption of the state's first constitution.

The next testing of constitutional attitudes had to do with national, not state government. In late 1777 New Hampshire was asked to ratify the Articles of Confederation. Partly because of the earlier controversy, the legislature decided to submit the document to individual towns before acting. The towns, although most reported general approval, made clear their commitment to state sovereignty. The citizens of Hawke (now Danville) complained that binding all states by a vote of only nine was "too prerogative"; Wilton argued that giving Congress the right to declare war bestowed "a power greater than the King of Great Britain in Council ever had"; numerous towns worried about New Hampshire's interests being compromised by insensitive central officials. Not a single town suggested that the Articles provided the Continental Congress with insufficient power. Complaints about the Articles granting too much power were concentrated in areas where antifederalism subsequently became strong.

Meanwhile two major and closely interrelated constitutional problems had begun to buffet the state. Both were triggered by dissatisfaction with the document so hastily adopted by the provincial congress early in 1776. A group of town leaders from the Connecticut River valley renewed complaints that the new form of state government left their communities underrepresented and demanded that a convention be called to rewrite the constitution. Portsmouth area critics of state government joined in the demand for a state constitutional convention. The legislature, after testing public sentiment, voted to hold such a gathering in the summer of 1778. By that time the western rebels had decided their towns would be better off joining the self-created state of Vermont across the river. Thus New Hampshire wrestled simultaneously with its own secession crisis and with a constitutional reform movement where existing authority supposedly was accepted. It took nearly five years to put down the western rebellion. Obtaining approval for a new plan of government took even longer.

The western rebellion was more than a constitutional conflict. It involved a complex mix of legal, demographic, geographic, and political factors all related to New Hampshire's colonial history. Constitutional questions, however, dominated the reasoning of the malcontents. They argued that the Revolution had severed all governmental bonds of allegiance except those of the individual to his town. Towns therefore had the right to join whatever state their voters chose. The New Hampshire Constitution, which classed small towns together for purposes of representation, had violated the fundamental right of each town to elect a member to the General Court, a right which towns in Connecticut enjoyed. Furthermore, the Constitution created a government with serious structural weaknesses which virtually guaranteed that seaboard inhabitants would dominate affairs. The Vermont Constitution, on the other hand, recognized the fundamental equality of all towns, accorded them representation, and in general seemed based on sound constitutional principles. In 1778 sixteen valley towns east of the river formally voted to join Vermont.

Constitutional issues were subordinated in the latter stages of rebellion. Vermont first accepted, then rejected the seceding towns. When community

Credentials from the town of Kingston to Josiah Bartlett to serve as Kingston's delegate to the New Hampshire ratifying convention. Courtesy of the State Archives. Photograph by Bill Finney.

leaders on both sides of the river launched a campaign to have all towns east of the Green Mountains become part of New Hampshire, the Vermont legislature reannexed the original sixteen plus twenty-two more. This "second union" lasted until leaders in both state governments withdrew support from the idea of any change in state boundaries. Meanwhile several spokesmen for the Continental Congress, including George Washington, expressed disapproval of the entire secession movement. The rebellion was over by 1783.

Acceptance of existing state authority by western leaders stemmed in part from constitutional reform within New Hampshire. The convention which met in 1778 had not accomplished much: its proposals were overwhelmingly rejected by the voters when submitted to town meetings for approval. But the existing Constitution had been enacted only for the duration of hostilities. As it became apparent the war would soon end the legislature called a second convention and ordered it to remain in session, amending its proposals until ratification by the citizenry.

That proved easier said than done. The convention first met in the summer of 1781. Dominated by Portsmouth area delegates—including John Langdon and John Pickering, who would play key roles in ratification of the Federal Constitution—it first recommended a constitution which eliminated town representation entirely and provided such high property qualifications for state officeholding that few supporting votes could be obtained. A second proposal, much more moderate in content, was similarly rejected. Finally, in the fall of 1783, the convention submitted a document which a majority of those voting accepted. The Constitution provided for a popularly elected president, a senate made up of county delegates, and a house of representatives which gave each town with 150 voters the right to choose a member. Smaller communities would be "classed," or combined, for purposes of representation. The rapidly growing western towns, then could see their influence increasing as the years passed. The following June a state government chosen under the new system met for the first time.

Thus, by the middle of the 1780s, the politically active portion of New Hampshire's population had extensive experience in constitutional matters. Citizens shared certain assumptions. They believed in representative government. They believed that such government should have separate executive, legislative, and judicial branches, and that the powers of each should be defined by a written constitution. Constitutions, in turn, should be drafted by individuals representing subunits of government—towns for state constitutions and states for any national constitution—and all proposed constitutions subject to close examination by voters in those subunits. They accepted the basic logic of a three-tiered system of local, state, and national authority. The whole arrangement they labeled "federated republicanism."

Within that pattern of shared assumptions, however, there was much disagreement. Individuals differed on how authority should be distributed among the three levels of power; until now controversies had concentrated on local and state relationships, but that would soon change. Two regions of the state—the eastern seacoast area and the western Connecticut River valley—had a long history of dissatisfaction with constitutional arrangements shaped largely by community leaders from central New Hampshire. Compromise had proved possible, but sectional differences remained. Finally, there existed both attraction to and deep distrust of the whole idea of constitutional reform. The past made clear that proposals for constitutional change should be carefully scrutinized to prevent loss of popular liberties.

Round One: Preparation for a Decision

New Hampshire, like other states, experienced serious economic and political troubles in the immediate postwar era. A short-lived commercial revival collapsed soon after mid-decade. The newly formed state government found itself torn by factional disputes, in part because it proved unable to combat the

John Sullivan (1741–1795) engraving by Thomas Hart, c. 1776. Shown here in the uniform of a Revolutionary officer, Sullivan had a stormy military career which included wintering at Valley Forge with Washington and defeating the Six Nations to free the frontier from Indian attack. He resigned from the army in 1779, and subsequently held many state offices. He was president (governor) of New Hampshire at the time of the ratifying convention, and served as its chairman. Courtesy of the N. H. Historical Society. Photograph by Bill Finney.

recession effectively. Accusations of corruption, favoritism, and insensitivity were leveled at public officials. In 1786 groups of irate citizens began meeting to pressure state government; one such group surrounded the legislative hall in Exeter and had to be dispersed by the local militia. Disillusionment became so great that the following spring nearly forty percent of towns in the state refused to send legislative representatives.

Given the context, it is not surprising that many citizens looked to the Continental Congress for help, and when efforts to beef up its powers failed, began discussing other forms of interstate cooperation. The legislature in 1786 appointed delegates to a convention on the subject to be held in Annapolis, Maryland. None of the appointees attended, but when that convention called for a general meeting of state delegates in Philadelphia, the legislature authorized any two of the state's four Continental Congress members to attend the meeting. John Langdon and Nicholas Gilman, both prestigious seacoast merchant-politicians, eventually made the trip south. Although they contributed little to the constitutional discussions, they supported the final proposals, then joined Congress to make certain its members did nothing to hinder ratification. Langdon and Gilman also promised to campaign for approval in New Hampshire.

The Federal Constitution was first published in Portsmouth on October 4, 1787. Even before then debate on its merits had begun; the debate continued unabated until ratification. New Hampshire's five newspapers printed article after article emphasizing the potential benefits of adoption. Ministers throughout the state devoted sermons to the subject; in general they too supported the Federalist position. Both Federalists and Antifederalists circulated pamphlets defending their stance and engaged in lengthy discussions in parlors, taverns, ship cabins and any other place an interested audience could be gathered.

Proponents articulated a variety of arguments. Ratification would be of immense economic benefit to merchants, landholders, mechanics, farmers and taxpayers. It would help solve the state political crisis by reducing interstate rivalries and circumscribing both the authority and responsibilities of state legislatures. It would give the United States a better international reputation. Ratification, in short, promised to solve all the problems of New Hampshire and its fellow states. "Many people look upon the adoption of the new constitution," wrote one newspaper correspondent, "as the millenium of virtue and wealth."

Critics saw no such millenium on the horizon. Deeply committed to decentralization, they worried about too powerful a central authority. Merchants might benefit from increased commerce, some argued, but New Hampshire's many farmers would not. If state officials responsible to their electors couldn't be trusted, what could be expected of national rulers? The proposed federal court system would put decisions in the hands of distant authorities insensitive to local circumstances. Lack of religious qualifications for national office holding—only

Protestants were eligible in New Hampshire—seemed fraught with dangerous implications. The proposed constitution, many concluded, provided much too radical a constitutional change. The state should vote against ratification.

There were no professional poll takers in the 1780s so it would be fruitless to attempt any quantitative assessment of public opinion. Several things, however, quickly did become clear. Federalist attitudes dominated only in areas with a long history of constitutional disaffection—the seacoast and Grafton County, the center of the western rebellion. Secondly, most critics of the constitution were not cowed by the fact that a very high percentage of the state's economic political and intellectual elite favored ratification. And finally, no one could be certain which side would win.

The proposed constitution itself dictated where the initial round of formal fighting would take place. Article VII stated simply that "Ratification of the Conventions of nine States shall be sufficient for the Establishment of this Constitution…." It was up to the state legislature to decide when, where, and with what membership the New Hampshire convention met. Actions taken by the legislature, leaders on both sides knew, would help determine the eventual outcome.

Individuals of known Federalist commitment controlled state planning for the upcoming convention. The next scheduled legislative session was set for late January. John Sullivan—seacoast resident, President of New Hampshire, a former revolutionary war general, and an outspoken unionist—decided that pro-constitution individuals would have a better chance of controlling a special legislative session than the regular one, hastily convened such a meeting, and urged his fellow Federalists to attend. The tactic worked. Of the ten senators who gathered, eight were from towns eventually voting for ratification. When the House had a quorum, attending members were evenly divided in sentiment even though the total membership contained a decided anti-Federalist majority. The speaker, Thomas Bartlett, strongly favored ratification.

Decisions made in December reflected the superiority of Federalist forces. Both houses agreed to form a joint committee to make recommendations for the convention. Bartlett selected an equal number of pro and anti members; the Senate, however, selected all Federalists. Not surprisingly, the committee recommendations had a pro-ratification flavor. The convention should be held at Exeter, in the heartland of Federalism. It would not convene until mid-February: by that time, it was hoped that six states, including neighboring Massachusetts, would have ratified. The state would pay expenses and each town or class of towns could send as many delegates as it had in the House. An apparently innocuous qualification stated that towns presently unrepresented could elect delegates if they chose. Finally, the state's exclusion bill, which prohibited most appointed state officials from simultaneously representing their towns in the legislature, would not apply to the convention. This made possible the participation of influential Federalists like Superior Court Chief Justice Samuel Livermore of Grafton County and State Treasurer John Taylor Gilman.

The Antifederalists in the House, led by Nathaniel Peabody of Atkinson, knew they had been bested and made one effort to change the joint committee recommendations. They tried to have the number of convention members doubled, hoping thus to dilute the influence of powerful Federalists like Sullivan and Langdon. Since that would also have doubled the cost of the convention to the state the motion failed badly.

The vote provided the last flurry of round one. Judge's decision: a clear Federalist victory.

Round Two: Decision Postponed

The election of convention delegates by the various towns and classes of towns came next. Copies of the Constitution were printed and distributed, selectmen began to post warrants for special town meetings, public curiosity about results intensified, and local leaders of both persuasions discussed strategy. Antifederalists, coached by men of like sentiment in Massachusetts and warned by returning legislators that the Federalists already seemed effectively organized, belatedly developed their own communication network. The network operated with the most effectiveness in the Merrimack River valley.

Antifederalist tactics dictated the internal dynamics of many town meetings. The plan was simple: elect Antifederalist delegates and bind them by written instructions so they could not at Exeter be talked out of voting "nay." It was inevitable that in some communities delegates chosen would object to binding instructions—after all, they could and did argue that the purpose of the convention was to discuss the constitution and make a reasonable judgement about its merits based on that discussion. In such cases instructions were especially important, for unwillingness to accept them indicated potential softness of commitment. The matter of instructions seemed more and more important as New Hampshire's Antifederalists watched an initial majority in the Bay State convention gradually slip away. Only a handful of delegates there had formally been instructed.

The Antifederalist tactics produced some elaborate and exciting local political contests. In Walpole, for example, Major General Benjamin Bellows was elected but refused to accept binding negative instructions. A few days before the Exeter convention, and shortly after news arrived of ratification in Massachusetts, a quickly convened town meeting replaced Bellows with an Antifederalist. Keene also held a second meeting but a Federalist majority voted both to keep the same delegate and to pass over the article warrant on instructions. Town after town either voted against the constitution itself or appointed a committee which advised against adoption.

Surviving records, however, are neither plentiful nor clear enough to calculate with precision the overall results. Contemporary estimates of instructed delegates reached as high as forty. A more likely figure is about twenty-five, all but two or three of whom were advised negatively. Whatever the exact total, the Antifederalists had a large base from which to operate. The total number of elected delegates would not be much over one hundred. With instructed delegates and a similar number of uninstructed but opposed delegates, the constitution might be defeated.

Federalists, meanwhile, prepared just as aggressively. They continued to flood newspapers with articles, including many critical of binding instructions. They also made every effort to maximize the number of pro-constitution delegates. The inhabitants of Newcastle, which hadn't elected a legislative representative for some time, chose a convention delegate when merchants in neighboring Portsmouth explained the need for more votes. Previously Canterbury and Northfield had shared a legislator: soon after the former chose an Antifederalist, the latter voted to send its own pro-constitution delegate. Up in Grafton County Samuel Livermore lined up support and convinced elected delegates they should make the long trek to Exeter. Bellows, Aaron Hall of Keene, Benjamin West of Charlestown, and other town leaders in Cheshire County fought successfully to limit the number of binding instructions.

The most important form of Federalist preparation involved the convention itself, not the local elections. The regular legislative session, which convened in Portsmouth January 23rd, provided the first good opportunity to gather accurate information about developments at the local level. What Sullivan, Langdon and their allies learned must have been distressing. Inhabitants in the interior apparently didn't share seacoast enthusiasm for ratification. The problem of binding instructions was more serious than anticipated. Antifederalists had found an effective leader in the influential legislator Nathaniel Peabody; who seemed confident of victory at Exeter. Given the uncertainty, the Federalist leaders decided they should have a contingency plan for Exeter. They should be prepared to engineer an adjournment if ratification couldn't be guaranteed.

The contingency plan, hatched in early February, involved tactics similar to those used in the December legislative session. It is not clear who coordinated things, but Sullivan, Langdon, Gilman, Livermore and West—all convention delegates and former Continental Congress members—undoubtedly knew beforehand what would happen. Federalists were told to arrive as early on February 13 as possible. As soon as anything close to a quorum appeared the convention would be called to order and a rules committee formed. This committee, chosen by the Federalists in attendance, would check the credentials of convention members. It also would prepare procedural ground rules which maximized the possibility of adjournment should that become necessary. By the time everyone arrived the procedures would be in place.

This bold plan worked to perfection. The convention journal for February

Hanover's credentials to Jonathan Freeman to serve as its delegate to the state ratifying convention. Courtesy of the State Archives. Photograph by Bill Finney.

13 tells the story. The first paragraph reads "about fifty members being assembled, they proceeded to the choice of a chairman, and the Honorable Josiah Bartlett Esq. was chosen." Of the "about fifty" recorded in attendance thirty-three voted in June for ratification. Five of these thirty-three had quietly left the nearby legislative session which Sullivan didn't adjourn until late that afternoon. Among the legislators remaining in Portsmouth were about two dozen delegates, a majority of them Antifederalists. The choice of Bartlett as temporary chairman may also have been preplanned. Bartlett was a highly respected judge, a close friend of Peabody, and uncommitted publicly on the issue of ratification. His election to the chair would give what followed the appearance of legitimacy among all convention delegates.

The second paragraph of the journal reports the choice of Livermore, Gilman and West as "a Committee to receive the returns of members elected; they were also appointed a Committee to prepare and lay before the Convention such rules as they shall judge necessary for regulating the proceedings in said Convention." The committee, in short, was to determine, not to recommend, the rules. Then the meeting broke up.

Attendance, swollen by legislative adjournment, had doubled by the next day. John Calfe, Federalist and long time clerk for the House of Representatives, was chosen secretary and President Sullivan won election by secret written ballot to the convention presidency. No doubt he received all the votes of those informed beforehand of the Federalist strategy. Early in the afternoon the committee reported. Three key procedural rules helped prepare for possible adjournment. No individual's vote would be recorded except on the question of adoption, which would enable those bound by negative instructions to vote for adjournment without their fellow townsmen ever finding out. Second, a motion to adjourn would take precedence over any other motion: this routine legislative provision could be used to prevent a final vote on adoption. And finally, no vote could be reconsidered without as many members present as made the initial vote. If the Federalists got in deep trouble they could sneak in a delaying vote, then walk out. Calfe reports simply that the report was "considered, received, and accepted." Antifederalists later regretted the acceptance.

Debate on the constitution began soon thereafter and continued until the following Thursday. Each section of each article in the proposed constitution was read, then discussed. The form of the debate quickly became routinized and predictable. Critics of the proposed union explained why they found the section unacceptable and Federalist spokesmen defended its logic. Joshua Atherton, a lawyer from the inland town of Amherst, spoke most frequently and effectively for the opponents, most of whom were content, as one observer wrote, "to remain silent…until the vote comes." Several Federalists shared responsibility for answering objections. Sullivan—who accepted the presidency only on condition he be allowed to participate in discussions—Langdon, Livermore, John Pickering, and two seacoast ministers, Benjamin Thurston and Samuel Langdon, played the most important roles as defenders of the proposed plan of union.

Only four parts of the constitution stimulated lengthy debate. Antifederalists objected strongly to two-year terms for congressmen and six for senators—in New Hampshire elections for both occurred annually. Section eight of Article I, on congressional powers, compromised state authority far too much according to several spokesmen. Atherton spoke at length against a federal judiciary. The debate on the last paragraph of Article VI, which stated that "no religious Test shall ever be required as a Qualification to any Office or public Trust under the United States," lasted nearly a full day. Its critics wanted officeholding limited to protestants.

While the discussions dragged on, leaders of both sides tried to count noses. Everyone agreed the Antifederalists had an initial advantage. Sullivan later estimated the difference at seventy to thirty but the best evidence suggests a much narrower margin, perhaps fifty to forty, with the rest—including some restricted by negative instructions—uncertain as to how they would vote. During dinner parties, convention recesses and whenever else the opportunity arose, the Federalists tried to add to their ranks. They also tested the willingness of delegates to vote for adjournment. By the twenty-first, when debate ended on the last article, no one could predict the outcome with confidence. "It is very doubtful how the numbers are," wrote Pickering's close friend Jeremiah Libbey. "Each party think they have a majority, and yet appear afraid of each other."

A proposal by eleven of the instructed delegates determined the next move.

Journal
of the
Convention
in New Hampshire,
which ratified
The Federal Constitution
1788.

Names of Towns and places Represented	Names of Delegates to convention	No of miles to Exeter					
Portsmouth	John Langdon Esq	30	1	1	1	1	1
	John Pickering Esq	30	1	1	1	1	1
	Pierce Long Esq	30	1	1	1	1	1
Exeter	John Taylor Gilman Esq	0	1	1	1	1	1
Londonderry	Colo Daniel Runnels	44	1	1	1	1	1
	Archib McMurphey Esq	50	1	1	1	1	1
Chester	Mr Joseph Blanchard	44	1	1	1	1	1
Newington	Benjamin Adams Esq	30	1	1	1	1	1
Greenland	Doct Ichabod Weeks	18	1	1	1	1	1
Rye	Mr Nathan Goss	24	1	1	1	1	1
New Castle	Henry Prescutt Esq	36	1	1	1	1	1
North Hampton	Revd Benj Thurston	12	1	1	1	1	1
Hampton	Christopher Toppan Esq	16	1	1	1	1	1
Hampton falls & Seabrook	Revr Saml Langdon	10	1	1	1	1	1
Stratham	Mr Jon Wiggin	8	1	1	1	1	1
Kensington	John Esq	8	1	1	1	1	1

State of New Hampshire
A Journal of the proceedings of the Honble Convention assembled at the Court House in Exeter on Wednesday the thirteenth day of February AD 1788 for the investigation discussion and decision of the Federal Constitution

Wednesday Feby 13. 1788. About fifty members being assembled they proceeded to the choice of a Chairman and the Honble Josiah Bartlett Esq was chosen

The Honble Saml Livermore the Honble John Taylor Gilman & Benjamin West Esqrs were appointed a Committee to receive the returns of members elected — they were also appointed a Committee to prepare and lay before the Convention such rules as they shall judge necessary for regulating the proceedings in said Convention

Adjourned to 10 oClock to morrow morning

Thursday Feby 14th 1788. The Convention met according to adjournment — About one hundred members present

Motion was made for the choice of a Secretary for the Convention, and the ballots being taken John Calfe Esq was chosen for that purpose, and sworn to the faithful discharge of the trust reposed in him

report being read and considered was received and accepted

Motion was then made by Mr Atherton seconded by Mr Parker. that this convention ratify the proposed Constitution together with the amendments but that said Constitution do not operate in the State of New Hampshire without said amendments

after some debate Motion was made by Mr Livermore seconded by Mr Bartlett & others, to postpone the motion made by Mr Atherton to make way for the following motion (viz) That in case the Constitution be adopted that the amendments reported by the Committee be recommended to Congress — which Motion of Mr Atherton being postponed

Adjourned to 9 oClock to Morrow Morning

Saturday June 21st 1788. The convention met according to adjournment

Resumed the consideration of Mr Livermores motion which being determined by the Convention in the affirmative — Motion was then made by Mr

Pages from the original manuscript of the convention journal showing the record of the first day of the convention in Exeter and the last day of the convention in Concord. Courtesy of the State Archives. Photograph by Bill Finney.

The group approached Langdon and said they would consider supporting adjournment, but couldn't vote for the constitution. Almost immediately Langdon made the motion for which he and others had so carefully prepared. By general agreement the vote was postponed until the following day. That evening a bargain was struck. If the adjournment motion passed the convention would reconvene in June at Concord, a more convenient site, although in the Antifederalist heartland. Whether Sullivan, Langdon and other Federalist leaders promised anything in the way of state appointments or other rewards cannot be determined. In any case the motion passed. According to Pickering, who seems to have been in charge of tabulating delegate sentiment, the margin was only fifty-six to fifty-one. Convention minutes note simply that after "some general observations were made" the "question was put and it was voted to adjourn to some future day."

Judge's decision on round two: a draw. Crowd reaction mixed. Federalists breathe a huge and collective sigh of relief. They know a vote on the constitution itself would have lost.

Round Three: Ratification

The vote on adjournment gave both sides hard information on which to plan strategy for the next four months. Antifederalists had about fifty solid votes, the Federalists about forty-five. Since the maximum number of delegates who might attend in June was around one hundred and ten, every vote counted. Momentum lay with the Federalists—they already had exhibited more skill in converting the undecided than their opponents—but the outcome was still in doubt. In late March one perceptive seacoast resident reported that there was a "probability" New Hampshire would ratify "although considerable danger" it would not.

The Antifederalists tried as best they could to prevent further erosion in their ranks. Led by Nathaniel Peabody, who had refused to serve as a delegate but remained active outside the convention, they convinced one town which had not yet chosen a delegate to elect an opponent of the constitution for the June session. Attempts were made in at least three towns to impose negative instructions on delegates who had voted for adjournment. Antifederalists in Boscawen convened a town meeting which voted to replace the elected delegate, who refused to promise a "nay" vote, with one who would. All in all, however, the Antifederalists were relatively quiet in the interim between sessions. They knew that had a vote been taken at Exeter the constitution would have been defeated. The majority, they hoped, would hold at Concord.

Federalist leaders could not afford to be complacent. To no ones surprise, they continued to flood the press with pro-ratification articles. The constitutional arguments differed little from those used before, but press coverage overall involved two fresh ingredients. One was widespread circulation in Cheshire and Grafton counties of the Hartford (Connecticut) *Courant.* The paper contained numerous articles explaining why Connecticut had ratified so readily and emphasizing the benefits of union to all Connecticut River valley inhabitants. Since many of the potential swing votes were from southwestern New Hampshire, circulation of the *Courant* had a large potential payoff.

Personal attacks on leading Antifederalists were the second new ingredient. Atherton provided a particularly inviting subject. At the beginning of the revolution he had been a loyalist. Now the Federalists accused him of "wishing to prevent the adoption of a system only because it will put it out of the power of Britain to subjugate us." Citizens were told that Peabody, still a major force in the legislature, opposed ratification primarily because it might undermine his influence over appointments to political office. Several writers linked Antifederalism to participants in the paper money riot of 1786 and to the well publicized personal financial problems of Peabody and others.

Federalists supplemented their publicity campaign with hard-nosed politicking at the local level. Benjamin Bellows somehow managed to regain the convention seat from Walpole: either a third town election was held or as town clerk he doctored the records to validate the results of the initial election. Whatever the reasons Bellows' credentials were accepted at the Concord session. Both Charlestown and Derryfield (now Manchester) repulsed efforts to force unwanted instructions on pro-constitution delegates. The Derryfield member, who had not gone to Exeter, showed up in Concord. Hopkinton held a special town meeting and released its delegate from binding negative instructions. Federalists in Boscawen drew up a petition which asserted that the recent town vote to change delegates had been illegal. Livermore produced two new supporters from Grafton County, one who had been elected but not gone to Exeter, the other representing Lincoln and Franconia which together had fewer than a hundred residents. The representative, Isaac Patterson, lived in Piermont, part of a class of towns which had chosen the county's one Antifederalist. All in all interim town meetings provided the Federalists with six badly needed new votes and prevented at least one potential defection.

Meanwhile the pro-constitution leaders worked on individual convention members trapped between the Antifederalist sentiment in the towns they represented and their personal willingness to support ratification. Not attending the Concord session was one possible solution to their dilemma. Four of the five elected delegates who failed to show in Concord had been at Exeter and probably were among those voting for adjournment. One of them had been given negative instructions and two others had been counted in the opposition camp by Federalist tabulators. The fifth non-attendee, Nathaniel Ladd from strongly anti-ratification Epping, missed both sessions.

All this made Sullivan, Langdon, Livermore and their associates optimistic as decision time approached. External factors added to the optimism. Since

Massachusetts two additional states had ratified, thus bringing the total to eight, just one short of the required nine. The New Hampshire and Virginia conventions both would meet in mid-June. If New Hampshire moved rapidly it could, as one writer put it, provide the "Keystone of the Federal Arch." It was an opportunity not to be missed. The Federalists gained further encouragement from the legislative session held in Concord early in the month. Langdon, who replaced Sullivan as state president, gave ratification a ringing endorsement in his inaugural and the legislative response suggested that resistance to the constitution had weakened. Even more important the session gave Federalist organizers an opportunity to gather additional information about how delegates were apt to vote. Victory by a thin margin looked probable, but much depended on who showed up, and when.

The first day, Wednesday, June 18, went well for the Federalists. Ninety of one hundred thirteen elected delegates attended and of the missing twenty-three, sixteen were from Antifederalist towns. Sensing a golden opportunity the pro-constitution delegates pushed through votes settling the Walpole and Boscawen disputed elections in their favor. Meanwhile the credentials of all members chosen during the interim—including those of Piermont the resident supposedly representing Lincoln and Franconia—were examined by the rules committee and accepted. Then the meeting adjourned.

Encouraged by these successes, Federalist leaders decided to push rapidly for ratification. Their plan was to forego the extensive debate and behind the scenes politicking which had been so necessary at Exeter. They would—like their counterparts in several other states—support a series of constitutional amendments to correct "deficiencies" pointed out by Antifederalists. The critical vote would come when someone, probably Atherton, moved for conditional acceptance, i.e., that New Hampshire ratify only on condition all the proposed amendments become part of the constitution. Federalists would seek postponement of that motion, substitute a motion for unconditional acceptance, and then vote to ratify.

Everything seemed in place by Friday. All but one of the known Federalists had arrived and four probable Antifederalists were still absent. Early in the day an amendment committee, chaired by Langdon, was appointed. It reported after the noon meal, at which point Atherton made his expected motion. The ensuing debate proved perfunctory, so Livermore, seconded by several delegates, tested sentiment by proposing postponement. He also announced that if postponement passed he would move unconditional acceptance. Postponement was voted and by common agreement the meeting dispersed until the following morning.

Saturday's events confirmed what by now everyone suspected. Atherton tried unsuccessfully to obtain an adjournment. As vote on the main motion neared at least one delegate torn between negative instructions and personal commitment left the building. He and three others—all in similar circum-stances—were recorded as in attendance but not voting. The final tabulation was fifty-seven yeas and forty-seven nays. The ten vote majority surprised even the most optimistic among Federalist leaders. Secretary Calfe recorded the pre-cise time at 1:00 PM in case Virginia ratified the same day and made claim to having been the ninth.

Round three required no judge's decision.

Epilogue

In the last century historians have exerted a good deal of energy analyzing votes in the various ratification conventions. Several generalizations can be made about New Hampshire. To begin with, the mutually reinforcing factors of geog-raphy and past constitutional experience correlate neatly with divisions on the proposed plan of union. Federalism was concentrated in the seacoast area and upper Connecticut River valley where inhabitants had a long history of attempted constitutional reform. Similarly, Antifederalism centered in regions whose inhabitants had resisted such reform. Secondly, Federalism was strongest among the upper classes. Of those listed in convention records as judges, esquires (justices of the peace), generals, doctors or reverends, thirty-three voted "yea" and only fourteen "nay"; misters, captains, and lieutenants, on the other hand, voted sixteen for and twenty-seven against ratification. Third, there was a clear Federalist bias among state citizens with "continental" experience: six for-mer representatives in the Continental Congress served as convention delegates and all worked hard for ratification. Finally, the eventual vote masked the close-ness of the struggle. Only the calculated and imaginative political maneuvering of men like Sullivan, Langdon and Livermore, made possible New Hampshire's claim to the label "Keystone of the Federal Arch."

Whatever historians make of the ratification conflict, adoption gained quick acceptance in New Hampshire. Portsmouth celebrated with a parade, fireworks, and free liquor. Ratification by Virginia, four days after New Hampshire, and by New York in July increased jubilation among citizens already optimistic about the newly established national government. Antifederalists swallowed their disappointment and advised acquiescence. Even Atherton gave up after New York. "The language" among New Hampshire opponents, he lamented to a friend there, has become "it is adopted, let us try it." Few, in sub-sequent years, regretted the attempt.

Nicholas Gilman (1755–1814) miniature portrait by an unknown artist. The son of an Exeter merchant who served as state treasurer during the Revolution, Gilman was an officer in the Third New Hampshire Regiment throughout the war. Afterward he worked briefly in his father's business, was active in the militia, and became involved in local politics. A protege of General Sullivan, Gilman won election to the Continental Congress in 1786, and to the Constitutional Convention in Philadelphia the following year. Later, he served four terms in Congress, ending his career as a U.S. senator. Courtesy of the Phillips Exeter Academy.

DRAFTING THE CONSTITUTION

*Address by Richard F. Upton to the Joint Convention of the Senate and
House of Representatives, State House, Concord, New Hampshire,
May 14, 1987, on the Bicentennial of the Meeting at Philadelphia of the
Convention to Draft the Constitution of the United States*

*T*o have a true appreciation of the difficulties which had to be overcome in
the drafting of the Constitution of the United States, one should read the first
seven Articles which remain today in the same form as when they were signed by
the assembled delegates on September 17, 1787. One will be struck by the great
care with which these Articles were prepared and the complexity of the subject
matter. To have obtained agreement by representatives of thirteen sovereign and
independent states was an enormous undertaking.

A famous American, Louis D. Brandeis, once said, "Most of the things
worth doing in this world have been declared impossible before they were
done." The creation of the Constitution of the United States, the great charter
of our national government, certainly qualifies under this statement.

The deliberations of the Convention which drafted it occurred at one of
the most difficult times in our history, and the conditions under which the delegates worked at Philadelphia would be considered intolerable today. The quarters occupied by the delegates were cramped and uncomfortable, and the heat
was unbearable at times. When the assembled delegates sought relief from the
heat by opening the windows of the hall, a horde of large black flies distracted
them. Slowness of travel, whether on horseback or by stagecoach, carriage, or
boat frequently held up the business.

It took twelve days to go from New Hampshire to Philadelphia in those
days, and thirteen days if you happened to come from Georgia. There were no
telephones, no overnight letters, no automobiles and no air travel.

Sectional jealousies between the thirteen states were often fierce.

The only national government at the time, located in New York City, was
the Continental Congress, a legislative body of one House, to which each of the
thirteen American States sent delegates. Each state had one vote. The New

19

(Left) Richard Upton delivering his address in 1987. Courtesy of the N. H. Bicentennial Commission. (Below) Program for the celebration of the Philadelphia Convention, May 14, 1987. Courtesy of the N. H. Bicentennial Commission.

PROGRAM

NEW HAMPSHIRE HOUSE OF REPRESENTATIVES
11:00 A.M.   MAY 14, 1987
IN BICENTENNIAL RECOGNITION
OF THE
CONVENING OF THE
CONSTITUTIONAL CONVENTION
IN
PHILADELPHIA
ON MAY 25, 1787

PRESENTATION OF COLORS
The First Newmarket Militia Company
Richard D. Longo, Captain

OPENING PRAYER
Rev. John B. McCall, Chaplain

SALUTE TO FLAG
Rep. Ednapearl Parr, D.A.R.

"THE CONSTITUTION SONG"
David Shepard, Composer
Accompanied by Tia Tesso

ORATION
Richard F. Upton, Esq.

"COMPROMISE"
David Shepard and Tia Tesso

WITHDRAWAL OF COLORS

BICENTENNIAL NOTES

Chronologically, the events leading to the United States Constitutional Convention were:

28 March 1785, Maryland and Virginia signed the "Mount Vernon Compact" settling outstanding issues regarding the use of the Chesapeake Bay and its tributaries.

The success of this meeting encouraged the invitation to all the States to gather in Annapolis in September 1786. Poor attendance resulted in no action except a recommendation to Congress that a convention be called to propose measures to strengthen the Articles of Confederation which had proven to be ineffective to meet the requirements of the new nation.

Congress endorsed the call for a convention to meet in Philadelphia on the second Monday of May 1787.

Representatives of the States began to gather in early May, but not until May 25, 1787 was a quorum present. This date is recognized as the beginning of the effort that resulted in the Constitution.

New Hampshire's delegates did not arrive until July 23. They were John Langdon of Portsmouth and Nicholas Gilman of Exeter. Both took an active role in the completion of the Constitution and New Hampshire's endorsement as the Ninth and Deciding State a year later on June 21, 1788.

CELEBRATION

Governor John Sununu, accompanied by a Delegation of five, will attend an opening weekend of celebration in Philadelphia on May 24, 1987.

Governors of all the Original Thirteen States will similarly attend with delegations.

New Hampshire's Delegation will consist of:
Rep. Russell C. Chase
Chairman of the New Hampshire Bicentennial Commission on the U. S. Constitution
Judge Thomas Donnelly
Historian
J. Bonnie Newman
Business Representative
Lorenca C. Rosal
Educator
Peter Kageleiry, Jr.
Student

England states tended to vote as a bloc. So did the Southern states. The Middle Atlantic states sometimes sided with New England and sometimes with the South. The charter of national government was then the Articles of Confederation, adopted during the Revolutionary War in 1777 and in its tenth year of existence, almost universally condemned for its defects, now that the war for independence had been won.

Could the American people somehow learn to think nationally rather than locally? That was the question.

George Washington, a delegate from Virginia, one of the first to arrive at Philadelphia, noted the problems. He said: "it is too probable that no plan we propose will be adopted...if to please the people we offer what we ourselves disapprove, how can we afterwards defend our work? Let us raise a standard to which the wise and honest can repair. The event is in the hands of God."

Washington was then fifty-five years of age and had retired to Mount Vernon after having led the American armies to victory in the Revolution. He had now come out of retirement to serve as a delegate and was to be chosen president of the convention.

Coming to Philadelphia, Washington first called on Benjamin Franklin, then serving as president of the Pennsylvania State Council. He was also a delegate. Franklin, the great American scientist and diplomat, was then eighty-one years old but still of keen mind. He showed that he well understood the difficulties in a letter he wrote to Thomas Jefferson, then serving as American minister in Paris: "The delegates chosen are men of character and ability so I hope good will come from their meeting. Indeed, if it does not do good, it will do harm, as it will show that we have not wisdom enough among us, to govern ourselves and will strengthen the opinion of some political writers that popular governments cannot long support themselves."

The convention, then scheduled to meet in Philadelphia, had been called by the Continental Congress to meet on the second Monday of May 1787, which was May 14, or two hundred years ago measured back from this very day.

Its purpose as stated in the call, was "for the sole and express purpose of revising the Articles of Confederation" to make them "adequate to the exigencies of government and the preservation of the Union."

The call of the convention, therefore, was couched in terms of a revision of the Articles of Confederation, but instead the delegates eventually produced a wholly new Constitution. It is fortunate that they were courageous enough to exceed their instructions when it became apparent that patching up the Articles would not do.

Unhappily, on that first day, May 14, 1787, there was no quorum present. Washington and Franklin were there but only two states had delegations present. Washington arrived at the place of meeting in a neat horsedrawn carriage, while

Letter of Nicholas Gilman to President John Sullivan, September 18, 1787. Gilman reported on the deliberations at the Philadelphia convention: "I hope to have the pleasure to lay this important affair before the State in a few days." Courtesy of the State Archives. Photograph by Bill Finney.

Franklin traveled in a sedan chair carried by several trusty convicts from the local prison. At eighty-one, Franklin's body was too frail to stand the jolting ride in a carriage over the rough streets of the city.

There being no quorum, the convention adjourned from day to day; ten days went by with a few delegates straggling in each day, until, at last on the 25th of May, there was a quorum of the states.

Washington was unanimously chosen president of the convention and William Jackson of South Carolina was elected secretary. A messenger and a doorkeeper were chosen just as is done today. Then a committee was appointed to draft the rules.

Among the rules was one, amazingly accepted without protest, that the proceedings be closed to the public. There was to be a journal which could be inspected only by members while the convention was in session. No copies were to be made and nothing communicated to the outside world. History records that there were few leaks.

Today this decision to proceed in secrecy seems startling. Most of us are accustomed to dealing with the "right to know" laws. The delegates of that day had not heard of such. Our minister in Paris, Thomas Jefferson, protested vigorously when he learned of the secrecy rule. In contrast, James Madison, a fellow Virginian and often called the "Father of the Constitution," later the fourth President of the United States, thought that secrecy was essential, so bitter were the disagreements among the delegates. Indeed, forty years later, Madison stated that if the proceedings had been open, the Constitution would never have been adopted. He reasoned that the delegates were proceeding on uncharted grounds with few precedents to guide them. As he put it, we will constantly be changing our minds as we go along and should feel free to do so without fear of being held inconsistent. Publicly stated views tend to become frozen. I mention this bit of history not with any idea of recommending it as an example for present-day legislative procedure.

A journal was kept by the secretary. When the Convention got ready to adjourn in September, a motion was made that the journal be destroyed. The adoption of this motion was narrowly avoided. Instead, it was voted to leave the journal in the custody of convention president Washington who kept it carefully for nine years and then, in 1796, deposited it with the State Department. Not until 1819, or thirty years later, was the convention journal published by direction of Congress. For some reason, the delegates were anxious to preserve the confidentiality of their discussions.

I should say a word about the delegates from New Hampshire. The State Legislature chose John Langdon and John Pickering of Portsmouth, Benjamin West of Charlestown, and Nicholas Gilman of Exeter, or any two of them. Our State was feeling poor so no money was appropriated to pay their expenses.

Cover of the proposed federal constitution as printed by John Melcher of Portsmouth in 1787 to comply with the General Court's decision in December 1787 to have 400 copies printed for distribution to the towns. This copy was received by the selectmen of Fishersfield (Newbury) and was recently found among the town's records. It is the only copy of this printing known to exist. Courtesy of the Selectmen of Newbury, N. H. Photograph by Bill Finney

Pickering and West never attended. However, Langdon and Gilman were already representing New Hampshire in the Continental Congress, then meeting in New York City. Langdon advanced the money for himself and Gilman to travel from New York City to Philadelphia. But New Hampshire's two delegates did not arrive until July 23rd, at which time the convention's work was entering its most important phase. History records that both of our delegates supported a strong and effective federal government.

Langdon was a prosperous Portsmouth merchant who had taken part in the early assault on Fort William and Mary in December of 1774, and had been Continental Marine Agent in charge of shipbuilding during the Revolution. He was later to be governor of the State, United States senator, and first president pro-tem of the United States Senate.

Nicholas Gilman was a member of the illustrious Gilman family of Exeter. He was said to be the youngest and most handsome delegate of the all-male convention. He later represented New Hampshire in the United States Senate.

In general our delegates to Philadelphia, as well as the other political leaders of our State, were keenly aware of the defects in the weak national government provided by the Articles of Confederation. There was no independent chief executive. During recesses of the Continental Congress, executive power was held by the "Committee of State," a committee on which each of the thirteen states had one representative. It is easy to see how such an instrument of government would have been an ineffective executive.

All states were equal in the Continental Congress, which had no control over finances and only feeble powers of taxation. To raise money required that the Congress send a requisition to each state legislature. Such requisitions were often dishonored.

There were no national courts. The highest appellate court of each state was a law unto itself. The central government could not regulate trade between the states. The several states imposed their own tariffs on goods coming in from their sister states. This was particularly true with reference to New Hampshire commerce coming into or passing through Massachusetts. Our country had no adequate national defense. This was illustrated when a merchant ship owned by two Portsmouth merchants was seized in the West Indies by Captain Horatio Nelson of the British Navy for some technical legal reason. The frustration of being unable to do anything about it was difficult to bear.

Each state could issue its own paper money, as could the Continental Congress. The unpaid debts of the states and of the Continental Congress from the Revolutionary War were a serious cloud on the national credit.

The Rev. Jeremy Belknap, of Dover, author of the first good history of New Hampshire, noted that the situation of the thirteen independent and sovereign states reminded him of a room containing thirteen clocks, all going at once, each ticking away to a different beat and ringing the hours on bells with different pitches of sound, a maddening bedlam.

The Constitution, as finally drafted, addressed the foregoing problems based on experience of the ten-year period under the Articles of Confederation.

We should never forget that in 1787 the thirteen American states, in seeking a stronger and more effective form of self-government at the national level, were an oasis of liberty in a world largely ruled by kings, emperors, and other despots, who would have been only too happy to see the American experiment fall on its face, thus discouraging the spread of democratic ideas among their own subjects.

The convention members themselves were none-too-confident that they would succeed and had some doubts that common, ordinary people were capable of self-government. They feared absolute power in whatever hands, and saw to it that power was dispersed, both by separation of powers and by federalism, which provided for a division of power between the Federal government and the several states.

They gave ground here and there in order to achieve unity, realizing their weakness as a national power as compared with England, France, Prussia and Russia, all of which maintained standing armies and navies.

They should be judged by the standards prevailing in their day and the conditions they faced, rather than by the 20/20 vision of two hundred years' hindsight. In the end, the Constitution was signed by delegates representing all the states present on the final day in September.

The Constitution lacked a Bill of Rights. This was to come two years later. The Constitution failed to deal with the issue of Negro slavery, postponing the issue to another generation which was equally unable to settle the matter by agreement.

However, the delegates did produce a Constitution which was eventually ratified by all the states and which has served well and effectively for the last two centuries and is still going strong. Machinery was also provided for amending the Constitution. The convention closed on September 16th and 17th and went through the process of final engrossment of the Constitution, much the same as our present-day procedure.

Franklin had reservations about several provisions but was convinced of the importance of a united stand. In a closing speech which he wrote but which was read for him, he said, in part:

> Mr. President, I confess that there are several parts of this Constitution which I do not at present approve, but I am not sure I shall never approve them; for having lived long, I have experienced many instances of being obliged by better information or fuller consideration, to change opinions even on important subjects, which I once thought right but found to be otherwise…for when you assemble a number of men to have the advantage of their joint wisdom, you inevitably assemble with those men all their prejudices, their passions, their errors of opinion, their local interests and their selfish views. From such an assembly can a perfect production be expected? It therefore astonishes me, Sir, to find this system approaching so near to perfection as it does…thus I consent, Sir, to this Constitution because I expect no better and because I am not sure that it is not the best. The opinions I have had of its errors, I sacrifice to the public good.

Upon the final adjournment of the convention, the convention secretary departed for New York City to deliver the engrossed parchment to the Continental Congress for submission to the several states.

Washington, at the close of the day, repaired to his lodgings for rest, where he made this entry in his diary, summing up the day's transactions:

Monday, 17th. Met in Convention, when the Constitution received the unanimous vote of 11 States and Colonel Hamilton's from New York (the only delegate from thence in Convention), and was subscribed to by Colonel Mason from Virginia, and Mr. Gerry from Massachusetts.

The business being thus closed, the Members adjourned to the City Tavern...dined together and took a cordial leave of each other; after which I returned to my lodgings, did some business with, and received the papers from the Secretary of the Convention, and retired to meditate on the momentous work which had been executed, after not less than five, for a large part of the time Six, and sometimes 7 hours sitting every day, except Sundays,...for more than four months.

There was a real leader! The next chapter of this epic is the story of the ratification of the Constitution by the several states. Therefore I will close this address on the following note: "To be continued."

Samuel Livermore (1737–1802) portrait by John Trumbull, 1792. An original grantee of Holderness where he was a large landowner, Livermore served as a judge, as a legislator, as a delegate to the Continental Congress, and later as a U. S. senator. A leading advocate of the new government, he used his considerable influence with the northern towns to win their support at the convention. Courtesy of the Currier Gallery of Art.

PLACING THE KEYSTONE
IN THE FEDERAL ARCH
Ratification by the States

Address by Richard F. Upton to the Joint Convention of the Senate and House of Representatives, State House, Concord, New Hampshire, March 17, 1988

This second chapter deals with the political struggle for ratification of the new Constitution and is a continuation of the address previously given to this body on May 14, 1987.

The prospects for the new Constitution were vastly increased by the support given it by George Washington and Benjamin Franklin. They were probably the two most famous and respected Americans of their day. Of a special importance was the kind of man Washington was. During the latter part of the Revolutionary War, in one of the dark periods, Washington's officers urged him to take control of the civil government. He immediately rebuked them and ordered that there be no repetition of such an idea. During the period in which the Constitution was under consideration there were suggestions that Washington be made king or president for life. All these ideas he rejected out of hand and without hesitation. No wonder he was trusted!

During this period there were published the "Federalist Papers" written anonymously but generally known to have been written by John Jay, James Madison and Alexander Hamilton. These essays were enormously influential in support of the new Constitution. To this day they are often referred to by the United States Supreme Court in interpreting the Constitution.

The Constitution, as drafted by the Philadelphia Convention, provided that the Constitution be submitted to special ratifying conventions to be selected by the people of each state, the method of election to be specified by each state legislature. When ratified by nine states out of the thirteen, the Constitution would take effect.

With relatively little debate the Continental Congress, sitting in New York City on September 28, 1787, directed that the process begin.

The Delaware convention ratified the Constitution unanimously on December 7, no doubt appreciating that the Constitution was a "good bargain" for the small states.

Pennsylvania followed suit on December 12 by a vote of 46 to 23. New Jersey was the third state to act, and on December 18 it too ratified the Constitution unanimously.

Georgia acted on January 2, 1788. The convention met behind palisades in an armed camp to guard against Indian attacks. The vote was unanimous. The fifth state was Connecticut which, on January 9, 1788, also ratified unanimously.

The sixth state, Massachusetts, which acted on February 6, had trouble dealing with the opposition. Such men as John Hancock, Samuel Adams, and Elbridge Gerry were among the opposition. After considerable debate, the Constitution was ratified by a vote of 187 to 168. That Massachusetts had difficulty reaching this result was a bad omen for New Hampshire.

Now only three more states were needed. On March 24, 1788, in Rhode Island, the various town meetings, on a trial vote, voted 271 to 243 against ratifying the Constitution. Accordingly the legislature saw no reason to call a convention. This was a setback. But on April 28 the Maryland convention voted "yes" 63 to "no" 11. This was the seventh state. The South Carolina convention met next and as the eighth state to ratify, it voted approval by a vote of 149 to 73 on May 23.

In New Hampshire the struggle was very close. The Governor (he was then called President) of the State was Major General John Sullivan of Durham, a lawyer turned soldier, who had served several years in the Continental Army during the Revolutionary War, under the command of Washington. His military record was mixed but his patriotism was unquestioned. He was a strong supporter of the Constitution and was to serve as convention president. At that time the State President also doubled as President of the Senate so General Sullivan had a voice in that body. Another strong supporter was the Speaker of the House of Representatives, Thomas Bartlett of Nottingham. Among the other supporters were John Taylor Gilman of Exeter, the State Treasurer; the senior State Senator, John Pickering of Portsmouth, a prominent lawyer; Josiah Bartlett of Kingston, signer of the Declaration of Independence and later president of the New Hampshire Medical Society; John Langdon of Portsmouth, merchant, Continental Agent, and himself a delegate to the Philadelphia Convention; the Sheafe and Long families; and most of the Protestant clergy.

Sullivan and Langdon were political rivals and each had served as the state's chief executive. Sullivan was later to be the first United States District Judge under the new Constitution, while Langdon went to the United States Senate and was its first president pro tempore. Both Sullivan and Langdon had taken part in the raids on Fort William and Mary at New Castle in December of 1774 in order to secure the powder from military control, an event well-remembered by the people of that day. Although political rivals, these two men worked together for ratification of the Constitution.

Sullivan decided to call a special session of the Legislature in December 1787. The Constitution itself had been first published in the Portsmouth *Spy* on September 29th.

During the interim before the convening of the Legislature, clergymen spoke from their pulpits and citizens debated in the taverns. Those who were in favor of the Constitution were called Federalists, and those opposed, Antifederalists. There were pamphlets and letters to the newspapers.

The meeting of the Legislature in special session was for the purpose of making provision for the election and convening of a ratifying convention. The calling of the special session in December during the winter months was not without purpose. Most of the Federalist sentiment was in the tidewater, and by calling the session to meet at Portsmouth, it would be less difficult for many Federalists to attend. The seacoast area was the center of Federalist support. When the Legislature met it was realized that the Federalists were not to have an easy time of it. The Legislature itself contained substantial Antifederalist sentiment.

A joint committee was appointed to draw up a bill. Exeter was to be the place for convening the convention, but it was not to meet until February 13 by which time the Federalists hoped that Massachusetts would have acted favorably. (This hope was realized.) It was provided that the state would pay the delegates instead of the towns. Significantly the law against plural officeholding was relaxed so as not to apply to the convention delegates. Thus President Sullivan, Chief Justice Samuel Livermore, and State Treasurer John Taylor Gilman, all Federalists, were able to serve as delegates by election from their respective towns. The delegates were chosen at special town meetings in the month of January. The strategy of the Antifederalists was to attempt to elect delegates opposed to the Constitution and then to bind them with written instructions to oppose it. These instructions were commonly drafted by committees chosen by the town meetings from those local residents known for their knowledge of political matters.

When the convention met at Exeter on February 13, only about fifty of the total number, expected to be in excess of one hundred delegates, were present, but those present proceeded to organize, choosing Josiah Bartlett as temporary president and a committee to produce a draft of the convention rules. It was realized that the opposition was strong but the Federalists controlled the rules committee as appointed. Realizing that it might be necessary to adjourn the convention, it was provided that there would be no record kept of the vote of each delegate, except on the main question of adopting the Constitution. It has been estimated that somewhere between twenty-five and thirty delegates attended subject to instructions from their respective town meetings, requiring

House of Joshua Atherton, Amherst, photograph c. 1900. As the town's delegate to the convention, Atherton was the most vocal opponent of the Constitution. Courtesy of the N. H. Historical Society.

them to oppose the Constitution. The local elections had in some cases been exciting. William Plumer of Epping, a lawyer and later several times governor and United States Senator, was defeated by his fellow townsmen in his effort to attend the convention because he was, in fact, in favor of the proposed Constitution. Major General Benjamin Bellows of Charlestown was elected but at first refused to attend when told he had to accept negative instructions.

Among the opposition was Joshua Atherton, a Tory during the Revolution, now a lawyer, of Amherst. Also in the opposition was Nathan Peabody of Atkinson who acted as a lobbyist, not a delegate. After several days of debate it appeared that the Antifederalists had fifty solid votes while the Federalists had about forty-five solid votes. Of the remainder there were eleven delegates who were not in sympathy with the negative instructions given them by their respective towns, and while not proposing to violate their instructions, they did inform John Langdon that they would support a motion to adjourn but if the main question were put, then they would vote against the Constitution.

Accordingly, on the day following this discussion, Langdon moved to adjourn the convention, since it was apparent that if a vote was then taken, the Constitution would lose. The motion to adjourn was strongly opposed, but on Friday, February 22, it was voted to adjourn to some future day and that when the convention adjourned it be to meet again at Concord on the third Wednesday in June next. There was no record vote taken but newspaper reports indicate that the vote to adjourn carried narrowly by a vote of 56 to 51. Thus the willingness of the instructed delegates to vote to adjourn carried the day.

The opposition to the Constitution came from delegates sent by towns situated mainly in the central part of the state. The population there was composed largely of persons engaged in agriculture. The Merrimack Valley was their principal means of communication with the outside world and meant that this area was influenced by what happened in Massachusetts. The opposition to the new Constitution also included people who were satisfied with the legislative supremacy and weak executive contained in the New Hampshire Constitution of 1783, then the fundamental instrument of government. Sullivan, in a letter to Nicholas Gilman, described the Antifederalist delegates thus:

> a motley mixture of Ancient Toreys, friends to paper money, Tender Laws, Insurrection &c.; persons in Debt, distress, & poverty, either real or Imaginary; men of blind piety, Hypocrites, & Bankrupts; together with Many honest men bound by Instructions to vote against the Constitution at all Events.

The arguments used by the Federalists were largely those which motivated the majority of the delegates attending the Philadelphia Convention. However, the arguments of those opposing the Constitution grew out of local views including the following: (1) that the new Constitution granted too much power to the central government and should have been modelled more along the lines of the New Hampshire Constitution of 1783; (2) that the two-year term for members of the House of Representatives and the six-year term for senators were too long (terms of office should have been one year as in the New Hampshire Constitution, making the elected members of the legislative body more accountable to the people); (3) that the federal court system proposed by the new Constitution would be too far removed from the public; (4) that the provision in the new Constitution granting the new federal government the sole power to issue paper money was too broad and the states themselves should retain a portion of this power; and (5) that the provision of the new Constitution contained in Article VI, that "no religious test shall ever be required as a qualification to any office or public trust under the United States," made the new Constitution unacceptable.

Those holding this view believed that there should be a Protestant qualification for office-holding as in the New Hampshire Constitution of 1783. Although most of the Protestant clergymen who were delegates urged their fellow delegates to reject this particular argument, a substantial number of the delegates persisted in opposition on this ground. Indeed, one delegate wrathfully made the point that "a Turk, a Jew, a Roman Catholic, and what is worst of all, a Universalist may be president of the United States."

This intolerant and bigoted attitude had deep roots in the New Hampshire of that day, and indeed a religious qualification for office-holding under the Constitution of New Hampshire was not removed until 1876, or nearly a century later.

During the interim between the first session and the reconvening of the convention on June 18, 1788, efforts were made by the Federalist faction to gain favorable votes. Several towns were persuaded to change their negative instructions at special town meetings called for the purpose. Some uninstructed delegates who appeared to be opposed were persuaded to change their views.

In the town of Hopkinton, Lt. Joshua Morse, the delegate from that town, who had been sent under negative instructions, was able to get his instructions changed so as to read that "Lt. Morse shall vote as he deems best for the public good."

When the convention was reconvened, in the Old North Church in Concord on June 18, it was evident that a change of sentiment had occurred. The conventions of New Hampshire and Virginia were both in session during June and it was considered important that New Hampshire's ratification occur before that of Virginia in order that New Hampshire might be the ninth state. By this time John Langdon had replaced John Sullivan as President of the State in an intervening election, and he sent a strong message to the Legislature endorsing the new Constitution. Two election contests were settled in favor of the Federalist delegates. A few towns also now sent delegates although they had not seen fit to do so at the Exeter meeting. The Federalist faction now believed that there was a majority present sufficient to carry the day. Thus on Friday, June 20, a committee of fifteen was appointed to consider and report such articles as they shall think proper to be proposed as amendments to the new Constitution and "lay the same before this convention." The convention then adjourned until 3 P.M. at which time the committee's report submitted by its chairman, John Langdon, was presented. Twelve amendments were recommended in the committee's report. These amendments were largely those which two years later became part of the Constitution now known as the Bill of Rights. Upon acceptance of the committee report, delegate Joshua Atherton of Amherst, an avowed opponent of the new Constitution, moved "that this convention ratify the proposed Constitution, together with the amendments; but that the said Constitution do not operate in the State of New Hampshire without said amendments."

The Atherton motion in effect made the adoption of the amendments a condition of New Hampshire ratification rather than an unqualified ratification accompanied by recommended amendments only. If adopted, the Atherton motion would have been ineffective to ratify. This motion was followed by debate pro and con. At the conclusion of debate, Judge Samuel Livermore, seconded by Josiah Bartlett, moved that the Atherton motion be postponed in order to give precedence to another motion, namely, "that in case the Constitution be adopted, that the amendments reported by the committee be recommended to Congress." The Livermore motion was intended to make the amendments take the form of recommendations to the Congress of the new government which, if approved, would then be submitted to the states for ratification. The Livermore motion was thereupon postponed until Saturday, June 21, 1788, at 9 a.m., at which time consideration of Mr. Livermore's motion was resumed and the convention voted to adopt it. At this point delegate Atherton moved that the convention adjourn. This motion to adjourn was defeated. The Federalists now clearly appeared to have the upper hand and Judge Livermore now moved, seconded by John Langdon and others, that the main question now be put for the adoption of the Constitution. The roll was thereupon called and 57 delegates having voted in the affirmative and 47 in the negative, the Constitution was ratified at 1 P.M. with the twelve recommended amendments, the same being recommendations and not conditions of ratification.

Thus New Hampshire became the ninth state required to put the new Constitution into effect. Messengers were dispatched on horseback to notify the Virginia convention and the Continental Congress then in session at New York City.

There still remained much to be done. Although nine states had ratified the Constitution placing it in effect, the states of Virginia and New York had not yet acted. The absence of either from the union would have greatly weakened the new government.

The debate in Virginia continued with Patrick Henry opposed to the Constitution and James Madison in favor. Finally, on June 25, four days after New Hampshire, Virginia ratified the Constitution by a vote of 89 to 79. On July 2, 1788, President Cyrus Griffin of the Continental Congress, declared the new Constitution in effect by virtue of New Hampshire's action.

The New York convention, which had begun its sessions at Poughkeepsie on June 17, appeared to be closely deadlocked with the Antifederalists having a slight majority. The Antifederalists were led by Governor George Clinton who presided over the convention as well. The Federalists were led by Alexander Hamilton. Shortly before the final vote, news reached the convention concerning the favorable votes in New Hampshire and Virginia. On July 26 the New York convention voted to ratify narrowly by a vote of 30 to 27.

Thus was demonstrated the truism that a few good men dedicated to a just cause can often make a difference in the course of history. And even more of a marvel, all this was accomplished within one year and one month after the convening of the Philadelphia Convention. Of great importance, too, was the attitude of the Antifederalists. They accepted the result, agreeing to give the new system a fair trial.

The United States Constitution has today become almost a civic religion, if such is possible. It is greatly respected by the American people. It is now the oldest written constitution of a federated nation.

The political theory of a constitution as the fundamental law superior to legislative, executive and judicial actions, proved to be an exportable idea, almost on a par with the Declaration of Independence. In the years since 1788, nation after nation have adopted constitutions, some less successful than ours to be sure. Most Third World countries of today have constitutions, many modeled on ours.

So I conclude by paraphrasing the eloquent words of the poet Emerson,

Neath the spire of the Old North Church,
Round and round the arguments swirled,
And then the embattled delegates stood,
And cast the vote heard round the world.

THE CELEBRATION
Commission Activities 1983
to 1988 and Beyond

William M. Gardner

*W*ith much foresight and due preparation, the New Hampshire General Court in 1981 approved the following resolution introduced by Senator William Sanborn of Deerfield, Representative Roger King of Deerfield, and Representative Maurice Levesque of Nashua, establishing the New Hampshire Bicentennial Commission on the United States Constitution:

**Senate Concurrent
Resolution No. 2
A Resolution**

establishing the New Hampshire Bicentennial Commission
on the United States Constitution

Whereas, the founding fathers signed the United States constitution on September 17, 1787, and the bicentennial of that signing will be on September 17, 1987, and

Whereas, New Hampshire played an historic role in the ratification of the United States constitution; and

Whereas, a joint resolution has been introduced in the United States Senate to establish the United States Constitution Bicentennial Commission which would plan and coordinate events commemorating the United States constitution bicentennial; and

Whereas, it is appropriate that New Hampshire be the first state to establish a state constitutional bicentennial commission to plan and coordinate state and local activities relating to the formulation and ratification of the United States constitution; now, therefore, be it

Resolved that the Senate, the House of Representatives concurring:

That there is hereby established the New Hampshire bicentennial commission on the United States constitution; and

That this commission shall be composed of:

I.   Five members of the senate appointed by the president of the senate;

II. Five members of the house of representatives appointed by the speaker of the house;

III. The secretary of the state or his designee;

IV. The attorney general or his designee;

V.   Eight New Hampshire citizens who are not officers or employees of the state appointed by the governor and council. The governor and council shall give special consideration to representatives of veterans' organizations and other patriotic associations;

That this commission shall encourage, plan and coordinate appropriate events and activities commemorating this historic event.

The resolution was approved on March 17, 1981. When all appointments had been made, the duly authorized members met on November 16, 1983, in the Legislative Office Building for organizational purposes. At that first meeting, veteran State Representative Russell C. Chase of Wolfeboro was voted chairman and other officers were selected to help carry out the mandate of the commission. Thus, New Hampshire became the first state to establish a commission and officially begin its preparation for the bicentennial of the Constitution.

During the commission's first year, Chairman Chase made contact with Vernon Morton of North Carolina, a member of that state's commission, and with North Carolina Lieutenant Governor Jimmy Green. A joint meeting resulted in several members of the North Carolina commission coming to Concord on October 17, 1984. Since New Hampshire and North Carolina were the only states of the original thirteen with established commissions, a resolution was adopted to be sent to the other eleven original states urging them to organize commissions to prepare for the bicentennial.

RESOLUTION

Adopted October 17, 1984

at

Concord, New Hampshire

WHEREAS: The Bicentennial of the formulation of the United States Constitution
occurs on SEPTEMBER 17, 1987, and

WHEREAS: The celebration of this National Event is a milestone in the life
of these UNITED STATES, and

WHEREAS: The Thirteen Original Colonies were involved in the formulation and
adoption of the Constitution, and

WHEREAS: It is essential that all freedom loving peoples around the world
recognize that these United States place a high value on the document
that prescribes their form of National Government.

BE IT HEREBY RESOLVED BY THE PARTIES MEETING THIS DAY, OCTOBER 17, 1984
FOR THE PURPOSE OF FURTHERING SUCH A CELEBRATION THAT:

Every effort be extended to encourage the Original Thirteen Colonies to
establish Commissions and join a group effort to celebrate the Bicentennial.

AND FURTHER, BE IT RESOLVED

that a copy of this Resolution be forwarded to the Governors and the Legislatures
of all of the States but with urgent encouragement for immediate action by the
Original Thirteen Colonies.

Signed in Concord, New Hampshire October 17, 1984

_____   _____
Chairman of New Hampshire Commission   Lt. Governor of North Carolina

_____   _____
Rep. Edna Pearl F. Parr   William Chamborn
Vice chr. N.H. U.S. Bicentennial Com.

_____   _____
Asst. 20th Chm. Holman Corporation   Natalie S. Flanagan State Rep.

_____   _____
H. David Stedman   Mary Louise Hancock
Chm. Holman Corporation

_____   _____
Exec. Dir. National Center for Constitutional   Wm. Gardner
Studies

                                     _____

Joint resolution with North Carolina urging the other eleven original states to form bicentennial commissions. Courtesy of the N. H. Bicentennial Commission.

When the commission was established, it looked forward to celebrating the bicentennial of New Hampshire's ratification on June 21, 1988. But several prior events in the development of the Constitution also deserved recognition, and the commission participated with others in those celebrations. The commission worked closely with the New Hampshire Humanities Council, jointly sponsoring several projects. Its first was "After the Revolution: New Hampshire and the New Nation," which studied the political, social and cultural lives of several New Hampshire towns for the decade before and after the ratification of the U.S. Constitution. This was an attempt to better understand life at that time in the various regions of New Hampshire and to grasp more fully the debate within the state for and against ratification. A workshop to encourage broad participation took place in the State House on January 26, 1985, for organizational and information purposes.

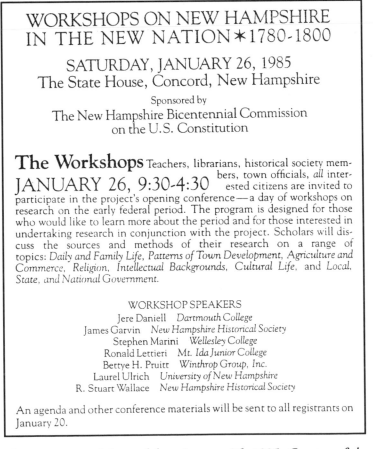

WORKSHOPS ON NEW HAMPSHIRE
IN THE NEW NATION ✳ 1780-1800

SATURDAY, JANUARY 26, 1985
The State House, Concord, New Hampshire

Sponsored by
The New Hampshire Bicentennial Commission
on the U.S. Constitution

The Workshops Teachers, librarians, historical society members, town officials, *all* interested citizens are invited to
JANUARY 26, 9:30-4:30
participate in the project's opening conference—a day of workshops on research on the early federal period. The program is designed for those who would like to learn more about the period and for those interested in undertaking research in conjunction with the project. Scholars will discuss the sources and methods of their research on a range of topics: *Daily and Family Life, Patterns of Town Development, Agriculture and Commerce, Religion, Intellectual Backgrounds, Cultural Life,* and *Local, State, and National Government.*

WORKSHOP SPEAKERS
Jere Daniell   *Dartmouth College*
James Garvin   *New Hampshire Historical Society*
Stephen Marini   *Wellesley College*
Ronald Lettieri   *Mt. Ida Junior College*
Bettye H. Pruitt   *Winthrop Group, Inc.*
Laurel Ulrich   *University of New Hampshire*
R. Stuart Wallace   *New Hampshire Historical Society*

An agenda and other conference materials will be sent to all registrants on January 20.

Announcement of the workshop, January 26, 1985. Courtesy of the N. H. Bicentennial Commission.

The several sessions presented the diverse views within New Hampshire during that time. Bettye Pruitt, an Associate of the Winthrop Group, analyzed eighteenth-century agriculture as it functioned on individual farms and within local and regional economies. In addition, she discussed the use of statistical data in general and tax lists in particular as sources for the study of the economy and social structure. R. Stuart Wallace, then director of the New Hampshire Historical Society, took a fresh look at New Hampshire's "Windows to the Past"—manuscripts, broadsides, newspapers, maps, and published volumes, noting in the process where they might likely be found. Stephen Marini pointed out the vast importance of religion in the life of eighteenth-century New Hampshire. Ronald Lettieri, of Mt. Ida College, analyzing the philosophical roots of the Constitution, explored those elements of antipathy between twentieth-century notions of democracy and eighteenth-century republicanism contained in the original constitution. He requested attendees to read *Federalist No. 10* prior to the workshop. James Garvin, also of the N. H. Historical Society, lectured with slides on the developments in architecture, engineering, furniture and other areas of material culture in New Hampshire in this period. Laurel Ulrich, assistant professor of history at the University of New Hampshire, presented the variety and complexity of female life in the period, from the genteel aspirations of Mary Yeaton of Portsmouth to the more traditional powers of "Old Mother Damnable" of Keene. All presenters discussed the location and availability of sources.

Other joint projects included a traveling display consisting of booklets, maps, state documents, and letters accumulated by researchers on the After the Revolution project and a speakers' bureau. Both the travel exhibit and speakers' bureau were established to bring the results of the accumulated research to local communities throughout the state.

Another result of the After the Revolution project was the Readers' Theatre, a play written by David Magidson based on the debates over ratification of the Constitution held at the two New Hampshire convention meetings of 1788 in Exeter and Concord. Called "A Collage for Town Voices," it dramatized the debate on the Constitution. The play climaxes as New Hampshire becomes the ninth and deciding state to approve the document and thus make it the basic law of the new country. The written text has been made available to schools, historical societies, and community organizations for use throughout New Hampshire. The commission sponsored a premier performance by drama students from campuses of the University System of New Hampshire at the State House on February 4, 1986, for the governor and other state officials.

Commemorative Souvenirs

The commission made several items available as commemorative souvenirs of the bicentennial. Three items in particular that deserve mentioning were the medal, stamp and ratification document.

Medal

The commission produced a commemorative medal for general sale and sent out a flier to publicize its availability. Included with the medal was a summary of New Hampshire's ratification written by commission member and Dartmouth Professor Jere R. Daniell.

Bicentennial Commission medal. On one side is the official seal of the New Hampshire Bicentennial Commission on the United State Constitution. The obverse contains the state motto and the formal commemorative inscription.

Ratification of the Federal Constitution in New Hampshire

New Hampshire became the ninth state to ratify the proposed federal constitution when, on June 21, 1788, a convention of town delegates meeting in Concord voted 57-47 to approve the document unconditionally. Since Article VII of the proposal declared that a national government would be established once nine (of the existing thirteen) states approved, New Hampshire was, indeed, the "deciding" state. Its inhabitants have long taken pride in their contribution to the founding of the national government.

Ratification did not come easily. Initially a majority of state voters and convention delegates were against approval of the constitution. These "anti-Federalists," however, were politically out-maneuvered by the pro-ratification, or Federalist, forces. The Federalists were also helped by developments elsewhere in the emerging nation.

The struggle began in the state legislature, which had the responsibility for calling the ratification convention. Federalists managed to have the date of convening set late enough to guarantee that Massachusetts would have made its decision beforehand. They hoped the Bay State would vote affirmatively—which it did—thus weakening resistance to ratification in New Hampshire.

The second and most dramatic phase of the conflict took place in the first session of the convention held in February at Exeter. It was clear well beforehand that anti-Federalist delegates outnumbered their opponents. Many of them—about forty percent of those elected—were bound by formal instructions from their constituents to vote "nay." The Federalists, however, arrived early, and with their temporary majority controlled the selection of convention officers. These officers set procedures which would allow them to adjourn the convention before any final vote was taken. After lengthy discussion, the convention did adjourn until June.

The intervening four months witnessed a gradual shift in the balance of power. Federalists bombarded the press with pro-ratification arguments. They convinced a few towns to withdraw instructions to elected delegates, or to select different men. When word arrived shortly before reconvening that South Carolina had become the eighth state to ratify, Federalists emphasized the opportunity at hand for New Hampshire to cast the deciding vote. There could be no delay, for the Virginia convention was already in session and might make its decision any time. On June 21, after brief debate, the New Hampshire convention voted approval.

Ratification Document

In addition to the medal, the commission decided to reproduce the original manuscript approval document announcing to Congress that New Hampshire had approved the proposed Constitution and recommended twelve amendments, which eventually became the basis for the Bill of Rights. The original manuscript was restored by the commission under contract with the Northeast Document Conservation Center, which surface-cleaned and mended the parchment. The original was photographed and reproduced in copies approximately half the size and made available for sale to the public.

UNITED STATES CONSTITUTION ARTICLE VII

"The ratification of the conventions of nine states, shall be sufficient for the establishment of this constitution between the states so ratifying the same."

NEW HAMPSHIRE
became that Ninth State.
On June 21, 1788, New Hampshire
approved the proposed Constitution
and it became the basic law
of the new country.

THE NINTH AND SUFFICIENT PILLAR RAISED.

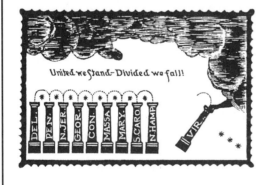

This original approval document, beautifully inscribed in script on parchment, has recently been found in an unused vault in New Hampshire's State House.

It also includes twelve proposed amendments which eventually became the basis for the

BILL OF RIGHTS

APPROVAL DOCUMENT

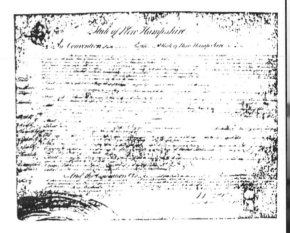

Copies of the NINTH and APPROVAL DOCUMENT in approximately half size (15″ × 13″) are available for sale.

No collection of constitutional historic documents can be complete without this reproduction, suitable for framing. It is dark, showing the maturity of age. A complete transcript is included. It is shipped, rolled in a protective tube.

Flier announcing the reproduction of New Hampshire's ratification document. Courtesy of the N. H. Bicentennial Commission.

Stamp

With the help of our congressional delegation, the commission made an effort to have a stamp issued by the postal service commemorating the New Hampshire ratification. On May 2, 1985, the New Hampshire House of Representatives approved Concurrent Resolution No. 12 as introduced by Representative Chase. The resolution petitioned the U.S. Postal Service for a stamp using the seal of the New Hampshire Bicentennial Commission on the United States Constitution, to be issued in the spring of 1988. A stamp was issued, although the design recommended by the legislature was changed by the postal service to a picture of the Old Man of the Mountain.

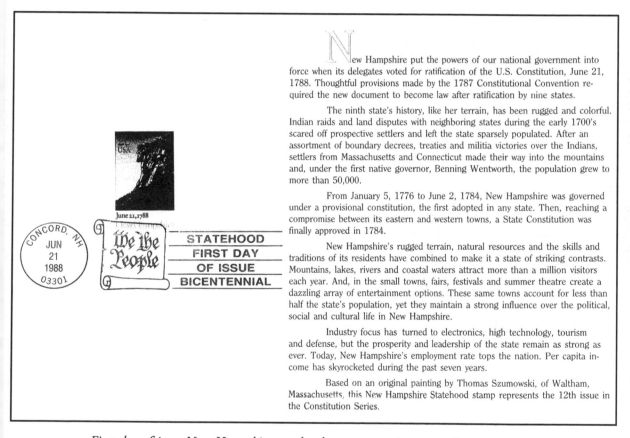

New Hampshire put the powers of our national government into force when its delegates voted for ratification of the U.S. Constitution, June 21, 1788. Thoughtful provisions made by the 1787 Constitutional Convention required the new document to become law after ratification by nine states.

The ninth state's history, like her terrain, has been rugged and colorful. Indian raids and land disputes with neighboring states during the early 1700's scared off prospective settlers and left the state sparsely populated. After an assortment of boundary decrees, treaties and militia victories over the Indians, settlers from Massachusetts and Connecticut made their way into the mountains and, under the first native governor, Benning Wentworth, the population grew to more than 50,000.

From January 5, 1776 to June 2, 1784, New Hampshire was governed under a provisional constitution, the first adopted in any state. Then, reaching a compromise between its eastern and western towns, a State Constitution was finally approved in 1784.

New Hampshire's rugged terrain, natural resources and the skills and traditions of its residents have combined to make it a state of striking contrasts. Mountains, lakes, rivers and coastal waters attract more than a million visitors each year. And, in the small towns, fairs, festivals and summer theatre create a dazzling array of entertainment options. These same towns account for less than half the state's population, yet they maintain a strong influence over the political, social and cultural life in New Hampshire.

Industry focus has turned to electronics, high technology, tourism and defense, but the prosperity and leadership of the state remain as strong as ever. Today, New Hampshire's employment rate tops the nation. Per capita income has skyrocketed during the past seven years.

Based on an original painting by Thomas Szumowski, of Waltham, Massachusetts, this New Hampshire Statehood stamp represents the 12th issue in the Constitution Series.

First day of issue New Hampshire statehood commemorative stamp, June 21, 1988. Courtesy of the N. H. Bicentennial Commission.

Cooperative Efforts

National, State, and Local

During the planning stages of our bicentennial celebration our commission worked closely with the national commission established by the Congress and President. Members of the New Hampshire commission in October 1986 attended a national conference of states on bicentennial planning in Orlando, Florida, sponsored jointly by the National Commission on the Bicentennial and by Disney World to help coordinate events throughout the country and share ideas for events in each state.

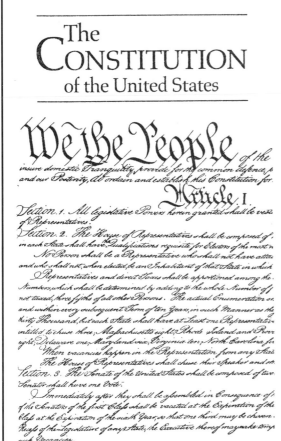

FOREWORD

In the last quarter of the 18th Century, there was no country in the world that governed with separated and divided powers providing checks and balances on the exercise of authority by those who governed. A first step toward such a result was taken with the Declaration of Independence in 1776, which was followed by the Constitution drafted in Philadelphia in 1787; and in 1791 the Bill of Rights was added. Each had antecedents back to Magna Carta and beyond.

The work of 55 men at Philadelphia in 1787 marked the beginning of the end of the concept of the divine right of kings. In place of the absolutism of monarchy, the freedoms flowing from this document created a land of opportunities. Ever since then discouraged and oppressed people from every part of the world have made a beaten path to our shores. This is the meaning of our Constitution.

This pocketsize book is one of a new series of copies of the Constitution by the Commission on the Bicentennial of the United States Constitution. The principal goal of the National Commission is to stimulate an appreciation and understanding of our national heritage—a history and civics lesson for all of us. This lesson cannot be learned without first reading and grasping the meaning of this document—the first of its kind in all human history.

Chairman of the Commission
on the Bicentennial of the
United States Constitution
Chief Justice of the
United States, 1969–1986

Cover and Foreword of the Constitution booklet published by the national bicentennial commission and distributed throughout New Hampshire. Courtesy of the National Bicentennial Commission.

The national commission also hosted a regional training conference in Boston during May of 1987. It was co-hosted by the six New England state commissions with many New Hampshire state and local commission members attending. The conference aimed to stimulate interest and coordinate plans for numerous celebration activities during the bicentennial.

One of the goals of the bicentennial was to get as many people in our state as possible to take notice of the Constitution and what it means. To begin that process of a civics lesson, thousands of small, booklet-sized copies of the Constitution were distributed across the state to school students and to the general public. It is estimated that 100,000 copies were distributed.

Many businesses helped in this endeavor. Weeks Dairy used the commission seal and a listing of upcoming bicentennial events on 350,000 half-gallon

NEW HAMPSHIRE...9th and KEY STATE to ratify the U.S. CONSTITUTION. June 1788

Article VII of the United States Constitution stated that the Constitution would become effective when nine states endorsed it. New Hampshire became the ninth on June 21, 1788.

The N.H. Bicentennial Commission on the U.S. Constitution is currently preparing a variety of programs of celebration and education that we all can share. Early programs include a research study of New Hampshire people and communities during the late 1700s, a traveling display, a Reader's Theater, commemorative coins and documents and the possibility of displaying the Magna Carta in our state during the summer of 1987.

We urge you to learn more about New Hampshire's role in this celebration and hope that you will take advantage of all upcoming activities, including a public celebration on the date of New Hampshire's ninth and deciding endorsement of the proposed constitution; June 21, 1988.

Very truly yours,

Russell C Chase

Russell C. Chase, Chairman
N.H. Bicentennial Commission
on the U.S. Constitution
State House, Concord, N.H.

Weeks Dairy in Concord spread the bicentennial message on milk cartons. Courtesy of the N. H. Bicentennial Commission.

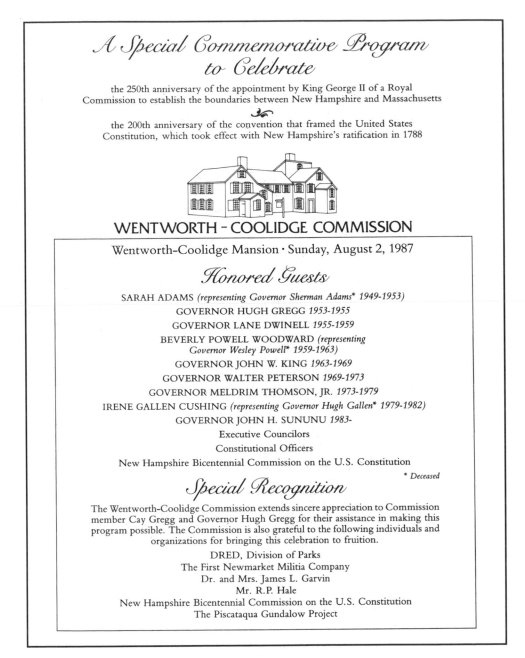

A Special Commemorative Program to Celebrate

the 250th anniversary of the appointment by King George II of a Royal
Commission to establish the boundaries between New Hampshire and Massachusetts

the 200th anniversary of the convention that framed the United States
Constitution, which took effect with New Hampshire's ratification in 1788

WENTWORTH - COOLIDGE COMMISSION

Wentworth-Coolidge Mansion · Sunday, August 2, 1987

Honored Guests

SARAH ADAMS *(representing Governor Sherman Adams* 1949-1953)*

GOVERNOR HUGH GREGG *1953-1955*

GOVERNOR LANE DWINELL *1955-1959*

BEVERLY POWELL WOODWARD *(representing
Governor Wesley Powell* 1959-1963)*

GOVERNOR JOHN W. KING *1963-1969*

GOVERNOR WALTER PETERSON *1969-1973*

GOVERNOR MELDRIM THOMSON, JR. *1973-1979*

IRENE GALLEN CUSHING *(representing Governor Hugh Gallen* 1979-1982)*

GOVERNOR JOHN H. SUNUNU *1983-*

Executive Councilors

Constitutional Officers

New Hampshire Bicentennial Commission on the U.S. Constitution

* Deceased

Special Recognition

The Wentworth-Coolidge Commission extends sincere appreciation to Commission
member Cay Gregg and Governor Hugh Gregg for their assistance in making this
program possible. The Commission is also grateful to the following individuals and
organizations for bringing this celebration to fruition.

DRED, Division of Parks
The First Newmarket Militia Company
Dr. and Mrs. James L. Garvin
Mr. R.P. Hale
New Hampshire Bicentennial Commission on the U.S. Constitution
The Piscataqua Gundalow Project

*Program for the celebration at the Wentworth-Coolidge House in Portsmouth.
Courtesy of the N. H. Bicentennial Commission.*

milk cartons, while Burger King, in conjunction with the New Hampshire Division of Parks and Recreation, developed a series of placemats used in their restaurants promoting the bicentennial celebration. An essay contest was held for students, in conjunction with the New Hampshire Bar Association, with three winners resulting. Newspapers, both dailies and weeklies, and radio and television stations all gave generously to increase awareness of the Constitution and its meaning to all of us, far beyond just reporting on the actual celebration events.

While the commission was preparing for the major celebration of the bicentennial, it also participated with other organizations, such as the Wentworth-Coolidge Commission and Common Cause, to bring attention to the Constitution. It also encouraged local communities to form their own com-

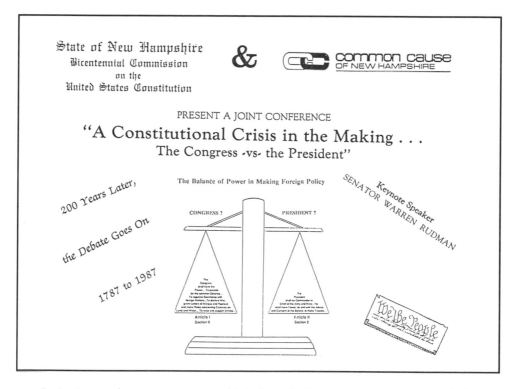

Invitation to the program sponsored jointly with Common Cause. Courtesy of the N. H. Bicentennial Commission.

missions. Sixty-five cities and towns received official designation from the national commission as bicentennial communities:

Alstead	Goffstown	Orford
Alton	Goshen	Ossipee
Amherst	Groton	Plaistow
Antrim	Hampton	Plymouth
Ashland	Hebron	Raymond
Belmont	Hillsboro	Rindge
Berlin	Holderness	Rumney
Bethlehem	Hollis	Salem
Bradford	Jefferson	Somersworth
Brentwood	Kingston	Sullivan
Bridgewater	Lancaster	Tamworth
Bristol	Landaff	Thornton
Campton	Londonderry	Unity
Canaan	Lyme	Wakefield
Candia	Manchester	Warren
Claremont	Meredith	Washington
Derry	Milford	Waterville Valley
Dorchester	Mont Vernon	Wentworth
Durham	Nashua	Whitefield
Ellsworth	New Castle	Winchester
Farmington	Newton	Wolfeboro
Gilford	Orange	

Scores of others held community events.

Philadelphia: We The People–200

The commission participated through its chairman, Russell Chase, at the bicentennial of the opening of the constitutional convention in Philadelphia on May 25, 1987. "We The People–200," the name selected by the Philadelphia organization established to plan and carry out the bicentennial celebration in that city, invited the 1987 governors of the original thirteen states to join in Philadelphia on May 24 and 25. Each governor was asked to bring a delegation to take part in portions of the program. Governor and Mrs. John H. Sununu attended with the delegation from New Hampshire that included Chairman Chase; Lorenca C. Rosal, educator; Judge Thomas Donnelly, historian; and Peter Kageleiry, Jr., student.

Each delegation was asked to prepare two subjects for discussion: a constitutional question of importance to your state 200 years ago, and one today. The delegation met, but, under time constraints, most of the discussion under

Delegates Thomas Donnelly, Peter Kageleiry, Jr., and Lorenca Rosal participating in the Philadelphia convention, May 1987. Photograph courtesy of Russell C. Chase.

question number one was curtailed. Under question two the proposals from the states (later to be voted on by the whole convention) covered items of general interest, including federal debt, costs of education, and questions of privacy.

The New Hampshire delegation, with guidance from Governor Sununu, had determined that the subject of states' rights was paramount in both periods. The proposal was made by educator delegate Rosal and discussed by student delegate Kageleiry. It was *resolved*:

> That Amendment #10 of the Bill of Rights should be revised to include the word 'explicitly' so it would read:
> "The powers not 'explicitly' delegated to the United States by the Constitution, nor prohibited by it to the States, are reserved to the States respectively, or to the people."

Delegate Rosal completed her presentation of it to the convention with the phrase, "And this time we really mean it!," which brought a roar of appreciative laughter from the delegates, who applauded the proposal and adopted it unanimously.

Under the sponsorship of "We The People–200," Philadelphia also set up a "State Day" for each of the thirteen original states. New Hampshire's State Day in Philadelphia was June 13, 1987. To highlight New Hampshire's State Day, the Timberlane Regional High School Band was invited to perform two concerts. Russell Chase describes the band's particpation as follows:

Timberlane had recently won national attention by representing New Hampshire at a contest against other regionally selected bands in Washington, D.C. Funds for the Washington trip had been raised by local subscription, and it was considered impractical to secure enough funds for the Philadelphia trip in this manner. Although the New Hampshire commission was not involved in the early planning of the event, it was considered imperative that we take part, and the commission helped fund the trip. A videotape of the concerts is a part of our record.

An interesting anecdote of the trip concerns the pressure of limited funds and a short period of time. June 13, 1987, fell on a Saturday. The band traveled by bus on June 12. They got a short night's sleep in a motel. Saturday was a busy day with the two concerts at different locations and the accompanying confusion—meals, recordings for the videotapes, etc. They finished late in the afternoon, loaded on to the buses, and slept their way back home.

Certainly finances demanded these economies, but the principal reason was that a portion of the band was seniors, and graduation was on Sunday. They made it.

Magna Carta

The state commission proudly joined with the U.S. Council of the Thirteen Original States in sponsoring a tour throughout New Hampshire of an original Magna Carta. Commission member and Deputy Attorney General Jeffrey R. Howard gives the following personal view of the event.

Early in the evening of a mid-July day in 1987 the justices of the New Hampshire Supreme Court stood on the plaza at the entrance of the State House, home to New Hampshire's 424 person citizen-legislature, its governor and its secretary of state. Behind the justices loomed the noble statue of one of the state's most famous sons, Daniel Webster. In front of them stood a line of school children, laborers and office workers, all awaiting entry to a 50-foot van. After finishing a long day of deciding important legal cases, New Hampshire's highest judges had joined the others who had come to Concord to see the document known as Magna Carta.

Magna Carta, the "Great Charter," along with several other documents of historical and constitutional significance, had been displayed in Concord for two days, and would that night be moving on for display in Portsmouth, Conway,

*Commissioner Natalie
Flanagan presenting cer-
tificates of achievement
to the Timberlane High
School Band members.*

*The Commission helped sponsor participation of the Timberlane Regional High School
Band in "New Hampshire Day" in Philadelphia, June 1987.*

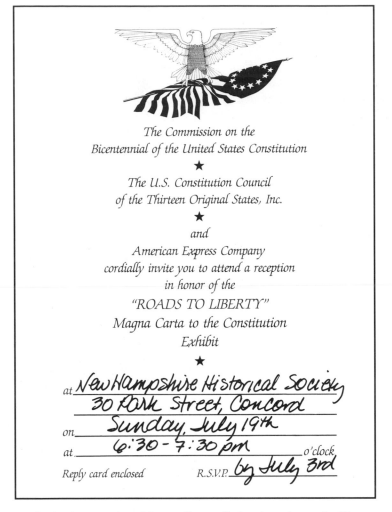

The Commission on the
Bicentennial of the United States Constitution

★

The U.S. Constitution Council
of the Thirteen Original States, Inc.

★

and

American Express Company
cordially invite you to attend a reception
in honor of the

"ROADS TO LIBERTY"
Magna Carta to the Constitution
Exhibit

★

at New Hampshire Historical Society
30 Park Street, Concord
on Sunday, July 19th
at 6:30 - 7:30 pm _____ *o'clock,*

Reply card enclosed   *R.S.V.P.* by July 3rd

Invitation to view Magna Carta during its sojourn in New
Hampshire. Courtesy of the N. H. Bicentennial Commission.

Hanover, and Keene. The exhibition had come to New Hampshire as part of its
tour of the United States, during which Americans would have the opportunity
to view an original of the first written instrument ever to contain several of the
constitutional concepts which we now consider essential to our liberty.

On June 15, 1215, more than seven and one-half centuries before the historic American tour of Magna Carta, the Barons of England met with King John
and presented him their grievances and demands. Failed military endeavors, the
difficulty of maintaining possession of lands on the European continent, and

other economic and political factors had led the king to ever more oppressive tax policies and arbitrary treatment of the Barons. They, in turn, became rebellious, steadily gaining more defectors to the cause as well as the support of the people of London. The result was the June 15th face-to-face meeting at a meadow called Runnymede, on the Thames River, southwest of London. There the Barons demanded and obtained from King John his agreement to abide by the written terms of the charter in his relations with them.

The provisions of Magna Carta were specific, they did not include much in the way of broad statements of government or individual rights. Taken as a whole, however, the sixty-one clauses of the charter stand as testament, as described by Levi Woodbury, a nineteenth century United States Supreme Court Justice from New Hampshire, to the sturdy spirit of the Anglo-Saxons, who were unwilling to let the liberties they had enjoyed be shackled by a code foreign to them.

Over the centuries, the importance of Magna Carta has been the subject of debate. It is beyond dispute, however, that two of its most significant contributions are, first, the concept of the rule of law and, second, that fundamental legal principles should be preserved in a charter or constitution. The United States Constitution, given life by the ratifying vote of the people of New Hampshire, owes much of its well-deserved respect to these two concepts expressed by Magna Carta. The framers of the National Constitution, as well as those who added to it the first amendments ensuring individual liberties, knew of Magna Carta and its periodic reissues. Their knowledge came from their study of the writings of the English jurist, Sir Edward Coke, as well as from having the great charter cited to them by such of their own number as John Adams. It is not surprising then that the Constitution and its Bill of Rights also embrace several of the specific ideas first set forth in their English ancestor. Not the least of these are the right of trial by jury and the principle that private property may not be taken by the government without just compensation.

The original Magna Carta displayed in the various New Hampshire towns in the Summer of 1987 is the copy dispatched by King John to Lincoln, which in the year 1215 was the third largest city in England. Through the generosity of the Dean and Chapter of Lincoln Cathedral, the perseverance of the "Magna Carta in America" organization in Oregon and the support of numerous public and private entities, the document's tour of the United States was made possible. And, as part of New Hampshire's celebration of the bicentennial of the United States Constitution, this state's most learned judges joined with wide-eyed school children in the unique experience of seeing the forebear of the Constitution, Magna Carta.

Events of September 19, 1987

New Hampshire Celebrates Bicentennial of the Philadelphia Convention's Final Approval of Constitution

Two hundred years ago on September 17, 1787, the delegates to the Philadelphia convention completed and signed the Constitution. National groups and New Hampshire communities celebrated that birthday on September 17, 1987, which fell on a Thursday. The New Hampshire Commission, with the Humanities Council, planned the state's celebration for Saturday, September 19, thus eliminating the competition for attention and making it easier for many to participate. The Humanities Council arranged the morning and early afternoon program, while the commission planned the musical presentation and the evening events.

Governor John H. Sununu opened the morning session in Representatives Hall with a review of the historic Philadelphia convention. He spoke particularly of the sectional problems and biases that were skillfully overcome by compromise and reason.

Commission Chairman Russell C. Chase presented Governor Sununu the Governor's Cup, the first of a series of pewter presentation pieces designed and donated by Hampshire Pewter of Wolfeboro. Chairman Chase took this opportunity to inform the governor and audience of the active participation of New Hampshire's business and industry organizations in support of the bicentennial. He also presented awards to the student winners of the National Bicentennial Writing Competition: Zephyr Rain Teachout, first  place; Amy Burnham, second place; and Richard W. Kim, third place.

The keynote address was delivered by Christopher Collier, co-author of *Decision in Philadelphia*. His learned dissertation was interspersed with anecdotes relative to the lives and habits of the Constitution's authors to the delight of the audience. Perhaps his best was the description of how Gouverneur Morris of Pennsylvania lost a limb and thereafter wore a wooden leg. The accident occurred while hurriedly leaving a tryst to which an angry husband returned earlier than expected. Morris, however, is best remembered as the author of the Preamble beginning, "We The People..." and his skillful wording of the document.

Following the keynote address was a lecture given by Charles E. Clark, a professor of history at the University of New Hampshire. His explanation of the

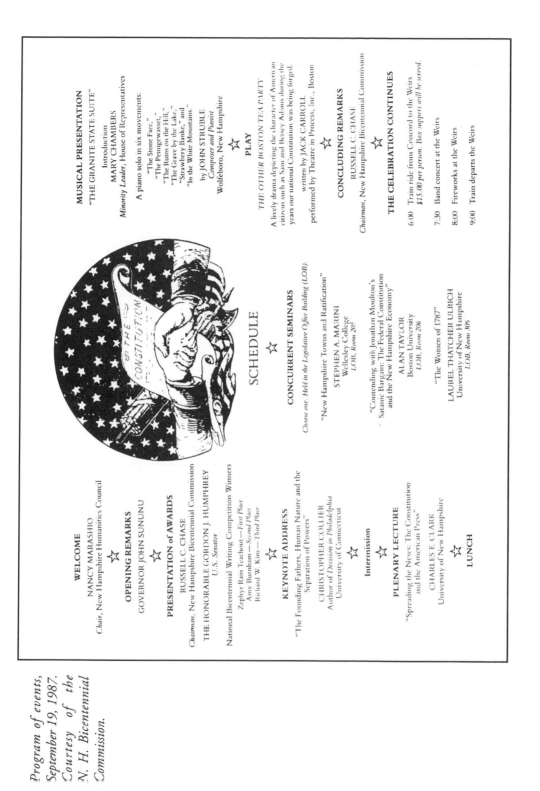

SCHEDULE

☆

WELCOME
NANCY MARASHIO
Chair, New Hampshire Humanities Council

☆

OPENING REMARKS
GOVERNOR JOHN SUNUNU

☆

PRESENTATION of AWARDS
RUSSELL C. CHASE
Chairman, New Hampshire Bicentennial Commission
THE HONORABLE GORDON J. HUMPHREY
U.S. Senator

National Bicentennial Writing Competition Winners
Zephyr Ram Teachout — *First Place*
Amy Burnham — *Second Place*
Richard W. Kim — *Third Place*

☆

KEYNOTE ADDRESS
"The Founding Fathers, Human Nature and the Separation of Powers"
CHRISTOPHER COLLIER
Author of Decision in Philadelphia
University of Connecticut

☆

Intermission

☆

PLENARY LECTURE
"Spreading the News: The Constitution and the American Press"
CHARLES E. CLARK
University of New Hampshire

☆

LUNCH

CONCURRENT SEMINARS
Choose one. Held in the Legislative Office Building (LOB).

"New Hampshire Towns and Ratification"
STEPHEN A. MARINI
Wellesley College
LOB, Room 205

"Contending with Jonathan Moulton's Satanic Bargain: The Federal Constitution and the New Hampshire Economy"
ALAN TAYLOR
Boston University
LOB, Room 206

"The Women of 1787"
LAUREL THATCHER ULRICH
University of New Hampshire
LOB, Room 305

MUSICAL PRESENTATION
"THE GRANITE STATE SUITE"
Introduction
MARY CHAMBERS
Minority Leader, House of Representatives

A piano solo in six movements:
"The Stone Face,"
"The Pemigewasset,"
"The Ruins on the Hill,"
"The Grave by the Lake,"
"Strawbery Banke," and
"In the White Mountains."
by JOHN STRUBLE
Composer and Pianist
Wolfeboro, New Hampshire

☆

PLAY
THE OTHER BOSTON TEA PARTY
A lively drama depicting the character of American citizens such as Sam and Betsey Adams during the years our national Constitution was being forged
written by JACK CARROLL
performed by Theatre in Process, Inc., Boston

☆

CONCLUDING REMARKS
RUSSELL C. CHASE
Chairman, New Hampshire Bicentennial Commission

☆

THE CELEBRATION CONTINUES

6:00   Train ride from Concord to the Weirs
$15.00 per person. Box suppers will be served.

7:30   Band concert at the Weirs

8:00   Fireworks at the Weirs

9:00   Train departs the Weirs

*Composer and pianist,
John Warthen Struble.*

crucial role played by the press during the ratification process was well received by the audience.

As part of the day-long program of activities, the commission sponsored a musical presentation by New Hampshire composer John Warthen Struble. It was the premiere performance of his work, *The Granite State Suite*, comprising six movements for solo piano, and was composed by him between April and December of 1986 in Wolfeboro to honor the state of New Hampshire and to celebrate its natural wonders. It is deliberately cast in a musical idiom designed to be maximally accessible to the general public without sacrificing musical integrity. A narrative description of the movements reveals the power of the composition.

I.   *The Stone Face* (The Old Man of the Mountain, Franconia Notch)
The suite opens with a stark musical portrait of this symbol of the state. The granite features of this natural rock formation, used as a central theme in one of Hawthorne's *Twice Told Tales*, are reflected in bare fortissimo octaves which weave a modal, contrapuntal texture whose principal theme will recur elsewhere in the suite.

II.   *The Pemigewasset* (Plymouth)
A pattering ostinato in the high treble sets off a lyrical, flowing melodic stream in the middle registers to suggest the flow of New Hampshire's central river, running from the White Mountains southward into the Merrimack. The Pemigewasset shares the varied moods and characters of other great rivers; at times deep and

placid, at others rushing briskly over shallow rapids. It flows past Plymouth, site of the Pemigewasset House, where Hawthorne died in 1864 while visiting Franklin Pierce, New Hampshire's only native president of the United States.

III.   *The Ruins on the Hill* (Salem)

A megalithic religious site in the southern part of the state, believed by many to be of pre-Columbian Keltic origin, these monuments have been a source of wonder and speculation since first discovered by Europeans in the 18th century, and have been cited as evidence that the North American continent was known and colonized by the ancients of Europe, Asia Minor and Africa thousands of years ago. The ruins include standing stones that mark the winter and summer solstices and the vernal and autumnal equinoxes as well as numerous underground chambers and a central altar stone. The music of this movement suggests a sense of the inscrutability of these ruins, as well as the pagan religious rites which may have been conducted in them.

IV.   *The Grave by the Lake* (Melvin Village)

Located on the ground of an old village church, where the composer served as organist, this grave site is commonly believed to be of Indian origin. According to local historian Marian Horner Robie, to whom the movement is dedicated, the grave was opened when the current road was cut that leads to the bay where the Melvin River empties into Lake Winnepesaukee, and the skeleton, since reburied, was discovered in a seated position. The music is a setting of an ancient Malecite Indian song collected by the famous ethnomusicologist Natalie Curtis around 1910. The grave is also the subject of a poem by John Greenleaf Whittier.

V.   *Strawbery Banke* (Portsmouth)

New Hampshire's principal seaport along its short Atlantic coastline is Portsmouth, site of the restored 17th- and 18th-century community pictured in this movement. The music suggests fleets of sailing ships on the windswept sea, bringing their cargoes to the old port.

VI.   *In the White Mountains*

The White Mountains occupy virtually the entire northern half of the state. This quiet, contemplative movement which ends the suite is intended to evoke the subtle atmosphere of these mountains, both in the silent grandeur of their topography and the unearthly silence of their snow-covered winter forests. There is, perhaps, suggestion of the first buds of spring breaking through as the snows begin their annual melt. The theme of this movement is a setting of the Anglo-American folk song "Barbara Allen," in a version sung in New Hampshire in the early 20th century.

☆ ☆ ☆ *SPECIAL* ☆ ☆ ☆
RAILROAD TRIP
Concord to The Weirs
September 19, 1987

For A
BAND CONCERT
at 7:00 P.M.
AND
For A Giant Display of
FIREWORKS
at 8:00 P.M.

TO CELEBRATE THE BICENTENNIAL
OF THE
U. S. CONSTITUTION

Round Trip and Box Dinner: $15.00

6:00 P.M. . . . . LEAVE CONCORD
7:00 P.M. . . . . BAND CONCERT
8:00 P.M. . . . . FIREWORKS DISPLAY
9:00 P.M. LEAVE WEIRS

TRAIN LIMIT: 400 (FIRST COME, FIRST SERVED)

—TICKETS—
NH BICENTENNIAL COMMISSION
UPHAM WALKER HOUSE, PARK STREET, CONCORD, NH 03301
(Make Checks Payable to: NH Bicentennial Commission)

With the completion of the musical presentation the day's activities were over and it was time for the evening finalé in Laconia. Statewide advertising brought upwards of 15,000 people to the Weirs at the west side of Lake Winnepesaukee for an evening of entertainment, climaxed by a gala display of fireworks. Most arrived by automobile, while a thousand boats of all sizes gathered from all corners of the "Big Lake." The view from the Weirs over the bay was spectacular, with a sea of boat lights spreading from the shore to Governor's Island.

George E. Letourneau of Allenstown with Ticket No. 1 for the "Fireworks Special" train ride. Letourneau is a 30-year veteran of state service. Courtesy of the State Archives. Photograph by Bill Finney.

Additional people arrived by a special fireworks railroad trip from Concord. The railroad had not been used for passenger traffic for several years, but this additional feature drew four hundred railroad and patriotic fans to endure a two and a half hour trip each way.

Chairman Russell Chase tells the 1987 railroad saga this way:

Organizing the celebration has been educational and frustrating, and I must admit I have enjoyed it. I am now informed and knowledgeable in several areas that I would rather have remained ignorant.

Railroading comes high on this list. Piano moving is a close second. More on this last at another time.

The railroad idea seemed a splendid way to get several hundred viewers to the fireworks without complicating the already horrendous parking problem.

The original Boston and Maine track (part of the line that ran from

Boston to Canada) still existed. A tourist railroad continues to use a short portion from Laconia north. It is called the Winnepesaukee Railroad, with headquarters in nearby Meredith. They have several passenger cars and a couple of diesel engines.

I talked with the owner of the Winnepesaukee Railroad over the next few weeks as we thought of possible problems. All looked great. The train would start in downtown Concord. There was plenty of parking. The railroad had plenty of insurance. They would add a box car to carry soft drinks, etc.

So, I talked with the New Hampshire Transportation Department, Railroad Division. They thought it would be a fine and practical addition to the celebration—but!

"You know you can't bring a passenger train all the way down to Concord?"

"What?" (There went my railroad trip and I have already been advertising it with enthusiastic acceptance.)

"Oh, no. There's a bridge over the river at East Concord and a trestle. Both have weak knees and have been declared unfit for passenger traffic by I.C.C." (Whoever they are.)

So, I drove up I-93 to look them over. They didn't look too bad to me, but I decided I didn't know how to get I.C.C. to change their minds, so I guessed I was stuck.

I drove to East Concord to find a parking spot where I could sit and figure out how to withdraw my advertising and cancel the trip without having to leave town—and there it was! In East Concord there used to be a foundry, right beside the track. The buildings are there, the property is surrounded by a chain link fence, and they must have had a lot of employees because there's room for two hundred parked cars—all paved and marked off.

"Aha!," I thought. "We will leave from East Concord!"

Back to the office. Who owns the foundry? Call the assessors. Call the owners in Nashua. "O.K. by us," they say, "but it's in the hands of a broker." Call the broker. No answer. Drive over to Epsom to see them. Can't find them. Ah, well! Eventually we get together and they agree to let us use the property.

So, I was all back together again, except—you have to have the engine on the front of the train. Normally, you drive one way, use a turn-table to turn the engine around, and use a side track to get to the new front of the train for the return trip. No turn-table or side track at East Concord. Stymied again. But... I called the railroad office in Meredith. They weren't even fazed: "Don't worry, we'll handle it."

"How are you going to do that?," I asked.

"We have two engines. We'll put one on each end of the train!"

Well, it went great. The tickets included a box dinner which the passengers were to pick up as they boarded the train.

The fireworks train en route *to the Weirs.*

"It's about forty miles to the Weirs," says the operator at the railroad office.

"I guess it will take us about an hour, then," I say.

"Oh, it will take a little longer than that."

"Well," I say, "we can leave at six o'clock and get there a little after seven."

The fireworks were to start after dark—about eight-fifteen or eight-thirty—and we would entertain those already there with a band concert. Timberlane Regional High School agreed to play. Everything fine!

"But," I thought. "What if it rains?" I decided not to worry, but my knees got sore from praying all week. No rain date. The fireworks people say they can handle anything but a downpour. Not to worry.

It's six o'clock, and we're off on time. Four hundred people with four hundred dinners, a diner in the middle of the train with a bar—how can you go wrong?

Slowly through the woods to the first crossing. The track has not been used so there is no signal system—no flashing lights, no "Ding, Ding!"

At the first crossing there is a man directing traffic and we cross without difficulty. As we leave, I look back to see the crossing attendant running to a truck. At the next crossing the same man directed traffic and hop-skipped the train to every crossing to the Weirs. It took us two and a half hours.

The fireworks were superb.

I didn't go back on the train. Probably that was a smart move. They didn't get back to East Concord 'til midnight.

And every report I've had gives the entire escapade top marks. It was great!

Events of June 21, 1988

Bicentennial of New Hampshire's Ratification of the
United States Constitution

The climax of New Hampshire's bicentennial celebration took place on the date of the state's ratification. The commission planned a day-long series of events plus an evening sit-down dinner on the lawn in front of the state house.

The day-long celebration started with an ecumenical service at St. Paul's Episcopal Church on Park Street just across from the state house. Among the highlights of the day was the morning parade consisting of military and school bands, marching units of military, scouts, and civilian groups, and floats coming from communities across the state. It was sponsored by the American Legion under the direction of M. Ray Olmstead.

Following the parade was a dedication ceremony in Representatives Hall. Participating as the keynote speaker was former chief justice of the U.S. Supreme Court Warren E. Burger, chairman of the National Bicentennial Commission. Throughout the day there were special exhibits, entertainment, craft demonstrations, and educational material available in and around the State House, State Library, and New Hampshire Historical Society Building, while the State Department of Agriculture hosted a special petting zoo for children on the back lawn of the Upham Walker House on Park Street.

Upon the completion of the dedication ceremony in the State House, the U.S. Military Academy Band from West Point entertained from a raised platform at the entrance of the Legislative Office Building. The band consisted of three officers and ninety-six enlisted members and fulfills all of the official musical requirements of the military academy. As the senior premier musical organization of the U.S. Army, it has performed for many historical events. Dr. Hubert Bird of the Keene State College music department composed "The Constitutional Overture" at the request of the band and directed the band while presenting the overture.

Following the band concert, former chief justice Burger led a group of school children in colonial costume with the ringing of the Liberty Bell replica located on a mobile platform at the intersection of Park and State Streets. It was rung thirteen times for the original thirteen states. The authentic Liberty Bell replica weighs 2,080 pounds and was cast in 1975 at the Whitechapel Bell Foundry in London, England, makers of the original Liberty Bell cast in 1752.

Next came the governor's reception, which was designed to thank those individuals and businesses that made contributions to support a fund to be used in New Hampshire for a continuing education program as a lasting memorial to the U.S. Constitution. The state Bicentennial Commission joined with the brokerage firm of Merrill Lynch in sponsoring this effort. Merrill Lynch helped to

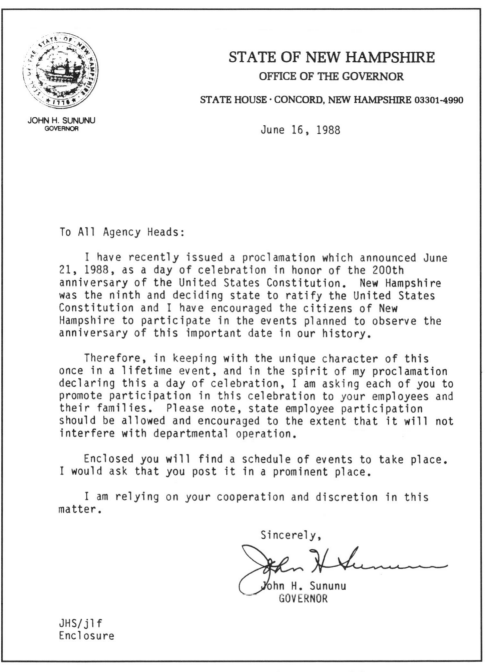

STATE OF NEW HAMPSHIRE

OFFICE OF THE GOVERNOR

STATE HOUSE · CONCORD, NEW HAMPSHIRE 03301-4990

JOHN H. SUNUNU
GOVERNOR

June 16, 1988

To All Agency Heads:

I have recently issued a proclamation which announced June 21, 1988, as a day of celebration in honor of the 200th anniversary of the United States Constitution. New Hampshire was the ninth and deciding state to ratify the United States Constitution and I have encouraged the citizens of New Hampshire to participate in the events planned to observe the anniversary of this important date in our history.

Therefore, in keeping with the unique character of this once in a lifetime event, and in the spirit of my proclamation declaring this a day of celebration, I am asking each of you to promote participation in this celebration to your employees and their families. Please note, state employee participation should be allowed and encouraged to the extent that it will not interfere with departmental operation.

Enclosed you will find a schedule of events to take place. I would ask that you post it in a prominent place.

I am relying on your cooperation and discretion in this matter.

Sincerely,

John H. Sununu
GOVERNOR

JHS/jlf
Enclosure

Letter from Gov. John Sununu allowing state employees to attend festivities on June 21, 1988. Courtesy of the N. H. Bicentennial Commission. (Following page) Map and program for events of June 21, 1988. Courtesy of the N. H. Bicentennial Commission.

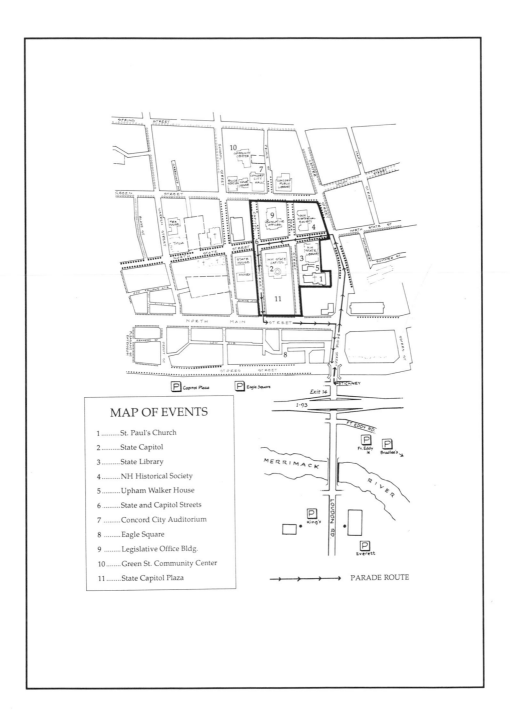

MAP OF EVENTS

1 .... St. Paul's Church
2 .... State Capitol
3 .... State Library
4 .... NH Historical Society
5 .... Upham Walker House
6 .... State and Capitol Streets
7 .... Concord City Auditorium
8 .... Eagle Square
9 .... Legislative Office Bldg.
10 .... Green St. Community Center
11 .... State Capitol Plaza

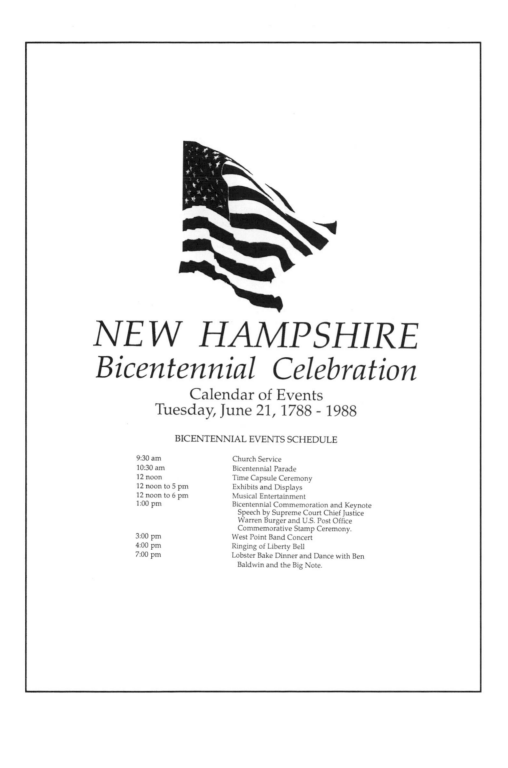

NEW HAMPSHIRE
Bicentennial Celebration
Calendar of Events
Tuesday, June 21, 1788 - 1988

BICENTENNIAL EVENTS SCHEDULE

9:30 am	Church Service
10:30 am	Bicentennial Parade
12 noon	Time Capsule Ceremony
12 noon to 5 pm	Exhibits and Displays
12 noon to 6 pm	Musical Entertainment
1:00 pm	Bicentennial Commemoration and Keynote Speech by Supreme Court Chief Justice Warren Burger and U.S. Post Office Commemorative Stamp Ceremony.
3:00 pm	West Point Band Concert
4:00 pm	Ringing of Liberty Bell
7:00 pm	Lobster Bake Dinner and Dance with Ben Baldwin and the Big Note.

*Invitations (left) hand-drawn by the Honorable Russell C. Chase and (right) R. P. Hale.
Courtesy of the N. H. Bicentennial Commission.*

CONSTITUTION DAY

JUNE 21, 1988 - 9:30 A.M.

St. Paul's Episcopal Church

A New Hampshire Service to Commemorate the 200th
Anniversary of the State's Ratification of the
Constitution of the United States.

Organ Prelude
Opening Hymn 716 "God bless our native land"

America

Opening Sentences and Invocation
The First Lesson: Hebrews 11:8-16
Choral Number: America the Beautiful   Ward
The Second Lesson: Romans 13:1-7
Choral Number: Brothers   Steubing
Address: The Rev. David C. Glendinning, Rector
          St. Paul's Episcopal Church
Litany of Thanksgiving for the Nation, p. 838
A Choral Presentation
     Shennandoah   Spivek
     Battle Hymn of the Republic   Steffe
     Abraham, Martin, and John   Lojeski
     God be with you, 'til we meet again   Tomen
Organ Postlude

+ + +

There will be a concert of tower bells offered by
the Tower Bell Guild of St. Paul's immediately
following the service.

The choral numbers will be presented by the Hopkinton Singers under the direction of Thomas Nerbonne.
Their accompanist is Gail Greenly.

Organ music is provided by Mr. Joseph Chapline,
organist/choir director of St. Paul's Church.

*Program for the ecumenical service at St. Paul's Church on June 21, 1988.
Courtesy of the N. H. Bicentennial Commission.*

Dr. Hubert Bird leading the West Point band in his composition "The Constitutional Overture," June 21, 1988. Photograph courtesy of Russell C. Chase.

fund several bicentennial activities and the lasting memorial. All individuals and firms sending donations were invited to the governor's reception held in the Legislative Office Building.

The grand finale of the day's festivities was a New England lobster bake with all the fixings on the State House lawn. Almost 2,000 New Hampshire residents and their friends took part, with music by Ben Baldwin and the Big Note during dinner and dancing afterwards.

Consumption of the dinner followed the presentation of toasts by six dignitaries using non-alcoholic drink:

Governor John H. Sununu:

"To George Washington and James Madison, and all the framers and ratifiers of the Constitution. May our leaders be guided by their genius, informed by their wisdom, and inspired by their virtue!"

The New Hampshire Bicentennial Commission
on the United States Constitution

and

Governor and Mrs. John H. Sununu

request the honor of your presence

at

A Ratification Celebration

for

"A New Hampshire Legacy"

on

Tuesday, June Twenty-First
Nineteen Hundred and Eighty-Eight
The 200th Anniversary of the Ratification
of the United States Constitution
By New Hampshire, the Ninth and Deciding State to Ratify

Special Guest Chief Justice Warren Burger

Founders' Reception   New England Lobster Bake
Five-Thirty P.M.   Seven P.M.
Legislative Office Building   State House Lawn

Colonial Costume Encouraged

Proceeds to establish "A New Hampshire Legacy," an endowment for Teachers' education and professional development

---

Two hundred years ago, on June 21, 1788, in Concord, New Hampshire, a convention of town delegates voted 57 to 47 in approval of the United States Constitution. Ratification by only nine of the original thirteen states was required for the Constitution to become the law of the land. Our state, New Hampshire, became that ninth state to ratify and in doing so, provided the key vote necessary to create one government of the people from a league of independent and sovereign states. On June 21, 1988, New Hampshire will celebrate the Bicentennial of the U.S. Constitution and our state's casting of the ninth and deciding vote for adoption of our nation's Constitution with **A RATIFICATION CELEBRATION** in Concord.

THE NINTH AND SUFFICIENT PILLAR RAISED

United we Stand, Divided we fall!

DEL • PEN • N JER • GEOR • CON • MASSA • MARY • S CARO • N HAMP

Please join in the celebration of New Hampshire's crucial role in the adoption and evolution of what is now the world's oldest living Constitution by sponsoring the Founders' Reception and Dinner on June twenty-first. By participating as a Founder, Benefactor, or Patron, you will be making an important contribution to our state and our future. Proceeds from this event will establish **A New Hampshire Legacy,** an educational endowment for teachers in New Hampshire to study issues relevant to the Constitution, the Bill of Rights, and our state's history. Ultimately, the beneficiaries of this endowment will be the students in our state, whose teachers will be well versed in techniques for communicating constitutional concepts and state history in their classrooms.

Contributors to the Founders' Reception and Dinner will provide funds for a lasting legacy in New Hampshire to insure that our teachers are equipped to promote interest and understanding of our Constitution and state heritage to each generation of citizens.

Celebrate New Hampshire, the state that made us a nation, on the evening of June twenty-first.

Invitation to the reception and dinner on June 21, 1988.

View of the State House lawn, evening of June 21, 1988, showing bunting on building and tents on lawn for lobster bake dinner. Courtesy of New Hampshire Bicentennial Commission.

Warren Burger:
> "To the rule of law throughout the world. May the protections of the law, wisely interpreted and honestly administered, remain the sturdy guardian of our happiness and well-being."

Russell C. Chase:
> "To the people of the United States and the Constitution which they have preserved for 200 years. May the year, month and day in which it was formed be ever held in grateful remembrance by every true American, and may we in turn pass on this precious heritage of freedom to the many generations of Americans to come.

John P. McMurray, assistant vice president of Merrill Lynch:
> "To the American spirit of enterprise. Two hundred years ago one person making this toast put it this way: 'To agriculture, manufacturing, technol-

Toast makers at the June 21st banquet: (clockwise from upper left) Miss Irene Hart, Gov. John Sununu, John P. McMurray, Christopher Kraybill, and Warren E. Burger around toast-master Russell C. Chase. Courtesy of the N. H. Bicentennial Commission.

State's Vote 200 Years Ago Praised

Burger: NH Made U.S.

By DONN TIBBETTS
State House Bureau Chief

More Stories, Photos on Pages 4, 5

CONCORD — "You in this state made the nation," declared Warren E. Burger, former chief justice of the U.S. Supreme Court.

He said New Hampshire "can and should take great pride in the fact you created the United States in the true sense of a nation."

Burger's comments were the focal point of yesterday's Bicentennial celebration dedication ceremony before a capacity crowd in historic Representative's Hall in the State House. It included the official presentation of a New Hampshire commemorative stamp depicting the Old Man of the Mountain.

A first day of issue album of that stamp was delivered yesterday to President Ronald Reagan at the White House.

The all-day celebration began in the morning with a prayer service at St. Paul Church. It was followed by a parade and was capped in the evening with an old fashioned New England lobster bake under colorful tents pitched on the State House plaza.

Later at a news conference Burger told reporters that if New Hampshire had not ratified the Constitution, making the document operative, the delegates "might have had to go back to the drawing board ... and it could have resulted in a Balkanized country.

"We could have wound up with not necessarily a disaster but certainly the great development of this country could not have occurred if we had not had that ratification 200 years ago today."

The 80-year old Burger, who for almost 16 years was charged with interpretation of the U.S. Constitution as chief justice, began his address by quoting George Mason from the Virginia declaration of rights: "If a free people do not from time to time look back at their freedoms and how they got them, they take the risk of losing them."

"That's why we are here today to look back," said Burger in his 12-minute oration. "The Constitution was the first of its kind in all human history and it has functioned for 200 years and has been copied by other people who wanted freedom and opportunity."

Burger was introduced by Gov. John Sununu, who recalled New Hampshire's key ratification. "New Hampshire not only voted right, it voted first," said Sununu.

William R. Cummings, regional postmaster general, presented the first issue of the New Hampshire commemorative stamp. Dr. Patrick Conley presented first copies of the Bicentennial book containing 13 chapters written by historians from the 13 original states.

Rep. Russell Chase, R-Wolfeboro, chairman of the state Bicentennial Commission, opened the dedication ceremony with the Most Rev. Joseph J. Gerry, O.S.B., delivering the prayer of thanksgiving.

BICENT   **Page 18**

Headline story from the Manchester Union-Leader, *June 22, 1988. Courtesy of the Union Leader Corporation.*

ogy and commerce. May they, in all their branches, flourish unrestricted under the protections of the United States Constitution.' And may we always remember both to guard the rights and to respect the obligations on which our great prosperity depends."

Irene Hart, New Hampshire Retired Teachers Association:
"As Abigail Adams once wrote to her husband, John, and I quote: 'Let us remember the ladies! Their wisdom and dignity, their labor and strength 'have been essential to our nation's success from its earliest days.' May the Constitution's third century bring American women their own golden age of accomplishment, equality and fulfillment."

Christopher Kraybill, president, Concord High School Student Council:
"James Madison and Thomas Jefferson both believed that 'the diffusion of knowledge is the only guardian of true liberty.' I would like to offer a toast, then, not just to learning and education, but to the many thousands of Americans who have marked this anniversary by bringing a fuller appreciation of the Constitution to our communities. May their efforts, and ours, continue long after this historic day."

Announcement of the establishment of the New Hampshire Legacy jointly with the N. H. Humanities Council. Courtesy of the N. H. Bicentennial Commission.

Those who attended some or all of the day's festivities were given a civics lesson and better understood and appreciated their Constitution and system of government. To continue this civics lesson in the spirit of the bicentennial, the commission decided to use the proceeds from the governor's reception and dinner to fund a lasting legacy. The $50,000 fund supports a permanent living legacy to strengthen New Hampshire citizens' constitutional awareness and appreciation by improving the constitutional literacy of teachers in the state. Annual weekly workshops and day-long workshops will better equip teachers to instruct their students on the Constitution and related subjects.

With the completion of the June 21 celebration and the establishment of the legacy, the New Hampshire commission was proud of what it had accomplished. With the guiding hand of Chairman Russell Chase during twenty-five separate commission meetings over a period of four and a half years, it lived up to the mandate given by the legislative resolution of 1981.

As a continuation of this full agenda of celebration, the commission's authority has been extended by the 1989 legislature to allow celebration of the bicentennial of the ratification of the Bill of Rights in 1991.

The bicentennial spawned many local celebrations, including those in Plymouth (left) and Tamworth (below).

Community observances in Orange (right) and Unity (below).

Orford (above) and Landaff (below) celebrate their designation as bicentennial communities.

Chairman Chase (left) hands proclamation to a young rider from the Granite State Morgan Horse Youth Club. Representatives of the group travelled to Philadelphia to participate in the "We the People" celebration in May 1987.

Independence Hall (below) provides an appropriate backdrop for the ceremonies marking the convening of the Philadelphia Convention, May 1987.

Edna Flanagan (left) and Ednapearl Parr with Rex Davis, Dean of Lincolnshire Cathedral, Lincolnshire, England, lender of Magna Carta for a touring exhibit.

(Below) Magna Carta attracted many visitors to the State House, July 1987.

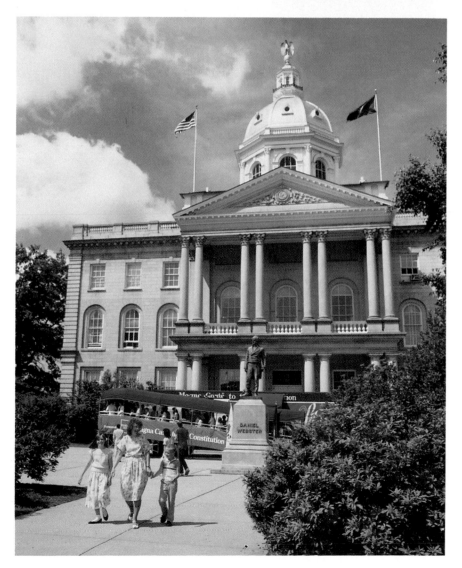

(Top) "After the Revolution: A Collage for Town Voices" reenacted the 1788 ratification conventions at Exeter and Concord in various locations throughout the state.

(Below) Exhibit panels for "Building a Nation, Building a State: New Hampshire, 1780–1800" circulated throughout the state as part of the N. H. Humanities Council's observance of the bicentennial.

Conductor and passengers enjoy the train ride from Concord to the Weirs for the Bicentennial fireworks display September 19, 1987.

Rep. Russell C. Chase, Chairman of the N. H. Bicentennial Commission on the U.S. Constitution, welcomes the June 21st celebrants in Representatives' Hall.

(Above) Two 18th-century gentlemen lead the parade past the Legislative Office Building. (Below) Representatives from each of the 13 original states carrying their state flag.

Bicentennial Parade.

Bicentennial Parade.

(Right) Postal Service employee obliges a customer with a first-day-of-issue cancellation of bicentennial commemorative stamp.

(Below) Bicentennial ecumenical service at St. Paul's Church, Concord, began the June 21st observance on a serious note.

(Left) Chief Justice Burger addresses the gathering in Representatives Hall, June 21, 1988.

(Below) Governor Sununu welcomes bicentennial celebrants.

The West Point Band performs to an appreciative audience.

(Right) Laconia school children ring the Liberty Bell with Chief Justice Burger (right) and Chairman Chase.

(Below) Young spectators, some in costume, line the parade route.

(Left) Governor Sununu chats with W. N. DeWitt, Chairman of the Founders' Committee, N. H. Legacy Program, and Chief Justice Burger at the lobster bake on the State House lawn.

(Below) Bicentennial celebrants eagerly await their servings of lobster.

749

In the House of Representatives Jan.ᵗʰ 25ᵗʰ 1790 –

of the next Session and that in the mean time the Peti:
tioners cause that a Copy of the Petition and order of Court
thereon be posted up in some public place in said Town,
three weeks prior to the sitting of said Court that any person
or persons may then appear and Shew cause if any they
have why the prayer thereof may not be granted, and
that the extent against said Town be stayed until the decision of the General Court ⟶ *Sent up by Mʳ Young*

alteration in the vote appt for Comtee to revise Laws &c   The vote appointing a Committee to Select revise and
arrange the Laws &c – came down from the Honᵇˡᵉ Senate
for the following amendment "That his Excellency the
President be one of the Committee in the room of John Sam
Sherburne Esqʳ – which amendment was read and concurred ⟶   *Sent up by Mʳ Duncan*

allowance to Chap lains ⟶   Voted that the Revᵈ. Doctʳ Haven the Revᵈ Mʳ
Buckminster and the Revᵈ Mʳ Ogden have and receive
out of the Treasury thirty Shillings each for attending
as Chaplains to the General Court the present Session
and that the President give order accordingly ⟶
     Sent up by Mʳ Emerson

Articles of Amendment to Federl Constitution accepted except one   Upon reading and maturely considering the proposed
amendments to the Federal Constitution Voted to accept
the whole of said amendments except the Second Article, which Article was rejected ⟶
     Sent up by Mʳ Copland

Adjourned to 3 oClock P.M – Met accordingly

*Ratification of the Bill of Rights on January 25, 1790, by the N. H. House of
Representatives. Courtesy of the State Archives. Photograph by Bill Finney.*

In Senate, January 20th, 1790. Voted that the General Court which by the Constitution is to meet on the first Wednesday of June next met at Concord in this state, was sent down for concurrence brought up, concurred.

Voted, to accept the whole of the amendments to the Federal Constitution except the first and second Articles which first and second Articles were rejected, was brought up, read and concurred with this Amendment that the second Article only be rejected and that all the other amendments be accepted, sent down, brought up, concurred excepting the following words in the latter part of the Article nor more than one Representative for every five thousand

Voted to accept the report of a committee appointed to receive and examine the accounts of the Board of War and that the President give order for the payment of the ballances, was brought up, read and concurred.

Extract from Senate Journal showing ratification of amendments which became the Bill of Rights. Courtesy of the State Archives. Photograph by Bill Finney.

AFTER THE REVOLUTION:
The Transformation of New Hampshire Towns, 1780–1800

Project Director
Karen Bowden

Project Coordinator
Quentin Blaine

Project Consultant
Stephen Marini

Site Historians

Wilfred Bisson
John W. Durel
John P. Resch
William L. Taylor

Helene-Carol Brown
Frank C. Mevers
Richard Schubart
R. Stuart Wallace

Sponsored by
The New Hampshire Bicentennial Commission on
the U. S. Constitution

Funded by
The New Hampshire Humanities Council
with additional support from
The University System of New Hampshire

Researchers

Patricia Andrews
Mary G. Annichiarico
Margery Arnold
Mal Bisson
Russell Chase
Carol Cole
Norene Cox
Jim Crabtree
Ellen Derby
Ester Fitts
Father Paul Fohlin
Elizabeth Hall
Howard Holt
Patricia Lottero
Lena I. Marchand

Paul Marashio
Robert Mitchell
Mary Pannell
Muriel Robbins
Walter Ryan
Lois Stabler
Barbara Sylvester
Andrew S. Taylor
Stephen D. Thomas
Kay Waterman
Joan Watts
Stephen Winship
A. Louise Wood
Katrina Yanizyn

The Project acknowledges with appreciation the assistance of the following:

Barbara Austen
Carl Bowden
Georgia Barnhill
William Copeley

Stephen L. Cox
Alan Rumrill
Jennifer Stearns

In Committee of Safety, April 16th, 1783.

A PROCLAMATION.

WHEREAS the Form of Government agreed upon by this State, in the year of our LORD one thousand seven hundred and seventy-six, was, (considering the then Situation of Affairs,) established to continue only during the unhappy and unnatural Contest then subsisting with Great-Britain :

AND WHEREAS the *General Assembly* of this State in their last Session, from Information they received, had a promising Prospect of a speedy and happy Termination of those Contests and Establishment of PEACE ; and taking into Consideration the fatal Consequences which might follow from being destitute of a regular Form of Government, did pass a Resolve recommending that the present Government be continued in its full force, till the tenth day of *June*, one thousand seven hundred and eighty-four, notwithstanding a general Pacification should take place in the mean time ; provided a permanent Plan of Government for this State should not be established antecedent to that Period : And it was recommended to the Selectmen of the several Towns and Places in this State to lay said Resolve before the Inhabitants at their next annual Meetings, if received before such Meetings were finished, if not so received, then at Meetings to be called for that purpose, and the Inhabitants were requested to signify, by vote, their Approbation or Disapprobation of continuing the present Government according to said Resolve, and the Clerks of the several Towns and Places were required to certify the same to the *Committee of Safety* on or before the 15th day of *April* then next. Which Returns having been made and carefully examined by the *Committee*, it appears clearly to be the Voice of the Inhabitants of this State, that the present Plan of Government be continued agreeably to said Resolve.

WE THEREFORE HEREBY MAKE KNOWN, That the present *Plan of Government* for this State, is continued in full Force and Effect until the tenth day of *June*, one thousand seven hundred and eighty-four, provided a permanent *Plan of Government* for this State, should not be established antecedent to that Period.

And all Officers, civil and military, and all Persons concerned, are to take Notice hereof, and govern themselves accordingly.

M Weare　　　　　　PRESIDENT.

BY ORDER OF THE COMMITTEE.

J Pearson

Deputy Secretary.

Printed at E X E T E R.

Broadside, April 16, 1783, proclamation of the Committee of Safety signed by President Meshech Weare continuing the "present Plan of Government for the State" to June 1784, at which time a new constitution giving greater recognition to the status of towns took effect. Courtesy of the N. H. Historical Society. Photograph by Bill Finney.

AFTER THE REVOLUTION
The Transformation of New Hampshire Towns, 1780–1800

Karen Bowden

Project Director

"Our government appears at last to be happily settled and every friend to virtue and good order must wish it permanency. I hope that twenty-five years of controversy and revolution will be sufficient for the space of time I have to exist on the globe. Were I to live to the age of Methusaleh, I should not wish to see another such period."

Jeremy Belknap

*A*fter the Revolution" sought to capture the peril and the challenge of the early years of the nation by taking a close look at life in New Hampshire 1780–1800. When the War for Independence ended, the victorious states faced a painful economic crisis: an enormous war debt, severe British sanctions against trade, rampant inflation. At the same time, citizens confronted perplexing political questions: How were the former colonies to govern themselves and establish stability and security? How would those who fought side by side in the war resolve differing ideas about the role of government and the extent and limits of liberty? The project set out to explore the ways in which the citizens of New Hampshire faced these issues, at the same time that they continued the work of building lives and communities.

The years 1780–1800 compel our attention not only because of their inherent interest but also because the period had a lasting and visible effect on the life of this state and its citizens. During this time state and federal constitutions took their essential form and many of the state's institutions—its schools, libraries and churches—were founded. The work of the people of the late eighteenth century also left its mark on the land—in field patterns, the layout of roads and towns, and the architecture of homes, churches and public buildings.

81

Because regional divisions were even stronger in the eighteenth century than they are today, the project undertook studies of eight towns in different areas of the state: the coast, the Merrimack Valley, the central highlands, the Connecticut Valley, and the northern frontier. The sites were selected to reflect not only the geographic range of the state but also the range of sentiment for and against the Constitution.

In observing the Bicentennial with this collection of parallel local histories, the Bicentennial Commission and the New Hampshire Humanities Council acknowledged the strong sense of place and past shared by many residents of New Hampshire. They also recognized that, after long ignoring local history, professional historians have over the past twenty-five years focused great attention on the local, and they drew on the techniques and topics of this "new history" in formulating the approach of the project.

Each study was to explore several related topics: the growth of the town or towns in question in the first twenty-odd years of independence, the impact of independence on the life of its citizens, and, in turn, the role of ordinary citizens in the establishment of state and national governments. An historian was assigned to each of eight sites, and local citizens were invited to participate in research on these communities. Other citizens throughout the state were also encouraged to undertake independent projects on the period 1780–1800. The collection presented here includes seven town studies and a biography of delegate Joshua Morse of Hopkinton. Included in the Appendix is "A Guide to Research in the History of New Hampshire Towns, 1780–1800" which was prepared for use within the project and beyond.

The interplay of geography and history was a dominant factor in the diversity which project scholars recognized in the formulation of the project. In the seventeenth and eighteenth centuries overland travel in the rocky hills and forests of northern New England was arduous. Settlement tended to cluster along the coast and the rivers; in the case of New Hampshire, along the Piscataqua, the Merrimack and the Connecticut. During the seventeenth century the Piscataqua Basin was the only settled area of what was later to become the state of New Hampshire. Not until the beginning of the eighteenth century did settlers move north along the Merrimack and the Connecticut. Because of the threat posed by the on-going French and Indian Wars, this stage of settlement was gradual, and it was not uncommon for fledgling farms and settlements to be abandoned in the face of recurring violence.

After the end of the French and Indian Wars in 1763, interior New Hampshire experienced remarkable growth. An influx of settlers from Massachusetts and Connecticut swelled the population of the towns of the Connecticut and Merrimack river valleys, and for the first time there was significant movement into the interior from both coastal New Hampshire and southern New England. By 1780 the population had increased from 52,700 to 103,129 and the number of incorporated towns had doubled.

When New Hampshire's scattered towns came together to function as a state during the Revolution, there were marked differences among them. Some like Portsmouth were already 150 years old and enjoyed vigorous activity in shipbuilding and commerce. Others, like Conway, were small agricultural or lumbering outposts, in their first generation of settlement and still struggling from harvest to harvest. Roads were few and rough in the extreme, and the great rivers remained the principal avenues of transportation and communication. As a result, many recent and not so recent settlers of inland and upland New Hampshire were tied by geography and history more to Massachusetts and Connecticut, and to their own still isolated regions, than they were to the political entity known as New Hampshire.

Until a generally acceptable state constitution evolved—and even beyond—politics reinforced geographical and historical divisions. Political domination by the long settled seacoast had alienated old and new settlers to the west and north, and the 1779 State Constitution, which was promoted by the growing towns of the Merrimack watershed, met opposition from the seacoast and the Connecticut. So great was resentment along the Connecticut that between 1779 and 1782 thirty-six towns attempted to secede from New Hampshire to join the newly forming state of Vermont. In some towns, there were two competing town governments, one with allegiance to Vermont and one with allegiance to New Hampshire.

Before examining more closely the interplay of local, state, and national issues and events as it is revealed in the studies collected here, we must of course take note of the differences among the studies themselves. Although the research teams began with the same set of questions, additional factors shaped their work, the range and quality of surviving records prime among them. A town like Portsmouth, with a long history and diverse economy and population, affords a remarkable range of records: three local newspapers, letters, diaries, histories written within memory of the late eighteenth century, as well as town, church, and court records. For Moultonborough, on the other hand, there are town and proprietors' records but little more. We must also bear in mind that the abilities, limitations, and biases of record-keepers necessarily influenced the accuracy and fullness of the accounts we receive. While today's historians strive for accuracy, their work is also influenced by their interests, experience, and methodologies. Each must decide the reliability and significance of the written record, and interpretations inevitably differ.

The several studies provide a sense of the sweep of events and movements in the last twenty years of the eighteenth century; at the same time they demonstrate the power of local concerns and problems. A fundamental reality for every town except Portsmouth and Exeter was rapid population growth, a continuation of the immigration which began in the 1760s. Between 1775 and 1800 the central New Hampshire towns of Concord, Hopkinton and Peterborough grew between fifty and seventy percent. On the frontier, Conway and Moultonborough doubled their populations to around 500. The southwest experienced the most striking growth: Keene increased its population by ninety percent to about 1,300. Chesterfield's population in 1800 was 1,915, an increase of 120%; Westmoreland's increased by 150% to 2,018.

Of all the challenges which faced the citizens of the newly independent state and its rapidly growing communities, the most dangerous were economic. During the war the New Hampshire economy was reassuringly brisk, but personal and public debt began to grow. Many towns struggled to meet their share of cash and goods to support the war, and accumulated debt which would take years to liquidate. Gold and silver became scarce, and the economy came to be based on highly unstable paper money issued by the continental government and by the several states. The war's end brought further hardship. The British restricted trade by American ships in British ports, and they completely prohibited American participation in the lucrative West Indies trade. Depression ensued, debt grew, specie became scarcer, and inflation prevailed. So great were the fear and anger of farmers from western Rockingham and Hillsborough counties that in 1786 they stormed the legislature in Exeter to demand the issuance of paper money.

Because Portsmouth was a port with a diverse, cash-based maritime economy, it appears to have suffered acutely from the depression of the 1780s. John Durel's essay draws on a wide range of sources, including eyewitness accounts by a number of foreign visitors, to describe the impact of the virtual cessation of trade on the mariners, tradesmen, and artisans of Portsmouth's riverfront neighborhoods. He also suggests, however, that the very age of the town and the relative complexity of its political and social structure maintained stability at a time when unrest was rife in several parts of inland New Hampshire. The town government's provision for the poor, well-established churches, and the memory of a once-vigorous economy seem to have sustained the town until a combination of factors, including the establishment of a strong central government, brought an economic revival in the 1790s.

There is evidence that the depression and inflation also had considerable impact on the Keene area. The contrast with Portsmouth is indeed telling. Wilfred Bisson's research reveals mob action against a money-lender, numerous prosecutions for counterfeiting and for fraudulent use of promissory notes and other financial instruments, as well as many suits by creditors against debtors. He notes that these transgressions were probably prompted by the postwar depres-

RICHARDSON's Tavern,
At the Sign of the United States
Arms ; KEENE :

		£.	s.	d.
1	Lodging,		0 ·	4
3	Meals,		3	
1	Horse-Keeping,		1	
	Oats,			
	Toddy,			
	Flip,			
	Punch,			
	Wine,		1	
	Gin,			
			5 · ·	4

Invoice from Richardson's Tavern, Keene, c. 1788. Courtesy of the State Archives. Photograph by Bill Finney.

sion, but he also argues that the violence and lawlessness with which at least some citizens responded to these difficult times was nothing new to Keene and its surrounding towns. Bisson characterizes the 1770s and early 1780s as disorderly times in which a rapid influx of new settlers, difficulty in reestablishing local authority after the expulsion of the British, and confusion and disorder of the Vermont controversy combined to frustrate the establishment of community.

The impact of the war and postwar depression is harder to gauge in frontier communities because most rural economies were still in large part agricultural and subsistence-based. Life was bound to be hard in upland towns like Moultonborough, Wolfeboro, and Conway as residents cleared land and built their farms, dependent on their own labor and health and the vicissitudes of crops and weather. Helene-Carol Brown's study makes clear that the process of becoming a community was slowed by the difficult economic climate. In Conway any surplus which might have gone to meetinghouses, schools and roads went to support the war and, later, to pay war debts.

In this context of regional isolation, rapid population growth and economic exigency, it is not surprising that the Constitution proved so controversial. Proponents engineered an adjournment at the February convention in Exeter when they confirmed their suspicions that the Antifederalists were in the majority. At the Concord convention the following June, the Constitution was approved by only ten votes.

Town records tend to be spare, and the records of local debates on the Constitution are no exception. There are no minutes, and typically we learn only something of the mechanism of decision and the decision itself. Portsmouth town records, for example, list only the names of those nominated to be delegates and the votes they received. There is no indication as to whether the document itself was discussed or debated, and no vote for or against ratification. From newspaper reports and from letters as well as from the final vote at Concord, we know that Portsmouth was strongly Federalist. Moultonborough, Wolfeboro, Ossipee and Tuftonboro, classed together, referred the Constitution to a committee which recommended in favor of ratification; the towns sent Nathaniel Shannon as a delegate without instructions; at the convention he voted aye. Peterborough also appointed a committee to study the document, and that committee recommended against ratification. Delegate Nathan Dix attended the Exeter convention but appears not to have made the trip to Concord. Conway, Eaton, Burton and Locations elected David Page as their representative, and then appointed a committee to write his instructions. The committee bound Page to vote nay: "As we find a great many good things in the proposed Constitution blended with what we cannot approve, and as there is not to be any alterations to be made in said Constitution, we Desire you to do all in your power to hinder the Establishment thereof."

The debate on the ratification of the Federal Constitution was of course embedded in the ongoing debate over the New Hampshire Constitution. Four different proposals were considered between 1779 and 1783, and dissatisfaction with the resulting document brought numerous changes in 1792. Because towns often voted provision by provision the records of these debates reveal much more about local thinking on constitutional questions than do records of the 1788 debates. Peterborough's support of the 1779 Constitution, which accorded primary authority to towns, and its rejection of the 1781 and 1782 plans, which strengthened state government, are at the heart of John Resch's analysis of the town's political culture. Resch makes understandable Peterborough's opposition to the Federal Constitution by illuminating the aspirations and principles of the town's Presbyterian founders, who in 1788 were still struggling to build a self-governing, self-sufficient agricultural community united in Calvinist belief. Indeed, adherence to this idea of community, which guided the settlement of New England from the seventeenth century, appears to have been a critical element in the Antifederalism of many New Hampshire towns, particularly the first and second generation towns of the Merrimack Valley and its adjacent highland.

As a group, the towns studied reflect the range of opinion on the proposed government, with six for, four against. They also fall within the regional pattern described by Jere Daniell in the essay which opens this volume. Coastal Portsmouth and Exeter, historically at ease with power and with much to gain from the regularization of commerce, voted for ratification, as did Moultonborough-Wolfeboro, frontier communities with historical ties to the coast. Concord and Peterborough, with most of their neighboring towns along the Merrimack and in the highland to the west, opposed the Constitution, much in keeping with their historical resentment of coastal power and their advocacy of local control. Conway's opposition may have been influenced by its ties to Concord and other communities in central New Hampshire as well as by the frustrations of raising scarce resources for a still remote state government. The towns of the southwestern corner of the state discussed by Bisson reflect the heterogeneity of the region. Chesterfield was Antifederalist. Keene, Walpole and Westmoreland voted in favor of ratification at Concord, although the latter two originally instructed their delegates to vote against.

Although New Hampshire towns divided almost equally for and against the proposed Constitution, it appears that in many cases there was little dissension at the local level, whether prevailing opinion was for or against ratification. Recorded votes reveal a strong majority, and in a number of cases unanimity. The fact that so many towns depended on committees and that two-thirds sent delegates without explicit instruction suggests both strong local consensus and high degree of trust, at least among the enfranchised. In towns like Exeter and Portsmouth ratification seems to have been a foregone conclusion. In others the decision proved more difficult, though it did not necessarily involve significant disagreement among the citizenry. Hopkinton first bound Joshua Morse to vote against, but just before the Concord convention the town meeting freed him: "to act as he should think best for the Public Good." There were, of course, exceptions. Bitter political manouvering resulted in contested elections in Walpole, as

☞ *THE NINTH AND SUFFICIENT PILLAR RAISED.* ☜

Graphic notice of ratification in the New Hampshire Gazette and General Advertiser *of June 26, 1788. Courtesy of the N. H. Historical Society.*

well as in Boscawen and Newington. An Antifederalist and a Federalist delegate from each of these towns presented themselves to the convention's membership committee; in each case, though by different means, the Federalist was seated.

Overall the towns of New Hampshire matured in this process of creating their state and national governments. When first confronted with the task, many were skeptical of the value of the enterprise. In 1779 Wolfeboro, like many towns, decided not to send a delegate to the constitutional convention, "presuming that the expense there will be greater than present circumstances of the town will afford, or even any advantages that are likely to arise from such a choice." In 1782 even fewer towns sent delegates than in 1779. In 1788 all but six towns participated, certainly moved by a sense of occasion but encouraged as well by the legislature's wise provision of an allowance for delegates to the convention.

Not surprisingly, our researchers found local records to be dominated by ecclesiastical issues and problems. The minister and meetinghouse of the established Congregational or, in a few cases, Presbyterian order were at the heart of every New Hampshire town in the seventeenth and eighteenth centuries, and provincial and, later, state law authorized the provision of tax money to their support. During the late eighteenth century a number of factors frustrated those attempting to implement this traditional pattern of community life. Internal theological differences between "Old Lights" and more evangelical "New Lights" within Presbyterianism and Congregationalism and a shortage of Congregational ministers were major factors. So too was the rise of a range of dissenting groups including Separate Baptists, Freewill Baptists, Methodists, Shakers, Universalists, and "Christians," the latter led by New Hampshire native Elias Smith.

The studies examine the impact of these ecclesiastical questions and problems and they suggest the role of religious change in the evolution of the state and its communities. Some of the problems were of course practical and economic. Most towns found it difficult to raise sufficient ministerial taxes in the postwar depression, and many were affected by the shortage of ministers. Concord spent six years seeking a successor to Timothy Walker who had provided moral, spiritual, and even political guidance for nearly fifty years. The Rev. Israel Evans who was hired in 1787 did not suit the community, however, and left after four years. Only in 1797 did Concord finally settle a satisfactory successor. Conway spent five years seeking a minister; the story of efforts to build and then to finish its meetinghouse covers nearly twenty years.

Some towns became embroiled in their ecclesiastical problems. Moultonborough and Peterborough both experienced consuming disputes centered on the minister. In Moultonborough the town divided against itself, with the majority refusing to settle the Rev. David Perley who was appointed by an Ecclesiastical Council and approved by a small but eager group of church members. Though the majority's objections were in part theological, the strength of feeling was fueled by anger at the want of democracy in the appointment process. In Peterborough the conflict was between the town and its ministers. The dispute with the Rev. John Morrison was a bitter but brief affair which took place just before the Revolution. Morrison's successor, David Annan, stayed on for ten years but was accused in meetings and various petitions to the Eastward Presbytery of triviality, drunkenness, and extorting land from the town. The conflict, which only exacerbated underlying differences between Old Lights and New Lights within the community, was intense and encompassing. John Resch speculates that the town did not send a delegate to the Concord convention because in the spring of 1788 the long battle with Annan was finally reaching its climax.

Hopkinton with its Separate Baptists, Wolfeboro with its Freewill Baptists, and Portsmouth with its Universalists and Sandemanians and the Keene area with its "Shaking Quakers," Baptists, Methodists and Universalists provide instances of the coming of new religious denominations. Although Congregationalists in Hopkinton and Portsmouth expressed concern over members and ministerial taxes lost, and though Wolfeboro took action by seizing Thomas Cotton's cow, the process of religious diversification in most of these

Display of documents produced by the State Archives for exhibition with Magna Carta in 1987. Courtesy of the State Archives. Photograph by Bill Finney.

communities seems far less bitter than the internal struggles which seized Moultonborough and Peterborough. In southwestern New Hampshire, where vacant pulpits and an atmosphere of disorder invited new sects seeking converts, the story was rather different. Religious dissent, particularly by the advent of the "shaking quakers," simply added to the already contentious atmosphere.

Stephen Thomas's biography of Joshua Morse follows religious revolution into the early nineteenth century, and provides a longer view of this process. Separate Baptists were already established in Hopkinton when Morse settled in 1772, and as a deacon of the Congregational church and a town official Morse dealt directly with the established church's loss of members and revenue. Thomas detects no bitterness or regret in the eventual incorporation of the Hopkinton Congregational Society as a private entity. Thomas' work, taken with the several other studies, suggests that the Toleration Act of 1819, which separated the town and the church throughout New Hampshire, resulted from a long, sometimes painful, but nonetheless inevitable process of social and religious diversification.

By the 1790s this diversification was underway, and an economic recovery was beginning which would further transform local society and culture. Though the war brought several years of hardship, it both forced and allowed Americans to become independent economically: to manufacture locally and to take charge of commerce. Once the postwar depression ended, local enterprise flourished and local economies became increasingly diverse.

Farming was still a central occupation in inland and upland New Hampshire. Many farms provided only subsistence, but productivity was slowly increasing. Between 1778 and 1797, tillage, mowing and pasture in Wolfeboro increased from 1,128 acres to 1,492 acres and orchard land from none to fifteen acres. At the same time access to markets was also improving. John Resch notes that Peterborough shifted to a market economy during the '90s, and Helene-Carol Brown describes Conway's dogged efforts to open roads to distant markets.

Even this early, however, New Englanders were admitting the difficulty of farming their rocky terrain and many were moving west to New York and beyond. Many, too, were entering trades, professions, and the beginnings of manufacturing. In Keene and Exeter, a range of water-powered industries grew up, and in Walpole, Keene and Concord central commercial districts developed, composed of stores, shops and offices. Merchants, artisans and professionals built their homes in these centers, and their Federal-style houses serve as a reminder that the New Hampshire town as we know it developed during the early years of the republic.

By 1800 the several communities studied were more different from each other than they had been twenty years before. Some remained primarily agricultural; others were transformed from small farming communities to bustling villages. Once knit by a common occupation and common religious beliefs and practices, citizens of towns like Concord, Keene and Walpole were now tied in many different ways: through trade or commerce; in fraternal and professional organizations; in a range of religious organizations, through newspapers. At the same time all seem to have become more prosperous and better able to meet communal goals: witness the completion of the meetinghouse in Conway and Wolfeboro, the numerous public improvements made in Portsmouth, and the increased attention to schools everywhere.

An important aspect of local growth was the development of a network of roads, turnpikes and bridges to unite once isolated communities. Some of these were community projects as was the case in Conway, but many turnpikes and bridges were private ventures. Recognizing the benefit to local trade and to their effort to make their town the state capital, citizens of Concord were particularly enterprising, investing in the Concord and Federal bridges as well as in the First New Hampshire Turnpike. Such efforts had political as well as economic impact. Some, like Governor Josiah Bartlett, argued that improved transportation was essential to the young state's efforts to overcome its historical disunity: "The advantage of good roads...is so great, that it is worthy your consideration whether the expense that will accrue will not be greatly overbalanced by the advantages...in giving citizens a better opportunity of being acquainted with the publick affairs of the state, and more effectually uniting them in one common interest."

The struggle to unite the citizens of New Hampshire in one common interest is, of course, ongoing. Within the state's towns and cities the work of building and sustaining community continues. Despite improvements in transportation and communication unimaginable in 1800, geography and history continue to shape the political culture of the state. New Hampshire's rivers, hills and mountains still enforce a strong sense of region and of place. Home rule is still a fiercely protected principle and practice, and questions of local versus state or federal power are subjected to lively ongoing debate in a discourse which first found voice in the War for Independence and in subsequent constitutional debates.

* * *

The essays collected here constitute just one aspect of "After the Revolution: New Hampshire and the New Nation, 1780–1800." A conference, exhibit, play, and speakers' bureau brought the work of the project researchers and other scholars of early American history and culture to the people of New Hampshire.

On January 26, 1985, more than 250 people gathered at the State House for the project's opening event, a day of lectures and workshops on sources and methods in the study of New Hampshire in the early republic. One year later, on February 4, 1986, once again at the State House, the Commission unveiled a fourteen-panel traveling exhibit, "Building A Nation, Building A State: New Hampshire, 1780–1800" and "After the Revolution: A Collage for Town Voices," a play by David J. Magidson. The exhibit combined reproductions of documents, broadsides, newspapers, maps, woodcuts, portraits and other artifacts to illustrate the tasks and achievements of the last two decades of the eighteenth century. The play, written for an ensemble of readers, focused on the Constitution by dramatizing New Hampshire's bitterly argued ratification debates.

Overview of Portsmouth, c. 1770, sketch from Joseph F. DesBarres: The Atlantic Neptune *(London 1780) of Portsmouth from an island in the Piscataqua. Courtesy of the N. H. Historical Society.*

The play and exhibit, complemented by a speakers' bureau, traveled to six communities in 1986. In recognition of the achievement of "After the Revolution," the National Endowment for the Humanities in 1987 awarded the New Hampshire Humanities Council an Exemplary Grant for "The Ninth State," a project which extended the tour of the play and exhibit, expanded the speakers' bureau and added two new elements: a symposium to observe September 17, 1987, the bicentennial of the completion of the Constitution and "The Constitutional Courier," a twenty-part newspaper series by Charles E. Clark on the way New Hampshire's five newspapers reported and commented on the events and issues of 1787–1788.

"The Ninth State" conducted more than ninety activities in forty-three towns over a two-year period. The resources of the project have been incor-

Exhibit panels for "Building a Nation, Building a State: New Hampshire, 1780–1800" circulated throughout the state as part of the N. H. Humanities Council's observance of the bicentennial. Courtesy of the N. H. Humanities Council.

ported into the Humanities Council's Programming Service for use in schools, libraries, historical societies, and other public settings. After the Revolution: A Collage for Town Voices was published by Peter Randall for the Bicentennial Commission in 1987. The "Constitutional Courier," introduced and expanded by Charles Clark, was published in 1989 by the Humanities Council as *Printers, the People, and Politics: The New Hampshire Press and Ratification.*

In addition to the site historians and researchers listed just ahead of this introduction, several others deserve recognition. The exhibit was designed by Susan Hamilton of Phineas Press, constructed by Thomas Greene, and mounted by William Hamilton. Edith Notman and Charles Coombs served as artistic directors of the play's inaugural tour; Marya Danihel was musical director. Susan Goldin and

Douglas Tilton, Jr., were its tireless producers. The cast, which was drawn from the Keene, Plymouth, and Durham campuses of the University of New Hampshire, included David Burland, Joseph Carlisle, Anthony Ejarque, Mark McKenna, John Seymour, Matthew Sheahan, Ruben Sierra, Carroll Tolman and Cathy Walker.

Etta Madden ably directed the varied activities of "The Ninth State" and Charles Bickford, Executive Director of the New Hampshire Humanities Council, oversaw the several years of humanities programming which New Hampshire enjoyed in observance of the Bicentennial

John Langdon (1741–1819) portrait by Edward Savage. A Portsmouth native and merchant, Langdon made a fortune in shipping during and after the Revolution. Active in politics, he served in the Continental Congress and was a strong supporter of the Constitution, having served as one of two New Hampshire delegates to the Philadelphia Convention in 1787. He was also one of three Portsmouth citizens chosen to represent the town at the state's ratifying convention. Courtesy of the Society for the Preservation of New England Antiquities.

PORTSMOUTH AFTER THE REVOLUTION

John W. Durel

Baltimore City Life Museums

*I*n August 1787 John Langdon, while in Philadelphia participating in the drafting of a new constitution for the United States, received a letter from his friend Eleazer Russell of Portsmouth:

> We are here in peace and plenty, waiting with ardent expectation the result of matters. To me there appears an agreeable humor in the people this way, to accept the plan that may be offered by a group of politicians whose abilities and integrity shine resplendent.

Deference to political leaders, as expressed by Russell, was a hallmark of the established view of social order in eighteenth century America.

Langdon was without question a leader. His courage and savvy during the Revolution had propelled him into a position of prominence. He had been in the vanguard of the group of local residents that on December 14, 1774, confronted the contingent of British forces at Fort William and Mary in New Castle, capturing gunpowder later used by the Americans at the battle of Bunker Hill. Following that incident the young Langdon—he was in his thirties—represented New Hampshire in the Continental Congress in 1775 and later supervised construction of ships in Portsmouth for the new Continental Navy. He emerged from the war a popular leader, serving at various times as speaker of the House and as president and governor of the state.

Thus Langdon was a natural choice to represent New Hampshire in Philadelphia. However, our concern is not so much with Langdon as it is with the community from which he came. Russell's letter suggests that Portsmouth enjoyed "peace and plenty" at the time and that her citizens were content to accept what the leaders of society offered. This essay will attempt to assess the accuracy of Russell's view.

In one sense, Portsmouth after the Revolution suffered from old age. Its

John Pickering (1737–1805) miniature portrait by unknown artist. One of three Portsmouth delegates to the convention, Pickering was trained in both theology and the law. At the time of his selection he was a state senator; subsequently he became chief justice of the Superior Court, serving until he lost possession of his faculties and was impeached. Courtesy of the N. H. Historical Society.

history stretched back over a century and a half to a small settlement called Strawbery Banke. The fields and pastures that were part of that settlement became, by the early eighteenth century, the site of a small seaport town with streets and wharves, houses and warehouses. By the 1780s the town was becoming a city, and the streets, wharves and buildings were showing signs of wear.

As early as the 1760s inhabitants had begun to distinguish between the "compact part of town" and the "outskirts." A map of the region published about 1770 shows that the two areas were clearly distinct. Open farmland spread to the south and west. As the Marquis de Chastellux wrote in his *Travels in North America* in the 1780s, "this country presents, in every respect, the picture of Abundance and Happiness. The road from Greenland to Portsmouth is wide and beautiful, interspersed with habitations...." Another traveler, Jacques Brissot de Warville, noted that "all the children I met along this road and in general in New Hampshire seemed to be in good health; they were plump and had healthy complexions, good color, and blond hair...."

This open, healthy countryside contracts sharply with the crowded conditions found within Portsmouth. Brissot left the plump children on the farms to find "a good number of women and children in rags" in a town where "everything show[ed] signs of being in a state of decline." Narrow, unpaved streets and old, dilapidated houses cast a dreary complexion on the place. Francisco de Miranda, yet another visitor, asserted in his *The New Democracy in America* that Portsmouth had "the saddest appearance one can imagine."

Almost all of the houses were built of wood, and many were then very old. The town had taken shape nearly a century earlier, at the end of the pre-Georgian period of architecture. By mid-century these early houses, many of them with steeply pitched, multi-gabled roofs, leaded casement windows, and exposed interior beams were decidedly old-fashioned. By the eighties even some of the Georgian houses, built in the 1740s or earlier, were becoming old. The major streets were only twenty-four to thirty feet wide, adequate for a small town but a problem for a growing city. By the 1790s there were local ordinances against blocking streets and alleys with carts, chaises, cordwood or rubbish. The smaller streets were irregular and crooked, often making passage from one part of town to another very difficult. All but one of the streets were unpaved, adding dirt and discomfort to the general inconvenience of travel.

Narrow streets and old wooden buildings raised fears of fire. More than once in the 1780s the inhabitants instructed the firewards to "see that no old ruinous Buildings be suffer'd to stand, which may expose the Town to fire...." Crowded conditions also gave rise to concerns over health. The practice of slaughtering animals within the compact part of town, open drains running through streets, the existence of numerous privies, including some with overflowing vaults, and the dependence on wells for drinking water combined to make dysentary and other diseases a serious threat. These conditions may have contributed to an unusually high fatality rate in September 1783, when the minister of the North Church recorded the deaths of seventeen children, more than in all the other months of that year combined. Such a tragedy doubtless con-

Foreshadowing their affirmative votes at the convention, this certificate for the Portsmouth delegates authorizes them to represent the town "for the Purpose of taking into consideration, and adopting" the Constitution. Courtesy of the State Archives. Photograph by Bill Finney.

tributed to the sense of depression about which contemporary travelers to Portsmouth commented.

Wartime and postwar economic conditions compounded the problems of overcrowding and old age faced by Portsmouth in the 1780s. The outbreak of hostilities had disrupted the normal course of overseas trade, which was the basis of the town's economy. Portsmouth merchant vessels bound for foreign ports fell prey to British warships, bringing financial loss to local merchants and danger to mariners. George Nelson's *History of the Custom Service* claims that in 1780 the

British captured nearly seven of every eight vessels sailing from Portsmouth. This loss of trade was offset to some degree by the practice of privateering, which began early in the war and continued until the surrender of General Cornwallis at Yorktown in 1781. Almost every issue of the *New Hampshire Gazette* during 1780 and 1781 reported British ships being brought into port by privateers, and their contents offered at public sale. These "valuable prizes laden with wine, rum, loaf and brown sugar, molasses, English goods, etc." kept many Portsmouth stores stocked and many Portsmouth mariners employed.

Far more detrimental to the local economy was rapid inflation and falling confidence in the paper money issued by the Continental Congress and the state. A merchant whose wealth was tied up in goods could withstand the onslaught of inflation, for as the value of currency fell his prices rose. But a person who earned a living by providing a service, and who was paid either with paper money or bills of credit, was especially vulnerable to rising prices. A shilling earned one day would not buy a shilling's worth of goods the next. On several occasions the town sought to control this problem by freezing prices of food and other commodities.

The unstable economy increasingly drove the most vulnerable people onto the rolls of the Overseers of the Poor. George Walton, in his old age, was one such victim. Walton had been a tanner and shopkeeper, and at one time had had sizeable landholdings within the town. By the late 1770s he still owned a parcel large enough to be divided into four house lots, but the sale of these did not yield enough to see him through his final years. In 1780 he gave the remainder of his property to the town in exchange for a place in the almshouse.

Portsmouth had to deal not only with its own poor but also with people from neighboring towns and from the Isles of Shoals who came to the port in search of employment or assistance. They were "no little burden" for the town which, in 1777, sought help from the state. By 1780 the number seeking assistance drove the Overseers to place a notice in the *Gazette* appealing to the indigent to go into the country "where they may find work." The situation was dire enough to cause the inhabitants, at a town meeting in April 1782, to agree not to spend money to illuminate the town when official word of peace arrived. Instead, they voted to use the money for the relief of the poor. Yet, when word of the peace treaty finally came a year later, in April 1783, the townspeople celebrated with church services, gun salutes, and illuminations at the State House and North Meetinghouse. The problems of the poor had not disappeared, but the joy of the moment overrode such chronic concerns. The celebration was but a brief respite from a mundane existence.

In this place, which Miranda described as sad and lonely, John Langdon built one of the finest Georgian mansions in America. While many struggled to survive during the postwar years, Langdon thrived. He had emerged from the war not only a popular leader but also a wealthy man, owing largely to privateering ventures. The Marquis de Chastellux described the house and the man thus:

> After dinner we went to drink tea with Mr. Langdon. He is a handsome man, and of noble carriage; he has been a member of Congress, and is now one of the first people of the country; his house is elegant and well furnished, and the apartments admirably well wainscotted.

In his elegant house Langdon entertained friends, acquaintances, and strangers who arrived with letters of introduction. This was the role of a man whose reputation extended far beyond the bounds of his home town. The Spanish envoy Miranda also recorded his visit at the Langdon mansion:

> After dinner, Mr. Langdon visited me and invited me for tea at his house. So I went forth, and Mrs. Langdon received me with great affability and attention. With some company that had gathered there, I spent the evening in society until eleven o'clock when I retired to the tavern.

The next day Miranda went to dine with the Langdons at two o'clock and again stayed until eleven.

Langdon's good fortune contrasts sharply with the lot of those on relief. Most Portsmouth residents, however, lived between these extremes of wealth and poverty, each coping with the economic distress of the times. Although the travel accounts which have come down to us do not record visits with such "middle class" people, historians can reconstruct their lifestyles through other means. We can enter the home of Mary Bettingham through the aid of a probate inventory. The elderly widow, whose husband had been a mariner, lived in half of an old dwelling on Buck Street, just a few blocks from Langdon's house. Her belongings were notable only for their age and poor condition. They included "6 Flag Bottom'd Chairs much worn," "1 old fashioned looking glass," and "5 old China Bowls some of them Cracked." Indeed, more than half of the items on her household inventory were characterized as old, worn or broken. Yet she was not destitute. She owned the half-dwelling where she lived, and amidst her old possessions could be found three gold rings and a pair of earrings. Unlike George Walton, Mary Bettingham was able to hold on to some of the treasures she had won over the course of her life.

Young Jack Wheelwright was not so fortunate. During the war he and his sister were raised by his father's mother; his own mother had died when he was very young. His father, a sea captain, was directly affected by the conflict. In September 1775 Captain Wheelwright sailed out of Portsmouth on the brig *Abigail,* bound for the West Indies, just as he had done eight times before. But this time the British seized his vessel and took it into Boston. Later, he was selected as an officer for the Continental ship *Raleigh* but became frustrated with the slow progress toward completing the ship. By 1776 he was master of the privateer Reprisal out of Boston, and thereafter he served on at least two other privateers.

In the fall of 1780 Captain Wheelwright's mother died, leaving him without someone to care for his children. In January 1781 he married Martha Davis. Eight-year-old Jack now had a twenty-two-year-old stepmother. At the end of the war Wheelwright resumed his former livelihood, as master of the ship *Hero*. In 1784, during his second voyage to Grenada, he died at sea. There is circumstantial evidence that Jack, then about eleven years old, was with his father on that final voyage.

Before the war Wheelwright had been in the top twenty percent of Portsmouth taxpayers; by its end he had fallen to the lowest forty percent. When he died he was heavily in debt, owing in excess of £400 to twenty-seven creditors. His young widow was forced to sell their house, which brought only £195. Jack was placed in the care of his maternal uncle. The boy had descended from a family that was neither wealthy nor poor. Both his grandfather and grandmother had been coopers and owned several properties in Portsmouth. His father had been well respected, described by Langdon as "an Excellent Master." Yet the younger Wheelwright in 1784 received no inheritance. He left Portsmouth and does not appear again in the records until April 18, 1790, when he died by accidental drowning in Newburyport, Massachusetts.

A third Portsmouth inhabitant fared far better. Cuff Whipple had been taken from his home in Guinea at the age of seven in 1767. His master, Joseph Whipple, a leading patriot, gave Cuff his freedom after the Revolution. In all probability Cuff remained in Joseph's employ, but as a paid servant rather than as a slave. In 1786 he married Rebecca Daverson, and over the next twenty years they had at least eight children. They became members of the South Parish Congregational Church and lived for many years as respected members of the community.

The different fortunes of a black man, an elderly widow, and an orphan reflect the heterogeneity of the Portsmouth population which, by the eighties, numbered 5,000 individuals. There were some very rich people, and some very poor, with many more in between. The faltering economy affected all, but the degree to which one suffered depended upon situation and circumstance.

If we follow the political activities of the town through the 1780s we find no sign of a crisis in government. Fifteen years earlier there had been a crisis, when, from 1766 to 1771, many people refused to serve as Overseers of the Poor. At the time the town was providing inadequate funding for relief, and many overseers found that they had to draw on personal wealth to help the poor. But, when economic distress was the major problem, there was no wholesale refusal to serve. Portsmouth's system of relief dated to the 1750s when the town constructed a

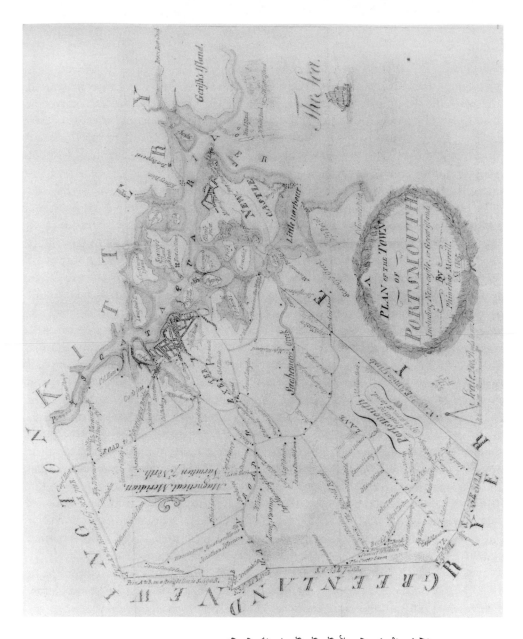

Plan of Portsmouth "including New Castle or Great Island," one of several town plans drawn by Phinehas Merrill in 1805 as part of the survey of towns mandated by the legislature. Courtesy of the State Archives. Photograph by Bill Finney.

workhouse. There had been an earlier almshouse, and also relief had been given to people cared for in private homes. But the prevailing emphasis was on providing work for the poor to alleviate the cost of relief. The precise nature of the work is not clear, but in 1785 the town appointed a committee to determine what was necessary to "furnish supplies to the workhouse...at the cheapest rates," and to make repairs that were "absolutely necessary" to the thirty-year-old structure. Not surprisingly the solution required an increase in taxes.

While poor relief was a major expense, so was education. The 1784 town meeting appointed a committee "to visit the public schools and enquire into methods practiced in them, to advise the masters to make such alterations as may be thought necessary, and to recommend and order such books to be used in the several schools as shall be judged best...." At the time there appears to have been four publicly supported schools in Portsmouth: a Latin school for boys, an English grammar school for girls, and two seasonal schools on the outskirts of town, one to the north and one to the west.

Also of concern and expense was road repair. As has been noted above, the streets were becoming overburdened with traffic. Ruts and poor drainage made passage extremely difficult at times. Each year the town allocated money for road repair, and allowed those who could not pay their taxes to meet the obligation by working on a road crew.

Roads, schools, and the poor were the major local concerns of Portsmouth inhabitants during the eighties. They approached these issues as a matter of course, using traditional methods. For example, the committee to evaluate the schools consisted of three wealthy men, one of them John Langdon's brother Woodbury, and the ministers of the North and South Congregational churches. The natural leaders of society were playing their proper roles, and the rest of the people accepted them.

Although there were no confrontations with authority in the political sphere in the 1780s, there were challenges to the established churches. The North and South Congregational churches had split from a single congregation in 1712, and although there were disputes at the time and for two decades afterwards, by 1780 the two coexisted peacefully. Together they claimed 449 ratepayers, or about 53% of all Portsmouth ratepayers. The South Parish was larger, with 266 contributing supporters; but the North Parish was wealthier, with 183 supporters raising about 25% more than the South Parish each year.

The community acknowledged the ministers of both parishes as leaders, not only in the spiritual sense but also, to some degree, in temporal matters. Samuel Haven, minister to the South Parish since 1752, had gained a reputation for his "plain, serious, and practical" sermons. The younger Joseph Buckminster, who had come to the North Parish in 1779, impressed the Frenchman Chastellux by the way "he introduced politics into his sermon, by comparing the

Christians redeemed by the blood of Jesus Christ, but still compelled to fight against the flesh and sin, to the thirteen United States...." Both ministers knew well Portsmouth's politicians: two of the delegates to the state convention on the Federal Constitution in 1788 were members of the South Parish; the other, Langdon, was a member of the North. These two parishes dominated the religious life of the town, but they were not alone. As a population center Portsmouth had long supported diverse points of view. By 1780 there were at least three other religious societies practicing there.

The Anglican Church had stood on Chapel Street since 1732, had kept a low profile during the war, and had gone for many years without a minister before engaging John C. Ogden from New Haven, Connecticut, in 1786. To the disappointment of many, Ogden proved "well meaning but erratic," made many enemies, and resigned under pressure after six years.

In 1757 twelve dissident members of the South Parish remonstrated against Dr. Haven, claiming that the minister's preaching encouraged "in a generall way" the notion that salvation depended upon one's behavior and not strictly on divine election. Other members of both the South and North parishes soon joined the twelve to form a third society, the Independent Congregational Church. By 1761 the congregation was large enough to purchase a lot on Pitt Street, move an old meetinghouse onto it, and engage Samuel Drown of Bristol, Rhode Island, as minister. After Drown's death in 1770 the Church went without a minister for many years. Joseph Walton, a cooper and elder of the Church, led the services until in 1789 the Church ordained him "without a Council or any other assistance."

A few years after the founding of the Independent Congregational Church Robert Sandeman, the leader of a small Scottish sect, arrived in Portsmouth. He apparently preached in all three Congregational churches, but soon ran into opposition. In 1765 he established a Sandemanian Society, with sixteen male and nine female members. Although the other ministers criticized Sandeman, there was no active persecution under the belief that persecution would only strengthen the resolve of the dissidents. The Sandemanian Society, small but active, survived into the 1790s.

These five churches made up the formally organized religious population of Portsmouth in 1780. Their existence established a general acceptance of pluralism in the town. For example, Langdon, who was a member of the North Parish, also supported and sometimes attended services at the Independent Church. He bequeathed money to both institutions in his will.

In the 1780s the two major parishes faced challenges on two fronts: decreasing financial support; and the formation of another sect in town. As the war came to a close, both the North and South Parishes increased the amount of money to be raised from members. However, as the reality of the post war depression set in, each parish experienced a steady decline in support. Taking 1782 as base year, over a ten year period North Parish support fell by 35% and South Parish by 49%. Both parishes raised funds through pew rentals and poll taxes. They sometimes had trouble collecting the money that had been assessed of members. At various times both parishes addressed the problem of delinquency of members.

The Reverend Buckminster's salary fluctuated with the amount of money raised, going from £135 in 1781 up to £195 in 1782, and down to £120 yearly plus incidentals such as a load of hay and pasturage for his horse. In 1791 his salary became an issue, forcing him to complain in a letter to his parishioners about the lack of punctuality in paying him. Dr. Haven's yearly salary remained at £93.6.8 throughout the period, and he too had trouble collecting it. In 1793 South Parish took pews away from delinquent members and sold the pews in order to settle its account with the minister. The parish owed him £210.6.11, more than two years' worth of salary.

After 1792, as Portsmouth's economy improved, North Parish income rose considerably. However, the money raised by the South Parish remained low. In the North Parish throughout the 1780s the number of people assessed for support remained about the same; it was the amount of assessment that declined. In the South Parish on the other hand, both the number of supporters and the amount given by each declined. By 1790 there were only 167 individuals assessed by the South Parish, a drop of ninety-nine people in ten years.

Some of these people had become Universalists. Local followers of John Murray, an itinerant preacher who had first visited Portsmouth in 1773, organized a Universalist Society in 1784. According to historian Stephen Marini, Murray's "forceful leadership and strict moral code provided a strong institutional framework for converts," and had a particular appeal for people in urban areas. Records of the North Parish show that in 1785 the church summoned one of its members, William Ham, Jr., who had become interested in the Universalists. Ham "appeared very obstinate and obstinately set against all attempts of the Church to recover him." The parish then voted to excommunicate him.

Not everyone saw Universalism as a serious threat. The Marquis de Chastellux noted that among people he talked with it formed "rather a subject of conversation, or even pleasantry, than a matter of dispute." Dr. Haven apparently tolerated the new sect. For example, he baptized eight children of Peter Coues between 1790 and 1797, even though Coues had served as moderator and held other offices in the Universalist Society since its beginning. The Universalists did not have their own ordained minister until 1799, so Coues turned to Haven for the sacrament, and Haven complied. It may be that Haven's tolerance worked against him, driving some of his parishioners to the more conservative Independent Church while he permitted others to become Universalists. For whatever reason, he saw his church's annual income cut in half and membership drop by a third.

The challenge that Haven faced was symptomatic of a time of economic distress and religious change. But neither the poor economy nor the appearance of the Universalists had an impact on Portsmouth's government. The challenge to a particular minister or doctrine was not a challenge to the authority of leaders like John Langdon.

Recall Eleazer Russell's letter to Langdon in the summer of 1787: "We are here in peace and plenty, waiting with ardent expectation the result of matters." Portsmouth was peaceful, but only a few people enjoyed plenty. Most were worse off than they had been before the Revolution. Russell went on to write that the people were inclined to accept a new plan of government, that they would readily support the work of able and honest politicians. Perhaps he was attempting to ingratiate himself with Langdon and, indeed, a few years later he became a Federal customs agent thanks to Langdon's patronage. Regardless of his motive, there was truth in what he said.

In spite of the diversity of wealth and of religious views, the vast majority—merchants and mariners, housewives and artisans, the elderly and the young—all depended upon a healthy overseas trade for their well-being. Langdon was convinced that the United States needed a strong central government to regulate commerce, and that once such regulations were in place and enforced, prosperity would return. Fortunately, his fellow citizens, his constituents, shared this view.

The degree to which the people agreed with Langdon is evident in the way they responded to the new Constitution's ratification in June 1788. They celebrated with a procession through the principal streets of town, organizing themselves by occupation. First came men employed in agriculture: husbandmen and laborers carrying the tools of reaping, threshing, mowing and haymaking. Then came those in maritime related occupations: sea captains, seamen, caulkers, riggers, blockmakers, and so forth. Next were other urban tradesmen: bakers, tallow-chandlers, hatters, and wheelwrights, to name only a few. Following the artisans came merchants and storekeepers, schoolchildren and teachers, the clergy and physicians, and finally politicians and office holders.

One observer, Nathaniel Adams, recorded that the organization by occupation was "intended to represent that in consequence of this union [brought about by the ratification of the Constitution], commerce, and all the arts dependant on it, would revive and flourish." The most elaborate report and commentary on the parade was printed in *The New Hampshire Gazette and Weekly Advertiser* on June 26, 1788. Clearly Portsmouth's citizens recognized their common dependence on trade and saw the Constitution as primarily a measure to improve the economy.

In time their hopes were realized. In the 1790s prosperity returned, greater than they had known before. Capital flowed in, enabling them to repair old houses and build new ones; to put in sidewalks and an underground aqueduct system; to construct a new pier, hotel and market house; and to make repairs to church buildings and schoolhouses. In short, they were able to address the problems that had plagued them earlier. Even poverty, which did not completely disappear, became less visible and less of a general concern.

The 1780s had been a difficult decade for Portsmouth. Economic hardship had touched most people. Perhaps, in an indirect way, the hardship had led some to reject established religious views. But there was no challenge to political authority. On the contrary, the poor economy appears to have brought people together, making them aware of their mutual dependence. Portsmouth—poor and lonely on one hand, rich and elegant on the other—came through the years after the Revolution without violence, united in its support for leaders like Langdon, and determined to overcome economic adversity and to regain the wealth it had once known.

John Phillips (1719–1795) portrait by Joseph Steward, 1794–1796. A native of Andover, Massachusetts and a Harvard graduate, Phillips settled in Exeter by 1740 where he was, successively, teacher, preacher, and merchant. Financially successful in both business and matrimony, his philanthropies were many including Dartmouth College and Phillips Andover Academy. Much of his fortune went to establish Phillips Exeter Academy and provide it with an endowment to underwrite scholarships. Courtesy of the Hood Museum of Art, Dartmouth College, Hanover.

EXETER AND THE NEW REPUBLIC, 1638–1788

Richard D. Schubart

Phillips Exeter Academy

$\mathcal{T}$he successful ratification of the Constitution in Concord on June 21, 1788, symbolized the gradual eclipse of Exeter's special prominence in the early colonial and revolutionary periods of New Hampshire's history. Though Exeter would continue to grow as a relatively prosperous town and retain importance as the county seat of Rockingham County throughout the nineteenth and twentieth centuries, its political stature was diminished with the moving of the capital westward.

By the time of the ratification in 1788 Exeter had already been in existence for 150 years as one of the three or four earliest permanent settlements in New Hampshire. The town was settled by John Wheelwright, a heretical minister who dared to back the case of his sister-in-law, Anne Hutchinson, against the ministerial hierarchy of Massachusetts Bay Governor John Winthrop. For his own advocacy Wheelwright was censored and banished from the Bay Colony, and with two dozen followers set out to found a new Puritan utopia well to the north of Boston.

On November 7, 1637, Wheelwright was formally disenfranchised, and he began to gather a group of supporters and supplies together in time for a hard winter excursion in a packet boat around Cape Cod and up the Massachusetts-New Hampshire coast to Portsmouth Harbor. Though no firsthand evidence is extant to provide the detail of his voyage, we speculate that his committed band survived the onslaught of winter in shelters established by Edward Hilton along the Piscataqua River about halfway between Dover and Portsmouth.

With the spring thaw, Wheelwright made his way down the Piscataqua through the Great Bay and down the Squamscot River until it reached the fall line where the tidal Squamscot meets the freshwater Exeter River. With several members of his party from Exeter, England—the furthest fortified city in the southwest of England, founded by William the Conqueror—Wheelwright decided to lay claim to this fortuitous spot by making treaty with the local Indians on April 3, 1638.

The original area has been estimated to be about thirty square miles surrounding the falls that took in the area of the present-day towns of Newmarket, Newfields, Brentwood, Epping and Fremont as well as Exeter. Here about 175 persons led by thirty-five heads of households proceeded to erect a settlement that ultimately survived conflicting rule and Indian attacks in the eighteenth century, prospered economically in the nineteenth century, and continues to know strong growth at the end of the twentieth century.

The primary advantages that enabled the successful growth—tidal transportation back to the open Atlantic through Great Bay; available water power on the fall line at the nexus of the Exeter and Squamscot Rivers; fresh water supply; saltmarsh hay; open meadows; a ready-made source of freshwater and saltwater fish as well as game; and great stands of tall white pines—are a tribute to Wheelwright's original choice of location.

Exeter's early development also owed something to John Wheelwright's original vision of a puritan community free of external authority from Massachusetts Bay. Wheelwright supplied the operating form of government under divine guidance with the Exeter Combination which was signed by thirty-five "freemen" of Exeter, and which proclaimed Exeter as an independent republic. The government consisted of three elders who had judicial and executive functions, chosen by the whole body of freemen who served as a legislative body.

The government functioned sufficiently well to create a roughly co-equal distribution of marsh, meadowland and wooded lots to each inhabitant, along with making regulations for effective pasturing of animals and lumbering of surrounding forests. The first homes were grouped along the west side of the river near the site of Wheelwright's first meetinghouse and church. The settlers busied themselves raising cattle and swine, making barrel staves and shakes, planting and fishing, and operating a grist mill.

In the meantime, however, as the early prosperity of Exeter attracted more settlers beyond those who made up Wheelwright's original compact, a certain dissatisfaction grew about the founder's vision. Particularly, questions arose as to whether Wheelwright's pact with God was sufficient to protect the settlement from Indian attacks. Several citizens therefore petitioned Massachusetts Bay to exert its jurisdiction over the town as it had earlier with Hampton, Dover and Portsmouth. This was done in 1643, whereupon John Wheelwright and a number of his followers voluntarily exiled themselves rather than submit to external authority.

The first major step forward economically was made in 1647 with the arrival of Edward Gilman, Jr., who was given a special grant of land to establish a sawmill. The lumber hewn from this water-powered mill would provide for enhanced building construction throughout the town, and would lead to Exeter's becoming a site of significant shipbuilding, in addition to providing an early example of successful entrepreneurship to others. Lumbermen who emulated Gilman's example would create such a demand on the majestic white pines that surrounded Exeter that an inevitable conflict of interest grew between local settlers and British agents who saw the main value of the straight and strong white pines in tall masts to be reserved for His Majesty's Royal Navy.

Though Edward Gilman, Jr., was lost at sea six years later, his father and brothers who had followed him to Exeter survived and prospered as lumbermen, shipbuilders and merchants. Together they laid the foundation for the most prominent political family in the future of the town. The Gilmans would provide much of the leadership of the town, state and region in the colonial, revolutionary and early national periods of American history.

A major change in Exeter's government came in 1680 when Charles II created the Royal Province of New Hampshire. Charles apparently hoped to weaken the growth of independent power in Massachusetts Bay as well as reward the loyal heirs of John Mason who held the original land patents in New Hampshire. This move was strongly opposed by local settlers and landowners. When Governor Edward Cranfield dissolved the Provincial Assembly, suspended several councilors, and raised rents and taxes, he was met with pitched resistance including a group of Exeter men and women who threatened the tax agents with scalding water if they persisted in their appointed rounds.

Though Governor Cranfield finally gave up his crude campaign to obtain local subservience and went home, the Crown was not through with its attempts to exert greater control. In 1686 Charles's successor, James II, established the Dominion of New England in an attempt to bring regulatory order out of local anarchy. New Hampshire was a primary target of this renewed effort at central authority in the colonies but the experiment was short-lived. The Dominion collapsed in 1689 with word of the Glorious Revolution and the opening of the reign of William and Mary.

Exeter resumed its governmental autonomy for a few years, then again became part of Massachusetts and finally a formal part of the Royal Province of New Hampshire in 1692. Throughout this period of governmental confusion, the town continued to realize a slow but steady increase in both population and economic prosperity. For seven years following Wheelwright's withdrawal the town was unsuccessful in attracting a ministerial replacement, but in 1650 Samuel Dudley arrived in Exeter's pulpit. Dudley was extremely popular and had an impact locally similar to that of the Gilman clan in the political realm. Dudley, like Gilman, operated a sawmill in addition to his ministry, and contributed to the town's financial as well as its spiritual well-being. Not surprisingly, then, the population grew apace from 300 in 1670 to about 600 in 1700.

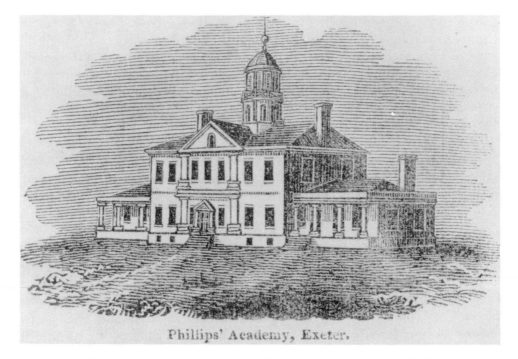

An early 19th century woodcut of the building that originally housed Phillips Exeter Academy. Courtesy of the N. H. Historical Society.

Although the population figures are not precise, substantial growth is reflected in the fact that the old meetinghouse was enlarged three times and finally replaced entirely in 1696 by a new and much larger building in a more central location on Front Street, near the present location of the Congregational Church. Similarly, the lumber from the old meetinghouse was used to construct a combined townhouse and courthouse building. Shortly thereafter, in 1707, Exeter voted to erect its first school building. As population increased in the outlying areas of Exeter, the inhabitants began to resent being taxed for support of ministerial and civic institutions that they rarely encountered or drew upon in person. The result was that, beginning in 1727, Newmarket, Epping and Brentwood formed separate parishes and towns as well.

Meanwhile, the original Exeter church split into two distinct parishes when the spiritual revival known as the Great Awakening reached Exeter in the 1730s. Many of the faithful were particularly influenced by the "fire and brimstone" preaching of George Whitefield who gave his last sermon in Exeter in 1770, shortly before his death. The converts to Whitefield's religious rhetoric in 1743 established their "new light" church, which included some of the town's most prominent leaders, in a building further up Front Street from the old parish.

There can be no mistaking the evidence in the first half of the eighteenth century of an increased readiness to resist the tendency of royal authority to interfere in local affairs. When what some historians have called the first significant colonial resistance to British imperial policy came to a head in the Mast Pine Riot of 1734, a group of Exeter men dressed as Indians roughed up ten agents of the King's Surveyor who was trying to reclaim valuable white pine boards and trees that were to be reserved for the Royal Navy.

The Mast Pine demonstration set a precedent for the Exeter citizenry to become prominent participants in virtually every other colonial protest over English rule and taxation. Matters grew increasingly heated after the Stamp Act, the passage of the Townshend Acts, and the Boston Massacre. While the city of Portsmouth was directly under the control of the Royal Governor with his troops situated in Fort William and Mary at the mouth of the harbor, Exeter was far enough down the Great Bay to be at a substantial distance from direct exertion of authority. Thus it was no accident that the revolutionary movement in the years from 1765 to 1783 was centered in the town of Exeter or that a number of its most prominent citizens became leaders in New Hampshire's rebellion.

When the Provincial Assembly appointed a Committee of Correspondence to coordinate New Hampshire opposition to the British closing of the port of Boston and the other "Intolerable Acts" of 1774, the Assembly was dissolved by Gov. John Wentworth. Finding itself unable to meet in the Portsmouth assembly rooms, the Assembly then reconstituted itself as the First Provincial Congress of New Hampshire and met in Exeter on July 21, 1774. Subsequently, Exeter men took the lead in the first military action against the British government in December 1774 when they forcibly removed the powder and cannon from Fort William and Mary.

Over the next year, from January to December 1775, the Second, Third, and Fourth Provincial Congresses met in Exeter to continue an alternative government to that of the Royal Governor and his councilors meeting in Portsmouth. When Governor Wentworth fled on board a British man-of-war in Portsmouth harbor in August 1775, the Fourth Provincial Congress asked advice from the Continental Congress in setting up a new government. As a result, New Hampshire drafted the first written state constitution which was adopted by the Fifth Provincial Congress meeting in Exeter on January 5, 1776. Five months later, on June 11, 1776, a joint committee of the Assembly met and adopted a declaration of independence from the British Empire nearly a full month before the rest of the nation.

The result of all this activity was that Exeter became the revolutionary capital of the state—state as well as local government continued to meet in the old townhouse downtown until 1782, when many of the sessions were moved to Concord. When the assembly was not in session the Exeter Committee of Public

Safety essentially ran the affairs of the new state. Moreover, all of New Hampshire's military endeavors during the Revolutionary War were managed from Exeter. Exeter's Nicholas Gilman, Sr., was State Treasurer from 1776 to 1783 coordinating New Hampshire financial contributions to the Revolution, while his son, Nicholas Gilman, Jr., led the state militia and later joined General George Washington's staff.

In the immediate aftermath of the war, Exeter was at the height of its political prominence though sessions of the General Court met alternately at Concord, Portsmouth, and elsewhere. That stature was enhanced further with the founding of Phillips Exeter Academy in 1781 by prominent Exeter merchant John Phillips.

Phillips was concerned that an educational institution be established that would express the new spirit of democracy in welcoming "youth from every quarter" even as it provided an education in both "knowledge and goodness" to future generations of leaders for the new American Republic. Using his own fortune to underwrite an endowment of some $60,000, John Phillips insured that for at least the first few generations there would be no tuition charge for any qualified student.

But if Exeter was enjoying considerable fame and fortune with the conclusion of hostilities and signing of the Peace of Paris in 1783, conditions inland and upland in the state were not as prosperous. Paper money that was issued by both state and local agencies during the war years produced a ruinous inflation that depreciated the currency so rapidly the General Court reestablished gold and silver as the only legal tender. However, the shortage of specie was so pronounced that large numbers of people, particularly farmers and debtors, began to clamor for the reissue of paper money. Unable to pay mortgage notes and fearing foreclosure on their farmland and property, farmers gathered into a mob in 1786 and marched on the General Court meeting in Exeter.

Though the paper money riot was quickly dispersed by a group of militia led by Nicholas Gilman, Jr., it was all too reminiscent of the much more severe uprising known as Shays Rebellion centered in Springfield, Massachusetts, which lasted for much of a year and with far more violence. It was these sorts of events together with other dislocations experienced under the Articles of Confederation that caused many to believe that a constitutional convention was necessary to plan for a more perfect form of union. When New Hampshire received the call to the Philadelphia Convention for May 1787 the General Court was in no hurry to send delegates as a result of monetary shortages and some suspicion as to the nature of the proposed proceedings.

Exeter was thrust into the limelight when the New Hampshire ratifying convention met in February 1788 to consider the new framework of government. But when it became evident that approximately two-thirds of the assembled delegates had definite instructions from their towns to vote against the proposed Constitution, Federalist proponents led by John Sullivan moved quickly for an adjournment, to reassemble at a future date in Concord. Though many of the most prominent Federalists like Madison, Knox and Washington were stunned by the turn of events in Exeter, it gave them added urgency to insure their lines of communication and organization were strengthened so as to leave little or nothing to chance the next time. Even then, the vote in Concord in favor of ratification of the new Constitution was by the slim margin of 57 to 47.

Though the first President of the United States, Revolutionary War hero, George Washington, came through Exeter in 1789 as part of a major trip to the states of both the northeast and southeast as a way of thanking the American people for their support in establishing the new republic, Exeter would not thereafter equal its initial political prominence.

Still the population and economic growth continued apace such that by the time of Exeter's 150th birthday in the spring of 1788 the town's population had increased to about 1,800 people. The lumber and mast trades had fallen off severely during the war, but thereafter the economy diversified into a number of new manufacturing areas including powder, paper, grist, and nails. This, plus more farming and animal husbandry, strengthened the resources of the local economy and made for greater resilience. In addition, Exeter became a thriving publishing center for both newspapers and books, as well as a banking center.

Over the next century diversification continued through the establishment of a major pottery works, a duck (sailcloth) factory, tanneries, saddlery, carriage manufacturers, hats, boots and shoes along with the Brass Works, the Exeter Machine Works, and the Exeter Manufacturing Company, all of which used water power. In politics Exeter continued to have some influence on the state and regional level as an important county seat of the most populous county in New Hampshire.

Petition to the legislature dated December 19, 1771, signed by John Sullivan as attorney "to Sundry of the Inhabitants of Peterborough," protesting the Rev. John Morrison's conduct, and "praying that they might be Set at Liberty to ordain & Support another Minister." Courtesy of the State Archives. Photograph by Bill Finney.

PETERBOROUGH AFTER THE REVOLUTION

John P. Resch

University of New Hampshire at Manchester

On January 28, 1788, the town of Peterborough "voted to reject the plan of government wholy as it now stands" and directed Nathan Dix to cast the town's vote against ratification of the Federal Constitution in the state convention. Peterborough's rejection of the proposed Constitution was part of widespread opposition to the new form of government among New Hampshire towns. In February of 1788 opponents nearly succeeded in rejecting the Constitution at the convention held in Exeter but were thwarted by supporters who adjourned the meeting before the vote was taken. When the meeting reconvened in Concord in June, Peterborough was one of four towns whose delegates did not return. "The people apparently felt," the town historian wrote years later, "that their action in January was final."

Peterborough's actions raise two questions: why did the town oppose ratification; and, why did Peterborough fail to send a delegate to the June convention to cast its vote against ratification. Answers to these questions lie deep within the character of the community and the substantial changes affecting it after the Revolution. The first part of the following account of Peterborough is intended to sketch the demographic, religious and economic character of the town from its founding to 1800 and the changes it underwent. These changes will serve as a context for examining the political culture of the community and the conditions which affected both its rejection of the Constitution and its apparent indifference toward its passage.

Peterborough was founded in 1738 by four speculators seeking profits from frontier development. They purchased the township from fifty Concord, Massachusetts, residents who fronted for them. The Massachusetts General Court had originally granted the township because the Concord residents "were all eager to leave the old home town and improve the wilderness for the public good." The proprietors surveyed the tract, divided it into ranges of 100-acre lots, split the lots among themselves, staked themselves to 500-acre farms of choice land, and promoted the sale of the rest. They attracted settlers through low prices for land and homestead agreements which guaranteed title to a 50-acre lot to anyone who built a house and raised a crop within five years of the agreements. Proprietors speculated that once the town's frontier was broken the demand for their land would subsequently increase its price. The investment turned out to be risky, however, for only a few people arrived, and in the 1740s the town was deserted because of its vulnerability to Indian raids.

In 1750, with the Indian threat removed, the proprietors promoted resettlement. They attracted young couples starting families and seeking economic independence by carving out homesteads. During the 1750s about fifty families settled in the town. Three quarters of Peterborough's inhabitants were under thirty years of age, half of them less than seventeen years old.

Despite their similarities in age and household composition, substantial differences existed among Peterborough's settlers. They varied in wealth: some of them being sons of well-to-do farmers; others apparently landless husbandmen or artisans anxious to homestead frontier land; and still others who were recent immigrants wanting to purchase inexpensive land. Three examples illustrate these differences. In the 1750s Samuel Miller of Londonderry purchased four Peterborough farms for his sons. Backed by their father, the four boys settled and assumed a prominent role in building the community. William Scott, on the other hand, was a homesteader who appeared to have little money and no backing. In the 1740s the proprietors promised Scott one hundred acres if he settled a family, built a house, and cultivated six acres. John Ferguson falls somewhere between the wealthy Millers and homesteader Scott. In the mid-1730s Ferguson immigrated from Ireland to Lunenburg, Massachusetts, where he took up "temporary residence." He purchased land in Peterborough at bargain prices and was among those who strived to settle in the 1740s. By 1750, after some fifteen years of temporary residence in Lunenburg, Ferguson returned to Peterborough with his wife and six children to re-establish his farm.

Settlers varied in background. One group, amounting to possibly a third of the settlers, appears to have been recent Scotch-Irish immigrants who lived more or less as transients moving back and forth between northern Massachusetts towns and Peterborough. They do not appear to have been deeply embedded in the communities where they resided while waiting to move to the frontier even though that temporary residence may have lasted for a decade or more. Another third came from Londonderry, New Hampshire, transplants from an established Scotch-Irish community which was founded in 1719. They carried the cultural baggage of a community which was deeply divided by religious differences. In 1739 Londonderry split into two parishes—"Old Light" Presbyterianism and

View of New Ipswich, 1850. Charles Barrett house at left. Courtesy of the New Hampshire Historical Society.

"New Light" Evangelicalism. "This unhappy division," the town historian noted, "continued for nearly forty years [and] was productive of evils long felt in the town, occasioning alienation of feeling, and often bitter animosities between members of these two religious societies." Since members of both groups settled in Peterborough, the town became a satellite of the religious conflict dividing Londonderry. Although the "Old Lights" prevailed in Peterborough, an undercurrent of religious dissent remained, emerging in the 1780s and 1790s to challenge the town church.

These differences produced neither a town nor a community but an aggregation of recent Scotch-Irish immigrants and young families from Londonderry engaged in subsistence farming. They faced the dual task of building a town and establishing a cohesive society. They accomplished the first in 1760 when they cast off the proprietors, incorporated the town, and assumed direct responsibility for self-governance. The community came later.

Between 1760 and 1790 marriage helped knit the aggregation into a cohesive society. By 1800, population growth and shifts in population structure eroded some of this cohesiveness and a more fluid and pluralistic society replaced the frontier community knit together by kinship. The population grew from 443 in 1767 to 1,333 in 1800 with a large portion of that growth having occurred after 1790. Around 1800 Peterborough's population stabilized at

5 June 1786

State of New hampshire } To the Honourable General Court of said State to be convened on the first wednesday of June next

Humbly Shews ⁂

The Subscribers inhabitants, of the Town of Londonderry in the County of Rockingham in said State; that your petitioners labours under many and very great difficulties on account of the great scearsity of a circulateing medium of trade; Also great uneasiness has arisen in the minds of your petitioners and manny others on account of a claim lately made to the uncultivated lands within this state; and as your Honours are the Guardians, of the rights and privilidges, of the people; and as we have no other regular way of redress, than by applying to you, therefore we Humbly request that your Honours, would take our case under your wise consideration and grant us relief by acting on the following Particulars. ⁂

1st. That you would not allow those Parsons purchasers of the Allen claim so called any part of their claim within this state. ⁂

2ly. That not any of those persons that are purchasers of said Allen's claim hold any commission of profit or Honour within this state for the space of one Year. ⁂

3ly. That the General Court take up the matter respecting the Masonian title, to the certain lands in this state, which we think their title to is not good; and that those lands claim'd by them be converted to the use of said state. ⁂

4ly. That there be a bank of paper Money made to redeem this States securaty. ⁂

5ly. That the General Court petition Congress to redeem the Continental paper currency that is in the Treasury in this state; the same being more than our proportion of the same. ⁂

6ly. That the Ports and Harbours in this state be opend and a free trade for all except the refugees. ⁂

Petition to the legislature dated June 5, 1786, from residents of Londonderry requesting protection of title to Masonian property and relief from the scarcity of paper money. Courtesy of the State Archives.

around 1,500 until into the 1820s. Growth occured through natural increase and settlement. Households in 1800 contained an average of six children, a third of the families having seven to nine children.

The town attracted many new families and lost a few. Federal censuses for 1790 and 1800 and local tax data for 1792 reveal more gain than loss. Analysis of the household heads appearing in the 1800 census indicate the presence of three distinct population strata. About a quarter were those who had been among the founders or early families of the town. About a third represented new families. The remaining 40% consisted of sons of household heads in the 1790 census. By 1800 the second generation of residents and the newcomers dominated the town's population structure.

Genealogical data provide another view of the shifts in age structure. From 1750 to 1770 the town remained a youthful community with the average age of a resident being 19, while the median age was 15, and more than 80% of the population was under 31. In 1770 the proportion of people under 31 composed nearly 77% of the population, a slight drop from the 1750 figure of 82.4%. Apparently the town was filling with more young families whose ages compensated for the aging of original settlers thus continuing to give the town an overall youthful character. From 1770 to 1790 the age structure shifted upward, the average and median ages jumping to 25 and 22 years respectively. The proportion of children under 10 dropped from 36% in 1750 to 26% in 1790. By 1790 the proportion of people 30 and under had fallen to 66% from 82% in 1750. By 1800 the share of 30 and under dropped further, to 60.9%. In summary, the period 1770–1800, witnessed a rapid population growth, a fundamental shift from founders to sons, the departure of many families for greener pastures, the migration of large numbers of people to the town, and a change in the age structure from a youthful to a more mature community.

These demographic shifts undoubtedly affected religious developments in the town. For most of this period Peterborough's religious life was one of constant turmoil. The town suffered from a vacuum in religious leadership because of a shortage of ministers and because of local contentions. The town quarrelled with and dismissed two ministers, John Morrison and David Annan, for various reasons prior to settling Elijah Dunbar in 1799. The vacuum weakened the authority of the town's founders and the doctrinal grip of "Old Light" Presbyterianism. In the late 1780s and 1790s younger men challenged that authority. By 1799, as a more fluid and pluralistic society replaced a community knit together by kinship, the struggle over church polity ended. Congregationalism replaced "Old Light" Presbyterianism; the religious preferences of the younger men and newcomers superseded those of the founders.

Efforts to create a stable church appeared to occupy more of the town's attention than political questions. As in other communities, Peterborough's town and church affairs were interwoven. Selecting a minister was probably a community's most important decision. The minister was expected to be the town's moral and spiritual guardian. In spite of its frontier position and the contention between old and new persuasions, the town, in 1766, settled the Rev. John Morrison, a twenty-three-year-old graduate of the University of Edinburgh who had arrived in Boston the previous year. Peterborough was his first pulpit.

In 1767 Morrison married Sarah Ferguson, daughter of John Ferguson mentioned above. Morrison lost favor in the town, was accused of swearing, drunkeness and lewd behaviour, and in 1771 the town appealed to the Londonderry Presbytery to relieve Morrison on charges of misconduct. The Presbytery advised the town to compromise with Morrison. But the town was adamant and in December petitioned the General Court for authorization to dissolve its agreement with Morrison. The Legislature rejected the petition on grounds that it was an ecclesiastic rather than a civil issue. The town prevailed for the following March Morrison resigned and left town without his family. He returned in 1775 to join the militia during the seige of Boston but deserted to the British during the battle of Bunker Hill. He died in 1782 still in British service. At Peterborough's request the General Court banished Morrison from the state thereby entitling the town to confiscate the ministerial property given to him by the community.

The town relied on itinerant ministers until David Annan, aged 24, accepted the call to its pulpit in 1778. Annan had left his native Scotland in boyhood, had graduated from Rutgers, and had followed his brother, Robert, who was then in the pulpit of Boston's Federal Street Church, into the ministry. In 1782 Annan married into the family of John Smith which extended to a clan of Morisons (no relation to the former minister), Moores, Mitchells and Ritchies, all of whom figured prominently in the community. By 1788 Annan's relationship with his in-laws had deteriorated to the point that church elders drew up charges against him which were presented that spring and summer as the political battle over passage of the Federal Constitution ensued.

The accusations against Annan revealed a deep and bitter controversy. He was charged with drunkeness, lack of preparation of sermons, unbecoming mannerisms, and attempted extortion of land from the town. The last involved two 50-acre lots to which the town denied Annan's claim. When Peterborough petitioned the Londonderry Presbytery to censure him, Annan left his pulpit, but did not resign until 1792. He tried to make a living as an itinerant minister. His situation deteriorated, and in 1800 the Londonderry Presbytery dismissed him from the ministry for intemperance, for abuse of his family, and for dishonor to religion in general. In 1801 he returned to Scotland where he died the following year.

The Morrison and Annan ministries help to illuminate the changes experienced by Peterborough during the revolutionary era. Town leaders were committed to a church which upheld traditional Calvinist doctrines and their social/political corollaries which supported local autonomy and rejection of a state established religion. Freedom of religion meant operating the town church according to the will of the majority. Officials had depended on Morrison and Annan to provide the moral leadership necessary to sustain their corporate view of the town. Instead of consensus, harmony and models of deportment which uplifted townsmen toward a greater accord with Christian ideals, the community was beset with drunken, lewd and grasping ministers who embroiled themselves in political and family quarrels. The ministerial failures were casting increasing doubt on the leadership capacity of the founders by the late 1780s.

For much of the period Peterborough was rudderless without a minister which encouraged division between generations about church polity and doctrine. Against this background the debate of the Federal Constitution took a back seat. The Annan affair in 1788 diverted attention from national politics. Peterborough, in short, was not in Concord to cast its vote against the Constitution apparently because it was wrapped up at home in an ecclesitical struggle which was helping to transform the community.

For the period from 1775 to 1790 Peterborough's political culture can be characterized as parochial, traditional and conservative. That culture included the principles of home rule, deference to men of wealth and piety, the ideal of a community where congregation and society were one, acceptance of the supremacy of God's laws in governing civil society, and a respect for freedom of conscience coupled with a conviction in the righteousness of Presbyterian beliefs. Some of those principles were challenged and defended as townsmen approved the 1779 State Constitution and rejected the proposed State Constitutions in 1781 and 1782.

The Constitution proposed in 1779, according to New Hampshire historian Jeremy Belknap, was "so deficient in its principles and so inadequate in its provisions," that it was easily defeated. Peterborough, however, overwhelmingly supported the proposal: Belknap's perceived deficiencies were virtues to Peterborough. Analysis of this attitude will help explain the town's decision to oppose ratification of the Federal Constitution.

The 1779 Constitution continued the form of state government which replaced royal authority in 1776. It created a General Court consisting of an assembly and a council. There was no provision for the office of governor. Representatives to the General Court were chosen either directly or indirectly by towns with each town of one hundred or more families entitled to send one representative to the assembly. Twelve counsellors were to be chosen at county conventions composed of town delegates. Towns were to be responsible for salaries and expenses of representatives thereby strengthening their accountability to their towns.

The 1779 plan enumerated rights and liberties which blended Lockean principles and traditional practices. It affirmed that the people were vested with "natural, inalienable rights of men," and "are entitled to life, liberty and property," "freedom of conscience," and the right to trial by jury. It insured extensive local authority over these civil liberties by granting towns discretionary powers to define "natural rights" and "traditional powers." Furthermore, the 1779 plan limited political power to Protestant property holders and upheld the right of local communities to establish tax-supported churches. It created a weak state government without an executive that was essentially a federation of towns. It protected smaller towns from the power of the larger ones by giving each an equal vote in the legislature—one town, one vote. The plan insured the domination of Congregational and Presbyterian interests in the General Court because they controlled a majority of New Hampshire towns and could use their power to continue their monopoly over local tax-supported churches.

During the struggle to adopt a State Constitution supporters of a weak and federated form of government confronted advocates of a strong, unified government. The concept of sovereignty was at the heart of this struggle. Advocates of both forms agreed, in theory, that the people, not institutions, were sovereign. They affirmed that individuals are the original and legitimate source of political power and that government derives its authority from the consent of the people. Subtle and significant differences emerged in the application of the concept, however.

The constitutional proposals made in 1781 and 1782, while varying in detail, largely incorporated the view that state government was based directly on the consent of the sovereign people and that the towns were a part of the whole government. The proposals broadened the electorate by eliminating the qualification that voters must profess the Protestant religion. They reduced the discretionary power of the towns to define "natural rights" and "traditional powers" through extensive statements defining the rights of the people. They forbade towns to tax for the support of a religious establishment those citizens who did not accept the "persuasion, sect or denomination" of the town-supported church. They weakened the grip of small towns over the legislature by reducing the number of towns represented and by making the state rather than the towns the paymaster for its legislators. They tried to strengthen state government by making the three essential powers of government—executive, legislative and judicial—independent of each other and by asserting state control over the militia, a traditional local prerogative.

The State Constitution as finally adopted in 1783 was a compromise which favored a stronger state government. Among its thirty-eight articles defining the rights of the people were liberty of the press, freedom of speech, prohibition against quartering troops in homes without the owner's consent, protection against excessive bail, protection against unreasonable search and seizure, guarantee of free elections for qualified voters, protection of property under due process of law, prohibition against standing armies without legislative consent, and freedom of worship.

The 1783 plan provided for the three branches of government but limited the powers of the executive by making him a voting member of the Senate and by creating a Council chosen by the General Court to advise the executive. The House of Representatives was to be composed of delegates from towns with 150 or more ratable polls thus replacing the principle of one town, one vote, with proportionate representation. Senators were to be elected from districts created for that purpose. The plan gave the state more control over appointment of militia officers thus breaking the tradition of their appointment by the towns.

Acceptance of the 1783 proposal revealed a decline of the traditional political culture based on town autonomy and a federated form of state government. The New Hampshire Constitution that took effect in June of 1784 introduced important changes. It gave larger communities more power than smaller ones. The grip of town majorities over the local religious establishment diminished because dissenters could no longer be taxed to support the local church. Towns became indissoluable parts of the whole rather than autonomous communities united in a federation.

Peterborough's acceptance of this compromise plan suggests that the community's political culture was not intractable. Its previous adherence to a federated form of government was a means rather than an end. The town's ultimate goals appear to have been a weak state executive, continuation of the community's right to have an established church of its own choice, and substantial local power in the General Court. Though lessened, these features appeared in the 1783 State Constitution.

Peterborough's opposition to the Federal Constitution in 1788 was consistent with its opposition to the 1781 and 1782 state plans. These proposals greatly strengthened a central government at the expense of local powers. The Federal Constitution rejected the federated form of national government then operating under the Articles of Confederation. It created a national government which embodied the application of individual sovereignty directly to the national government creating a single political authority in which state and local governments were constituent parts. It contained a potentially powerful executive. Furthermore, the 1788 proposal neither prohibited the creation of a national church nor guaranteed protection of local church establishments.

The similarities between the proposed Federal Constitution and the earlier state plans opposed by Peterborough was probably apparent to the town committee responsible for reviewing the federal plan. Five of the committee's nine members reviewing the Federal Constitution had served on town committees in 1781 which recommended rejection of the state proposals. The other four members were close relatives of one or more of the other five. Together, they represented the guardians of the traditional political culture which was threatened by these plans. Most members of the 1782 and 1788 committees were among the founders of the town and had served in the militia during the Revolutionary War. They were church leaders, such as Elder Samuel Moore, John Morison, and William Smith, all of whom were in their fifties and were among the towns highest taxpayers. In part, Peterborough's opposition to the Federal Constitution reaffirmed their concept of sovereignty which made local government the foundation of a federated form of national government.

In 1789 the ministers of the Eastward Presbytery, with which Peterborough was associated, expressed concerns which might also have been an additional factor in the town's opposition to the Federal Constitution. In a letter to President George Washington the ministers objected that the Constitution did not contain "some explicit acknowledgment of the only true God," and that it had not prohibited the creation of a "religious establishment." The proposed Bill of Rights, introduced in September of 1789, which insured religious liberty, eradicated their objection.

This revolutionary period, 1775–1790, reveals two major conflicting forces within Peterborough. On the one hand, the Revolutionary War, opposition to strong state government, and rejection of the Federal Constitution united the community behind its parochial, traditional and conservative political culture. On the other hand, a vacuum in religious leadership weakened town authorities and their principles, especially among the younger generation and newcomers. In 1788 these two forces appeared to intersect. The town's controversy with its minister in 1788 appears to have diverted attention from national politics to local church polity and doctrine. By 1790 a new spirit of enterprise which linked the town's economy to market opportunities competed with subsistence farming. New men with ambitions more compatible with the wider political and economic horizons afforded by increased state and federal power emerged as Peterborough's leaders.

During the 1790s contention continued between the elder citizens and the new generation who cared less for form and more for substance in their religion than had their fathers. Following Annan's resignation the town offered the pulpit to Rev. Zephaniah Swift Moore who rejected it to accept a calling to a community even more divided than Peterborough. Frustration increased as the town appeared to be abandoned by spiritual leaders. Only with Dunbar's acceptance in 1799 did the town settle into a period of stability. In a lengthy sermon on January 4, 1801, welcoming in the new century, Dunbar reassured old and young that the emergence of the new social order had a larger meaning which conformed with fundamental Christian beliefs and promise for a millenium.

SOUTHWESTERN FRONTIER: KEENE, CHESTERFIELD, WALPOLE & WESTMORELAND, 1780–1800

Wilfred Bisson

Keene State College

During the decades of the 1780s and 1790s Chesterfield, Keene, Walpole and Westmoreland were still being settled. In 1780, they were in their first or second generation and had scarcely changed the aspect of the land; settlers had made little change in the environment. By 1800 the population, by birth and, more importantly by immigration from southern New England, increased to about three times its 1780 figure. Chesterfield increased from 874 in 1775 to 2,161 in 1800, Keene from 435 to 1,645, Westmoreland from 758 to 2,066, and Walpole from 549 to 1,743.

The two tools by which the early settlers of Cheshire County subdued the wilderness, the axe and fire, were zealously applied, and, by 1800, much of the forest was transformed into farms. The moving water of the Ashuelot, the Cold River, and other streams provided the energy for an industrious people. Mills were constructed, dams were built, and the spawning grounds of the Atlantic salmon and shad narrowed and eventually disappeared.

The Keene historian Salma Hale, writing in the 1820s, lamented the disappearance of these food sources: "It is much to be regretted that the inhabitants...living near the sources of the large rivers...did not...take care that regulations were made and adhered to...for preserving the fish.... In the early settlements of the country, vast numbers of salmon and shad were caught yearly at the foot of Bellows Falls in Walpole."

The change in these towns was remarkable: from unkempt frontier settlements they had evolved into prosperous villages. The small timber dwellings had been replaced by substantial two-story structures built in the new Georgian and Federal styles. What had been a ragged, asymmetrical appearance gave way to a

Petition to the governor dated February 2, 1753, from citizens of Upper Ashuelot requesting the grant of a charter to legally form a town. The place granted became Keene. Courtesy of the State Archives. Photograph by Bill Finney.

sharp trim solidity. The physical transformation of the landscape was paralleled by the evolution of an ordered society.

According to Salma Hale, in 1800 these four towns presented "the fairest evidences of the benign effects of a regular government and free institutions," but decorum had not been among the ingredients of the original social polity of these towns. Rather it grew slowly, grafted onto a somewhat abrasive and internally contentious social order. The most basic social institution, the family, suffered instability largely because of the capriciousness with which death struck down parents in their prime. It was not uncommon to spend one's childhood with more than one set of parents. The resulting family fragments, although they always sought to coalesce into complete families, undoubtedly gave life a sense of insecurity.

The Congregational Church, which served as the social and moral center of New England communities, remained weak until the mid-1780s in Keene, Walpole and Westmoreland. In Chesterfield the Church never did achieve the status of a commanding social arbiter such as it is known to have had in most New England towns.

The causes for this weakness as a cultural institution can be found in factors such as the diverse and individual origins of the settlers, the individualistic character traits fostered by movement of these settlers from their natal towns, the poverty and consequent inability to support a minister in these towns, and the short supply of educated orthodox ministers. The Walpole church records, for example, note that new settlers are maintaining their connections in the towns from which they came rather than tranferring to the Walpole church.

In the early years of the Revolution, the destruction of the traditions by which authority was established further compounded the problem. Before the Revolution, governmental authority had rested on the prestige of certain influential residents, such as Josiah Willard and Elijah Williams, who had appointments from the royal governor. These appointments, as militia officers and as justices of the peace, represented the most conspicuous means of legitimating political authority. When the Revolution denied the authority of the crown and its agents, the principle of communal authority was temporarily weakened. As a case in point, Williams, a justice of the peace, was forcibly dissuaded early in 1775 from carrying out his duties by a mob. It was not the last time Williams would be the object of mob attack.

During the Revolution disorder increased, church attendance became sporadic, riots were frequent, and prostitution was practiced. Hale mentions few riots in Keene but refers to "the agitations which were once too common" and speaks about compelling "the restless and discontented to engage in the quiet occupations." The Cheshire County court records for 1781 note that Ebenezer Swan, Isaac Bundy, Namoah Drury, Antipas Harrington and Elias Bundy, were indicted for "riotous disturbance" for mobbing the constable and liberating a prisoner. From Abner Sanger's journal description we can infer that Josiah Willard's house was a bordello.

The authority of New Hampshire suffered, owing largely to the distance of these towns from the seat of state government. Taxes often went unpaid. Chesterfield failed to provide schools. All towns were reluctant to meet their beef and continental requisitions for the army. In the early 1780s these towns experienced internecine division as rival parties disputed whether they should remain with New Hampshire or join the new state of Vermont. All records appear to have been revised later to obliterate the towns' flirtation with secession from New Hampshire. All did join Vermont for a time, but all retained strong New Hampshire elements. Keene, and probably Walpole and Westmoreland as well, had rival Vermont and New Hampshire town governments. Competing militia companies drilled and dual courts met in the same building although at different times. Occasionally, riotous mobs attempted to stop the courts. Diarist Sanger noted that "the street is full of tilts" during a meeting of the Vermont court and cited the "hubbub about the Vermont Proclamation," and "much bluster," and "quarreling."

The situation became tense in December 1781 when the sheriff of Washington County, Vermont, arrested the New Hampshire sheriff of Cheshire County and incarcerated him in Charlestown, another New Hampshire town that had seceded to Vermont. (At that time Washington County, Vermont, included the same area as Cheshire County.) In retaliation, a New Hampshire force came to Keene and arrested the Vermont sheriff, but was itself taken into custody by an enraged pro-Vermont mob.

At this point, the New Hampshire partisans, who included many of the old Keene leaders, demanded that New Hampshire send troops to enforce its authority. While the New Hampshire partisans were appealing for armed assistance, Vermont deserted its supporters. Responding to prodding from the Continental Congress, the Vermont legislature renounced its jurisdiction over the secessionist towns in early 1782. However, when the New Hampshire Superior Court met in Keene that September, a mob tried to stop it. Another mob put an end to the troublemakers.

New Hampshire granted amnesty to Vermont supporters, and reconciliation went smoothly except in Chesterfield, where a vast majority had supported Vermont and succeeded in holding local power for a number of years. This is evidenced in a petition to the General Court dated March 5, 1783, in which Chesterfield citizens of the Vermont party requested the decommissioning of both of the town's justices of the peace. This granted, leadership of the town fell to Samuel King who had served as sheriff for Vermont and who served as town moderator for some years thereafter. In 1783 King was elected to represent Chesterfield in the New Hampshire Constitutional Convention.

Wyman Tavern, c. 1762, a Keene Revolutionary landmark. Courtesy of the Historical Society of Cheshire County.

Information on the period from 1783, when Abner Sanger's journal ceases, to 1787, when the region's first newspaper, *The New Hampshire Recorder,* began publication, is scarce. This was a cash-starved time in which barter was the principal means of doing business, with grain potash salts, flaxseed, hog's fat, and beeswax being the common items of exchange. When the newspaper was established, numerous advertisements called for payment in commodities. After cash again became available in the late 1780s, the ads began insisting on payment in cash.

Counterfeiting was common. In 1782 the Superior Court returned an indictment for a certain Carlyle, who was counterfeiting fifty-dollar bills in Continental currency, and in 1789 a notorious counterfeiter violently escaped incarceration on Prison Street in Keene. In the Cheshire County court records for the early and mid-1780s there are numerous cases of fraudulent use of promissory notes, bills of sale, and other financial instruments. Keene, Westmoreland and Chesterfield voted to have their representatives to the General Court support the State's issuance of paper money. Court records are full of suits by creditors attempting to collect from delinquent debtors. Echoing Shays' Rebellion in this region was a violent outbreak in the town of Marlborough in which a mob destroyed the orchard, crippled the livestock, and gagged the horses of an apparent money lender and tavern keeper. The advertisement in *The New Hampshire Recorder* offering ten silver dollars reward for information about this mob asks "Shall such things be tolerated in a Christian land, that would make a Mehamitan blush?"

Other indications of social disquiet included outbreaks of religious dissension. In 1784 Chesterfield refused to exempt Universalists from the ministerial tax. A group of Baptists had resided in Westmoreland since the early 1770s, and by the mid-1780s they were accepted with equanimity and received a division of the ministerial tax. Yet another more radical group of dissenters—the "shaking quakers"— disturbed the communal harmony. In 1783 the town voted that "parents and masters [must] keep their children from seeing the shakers on Sundays." To prevent the townspeople from harboring religious dissidents, Westmoreland also voted that no shaking quaker be allowed to stay in town more than one night except at a public place. From Keene there is a report of an escape from the town gaol of a malefactor "who was much addicted to new-light preaching."

From an economic point of view the mid-1780s seems a paradox. There is much impressionistic evidence which suggests economic hard times. Yet, despite the cash famine, speculation in land continued, and settlers continued to move northward to and through these towns. More land was being cleared. Sawmills, gristmills, a linseed oil mill, a potash works, and carding and paper mills made their appearance toward the end of the 1780s, indicating that economic growth was occurring even in the absence of abundant cash.

Town pounds were constructed in the mid-1780s, and some towns began to employ fulltime poundkeepers in the early 1790s, indications that the wilderness was being subdued and that an economic revival was taking place. New and more detailed regulations about confining rams attest to the growing importance of the sheep industry, as did greater emphasis on the maintenance of proper fencing, as well as increasing bounties on wolves and other predators.

Chesterfield's development after 1782 diverged from that of the other three towns. By 1800 it was the most populous but it remained divided. With taxes unpaid, schools unsupported, and no strong minister it became a hotbed of religious heterodoxy. In contrast, strong willed, articulate, and long-lived ministers in the other towns—Fessenden in Walpole, Pratt in Westmoreland, and Hall in Keene—used their influence to curb profanity, sexual immorality and other vices and to inculcate habits of respect and obedience to legitimate authority, both secular and ecclesiastical. These towns curbed religious dissent, enforced payment of ministerial taxes, and jailed dissenting preachers.

Strengthening the forces for social control was the establishment of two Masonic Lodges, the Rising Sun Lodge in Keene, established in 1782, and the Jerusalem Lodge in Westmoreland which was formed a decade later. In bringing together local merchants and professionals, the Lodges played a role in their

Park Hill Meetinghouse, Westmoreland. Built in 1762, with early 19th-century alter-ations. Courtesy of the N. H. Historical Society.

communities which was not unlike that of churches, militia companies, and town governments.

The press also strengthened the forces for social control. In Keene, the *New Hampshire Recorder* was established in 1787, and the *Columbian Centinel,* the *Rising Sun,* and, the *New Hampshire Sentinel* began publication prior to 1800. *The Farmers Museum* was founded in Walpole in 1793. All in all, by 1787 social control and decorum had smoothed much of the roughness inherent in an earlier frontier society in Keene, Walpole and Westmoreland.

In 1788, the ratification of the United States Constitution lacked the significance that it was to assume for later generations. This step, which to us seems an important milestone in human history, took place in an atmosphere of political serenity, without rancorous debate and with little comment.

Representatives to the ratifying convention from Keene, Walpole and Westmoreland voted to accept the Constitution with the understanding that a bill of rights would be added later. The Chesterfield representative voted to reject the new government proposed, although he does not seem to have opposed federal union, per se.

There is evidence of strong, if not vociferous, support of a more powerful national government. In a discussion of the work of the Federal Convention in

Selection of a delegate to represent Walpole at the state ratifying convention necessitated several town meetings. The second, on January 28, 1788, was "to See if the Town will give Benjamin Bellows Esqr. Instructions," while the third voted first to rescind the vote, and subsequently, to reconsider his election in favor of Lt. Aaron Allen. Ultimately, however, Bellows served, and voted in favor of the Constitution. Courtesy of the State Archives. Photograph by Bill Finney.

Philadelphia, a writer in *The New Hampshire Recorder* on October 30, 1787, remarked: "The Tories [during the Revolution] despised the proceedings of the conventions and town meetings and called them mobs—the antifederalists despise the convention of the United States and call [it] the acts of mobs and fools." On January 8, 1788, the newspaper reported that a town meeting had "by a large majority" elected the Rev. Aaron Hall as delegate to the Exeter Convention called to ratify the Constitution and "no self interested antifederalist appeared to retard this important business."

Almost all of the early historians agree that after the new government's ratification in June 1788 the history of the area was uneventful. Annalist Salma Hale wrote:

> After this period, but few, if any, events have occurred which would be interesting or instructive. The adoption of the National and State Constitutions, and the regular administration of the laws, have calmed the agitations which once were too common, and compelled the restless and discontented to engage in the quiet occupations of productive industry. Society has improved, the town has prospered, and now presents one of the fairest evidences of the benign effects of a regular government and of free institutions.

With the growing prosperity of the 1790s, ferries across the Connecticut River were allowed, the Great Bridge was constructed over the Connecticut River in North Walpole, and dams were built on the Ashuelot River to provide power for the mills.

Chesterfield Academy was founded and the Walpole Wits enriched America's literary heritage. The sermons and orations of the time in celebration of being American contrasted sharply with the jeremiads of a century earlier. The Rev. Aaron Hall in Keene noted that "happiness is ours, if we will make it so."

Ministers of the Congregational Church, particularly Aaron Hall in Keene and Thomas Fessenden in Walpole, enjoyed an enhanced status as moral arbiters of their communities which has probably never before or since been equaled. Hall's "Oration on the Adoption of the Constitution" was sold in several editions. Fessenden's articles, under the by-line "The Religionist," published in the *Farmers Museum,* contain the classic arguments for the necessity of a state religion and the importance of public taxation for the support of religion.

The harmony of the early 1790s began to fade by mid-decade. Newspapers spoke darkly of plots and secret societies which would undermine the republic. On May 13, 1793, the *Columbian Informer* carried an article warning of the subversive nature of the "Jacobinical" democratic clubs springing up in the cities.

Religious pluralism increased as Methodism made inroads in Chesterfield. In 1797, however, the town of Winchester voted to invite nonconforming ministers to preach in their new meetinghouse, and there was an outburst of wrath from the Western Association, the body to which the area's orthodox clergy belonged. Later, Dr. Ziba Hall, a leader of the Rising Sun Lodge, refused to pay his ministerial tax on the plea that he was a Universalist. Although Hall was ultimately forced to pay, these events foretold the shattering of a glacial harmony in the first decade of the new century. But that is another story.

YEARS OF REVOLUTION, YEARS OF DECISION
Attitudes and Reactions in the Lakes Region during the 1770s and 1780s

William L. Taylor

Plymouth State College

*U*nderstanding why our forebears reacted to events in ways we find unexpected is a challenge to the historian of two hundred years later. The decades of the 1770s through the 1790s are considered momentous ones by scholars and laymen alike but, as we shall see, the inhabitants of Moultonboro and Wolfeboro seem to have had minimal concern with events that we deem pivotal in our nation's history. The narrative that follows examines the issues which surviving records suggest occupied the citizens of these struggling communities during the late eighteenth century.

Although they were not then on the edge of settlement, the towns of Moultonboro and Wolfeboro must share the designation "frontier" towns since each was located in the northern tier of development and since each seems to have faced similar problems in its effort to overcome the difficulties of pioneering. As proprietary towns, their history represents a common trend that began in the late colonial era and continued into the early years of the republic: the treatment of land as real estate to be bought and sold for profit. As in many speculative ventures, the expectations relating to land did not necessarily match reality, but in the mid-18th century hopes for the profitability of New Hampshire's interior were high.

During the governorship of Benning Wentworth, Wolfeboro (originally spelled Wolfborough, Wolfsborough, or Wolfboro) was granted by the Masonian proprietors in 1759 to a group of proprietors including some prominent members of the colony's elite. Wolfeboro's history reflects the growth of settlement that occurred when it became common knowledge that French

Petition of Jonathan Moulton of Hampton to the Governor and Council, filed March 30, 1771, requesting incorporation of the town of Moultonboro, "to which place many more would soon be Transplanted & Settled if they could Enjoy those advantages common in Towns Incorporated." Courtesy of State Archives. Photograph by Bill Finney.

power in North America was coming to an end. Victory of the British at Quebec and the successful raid by Robert Rogers on St. Francis meant that the French and their Indian allies could never again mount raids into British territory as had been so common since the wars began in 1689.

Henceforth, new settlements on the frontier would be safe from such depradations and the only perils for settlers would be those associated with pioneering. A quick survey of town charter dates indicates the significance of the impending British victory, formally acknowledged in the Treaty of Paris of 1763. News of the British success brought a rush of settlement in the central and northern sections of New Hampshire. Many wished to come to these areas since they were in such close proximity to existing settlements. And proprietors recognized the potential for making money in the northern wilderness.

Moultonboro was also granted by the Masonian proprietors; its sixty proprietors received their grant in 1763. The town grew slowly but steadily, and its history has similarities with Wolfeboro because of the common access to Lake Winnipesaukee and because the two towns shared a representative to the legislature and to the Constitutional Convention in 1788.

Wolfeboro's history during the late colonial era was particularly rich because of its association with Gov. John Wentworth between 1767 and 1775. By all accounts, Wentworth was a man of vision, a man who saw beyond the obvious and the immediate. As a proprietor of Wolfeboro, he had a definite interest in the development of the northern towns. This dovetailed nicely with his other offices, those of provincial governor and Surveyor General of His Majesty's forests in North America. All three roles put John Wentworth in the position of desiring growth in Wolfeboro and in the northern regions of the province. Significant growth would enhance his own proprietary interests as well as embellish his standing as governor and surveyor general.

According to his biographer, Lawrence Shaw Mayo, "one of John Wentworth's youthful dreams had been to possess a country estate in the upland regions of his native province." Originally he seems to have preferred the "lower Cohoss [Coos]" region, but as an original grantee of the township of Wolfeboro his interest was drawn there. It was closer to Portsmouth, the provincial capital, than the Coos region and was therefore more accessible, being only fifty miles from Portsmouth.

Wentworth's commitment to country life on the frontier was in striking contrast to the lack of interest his uncle and predecessor had in such matters. Benning Wentworth (governor from 1741 to 1766) was oriented toward Portsmouth and its environs. Although he had granted many interior frontier towns, had sought to extend the territorial claims of the colony to the Hudson River watershed, and (after 1759) had recognized the long suppressed desire to settle the northern regions, he seems to have been minimally involved in frontier

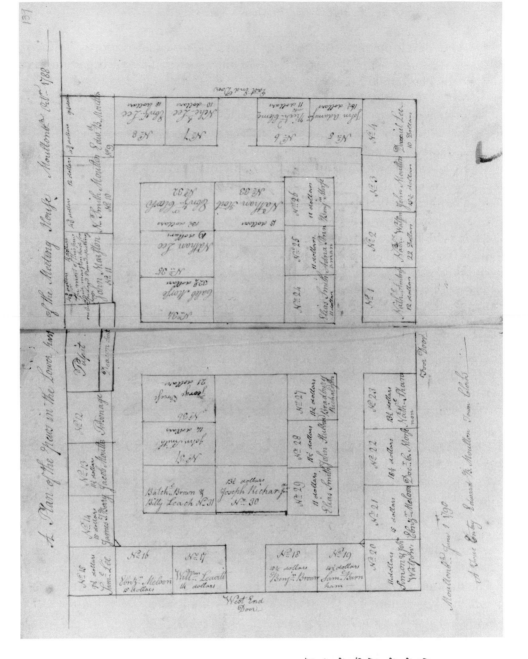

"Plan of the Meeting House, Moultonborough, 1790." Note that the costliest pews were those located directly in front of the pulpit. Courtesy State Archives. Photograph by Bill Finney.

life and development after making individual township grants. Thus, the country estate of John Wentworth marks an important step in the evolution of the New Hampshire frontier.

By 1768, when Wentworth commenced work on his estate, the situation in New Hampshire had changed considerably since the incumbency of his uncle. All claim by New Hampshire to what is today Vermont had been lost, thus considerably reducing available frontier lands. Wentworth may well have thought that Wolfeboro would be a suitable location as a focal point for development of the northern region, or perhaps as a settlement on a future post road connecting Portsmouth with Canada.

Whatever his ultimate goals, Wentworth's estate must have been a most impressive sight to ordinary settlers of the region, for they had likely never seen such large structures with such fine furnishings and facilities. Unfortunately for the governor, Frances Wentworth, his wife, was not nearly as enamored of country living as was he. A letter surviving from 1770 indicates that she could hardly wait to get back from "this solitary wilderness" to the more civilized and sophisticated lifestyle found in Portsmouth. Despite his wife's lack of enthusiasm, Wentworth continued to lavish much time and money on his estate, which he valued during the Revolution at 20,000 pounds.

The presence of the governor's country estate in this frontier grant appears to have had the desired effect. In 1766 no permanent residents lived in Wolfeboro, whereas in 1769 the governor estimated the population to be 150. The census of 1775 counted more than 200. Other members of the Portsmouth establishment likewise saw the area as a place for building summer residences. These included Jotham Rindge, the governor's uncle, who built his summer house just over a mile north of Wentworth's house; Peter Livius, a Portsmouth merchant and member of the Executive Council who constructed a residence five miles distant in Tuftonboro; and Samuel Livermore, the attorney general of the province, who selected Holderness for his country residence.

In addition to building his large estate, Wentworth took great interest in improving communication in frontier areas. Construction of the road from Portsmouth to Wolfeboro occupied much of his attention in 1769–1770. Had he remained governor after 1775, transportation throughout the region might have been much enhanced. He seems to have had a clear recognition of the relationship between growth on the one hand and good transportation on the other.

The coming of Revolution in 1775 irreversibly altered the concept of the northern towns as a place for country estates of the Portsmouth elite. It also doomed any possibility that the region would have significant developmental assistance from the provincial governor. After 1774, the last year of Wentworth's residency, Wolfeboro and Moultonboro were forced to rely on their own ingenuity and resources. Both towns were inhabited primarily by farm families struggling to establish homes on the frontier. Whereas Wolfeboro had been an atypical frontier town with at least two large estates, it now became just another frontier town trying to cope with the myriad problems arising from the crisis of revolution and, later, struggling to address problems associated with establishing a new state and a new nation. Moultonboro and Wolfeboro thereafter traversed similar paths.

Beginning in 1775, the Revolution brought all kinds of difficulties to New Hampshire. The northern towns did not have to worry about fighting in their area, but they did have to contribute to the war effort and send some of their men to the army. Town documents reveal that Moultonboro and Wolfeboro coped as best they could with the travails of war, and that each was often taxed beyond its ability to pay. Both also had to face the special problems of proprietary towns, including those created by absentee proprietors. Events in Moultonboro reveal that becoming an incorporated town could be a difficult process, and that disputes over religious matters could be bitter and time-consuming.

In March 1771 Col. Jonathan Moulton of Hampton, a proprietor of Moultonboro, requested in a petition that Governor John Wentworth make it an incorporated town. He noted in the petition that forty families had already settled there. The petition continued:

> many more would soon be Transplanted & Settled if they could Enjoy those advantages common in Towns incorporated of Gospel Institutions, schools & other Privileges of Societies Legally constituted the want of which discourages the best sort of settlers, Sober Serious People who have a proper Sense of the Ends of such Society.

However, for reasons unknown, the town remained unincorporated until 1777.

Within months of incorporation Moultonboro was racked by a crisis that split the town over whether the Rev. Samuel Perley was in fact its legally settled minister. Records of town meetings use extremely strong language in documenting the matter. The dispute occupies more space in the official records than any other during the period examined, 1770–1790. Apparently the Reverend Perley was voted to be the settled minister by an ecclesiastical council—likely the town's search committee—in 1777. On December 25th the freeholders voted to renew his call. However, some residents did not concur, and the controversy came to a head the next summer. Perley had been scheduled to be installed in July of 1778, but a town meeting held on August 25th voted to remove him and denied that the town had ever officially decided to settle him as its minister—"pretended settlement" was the term used in the minutes. The animosity and bitterness dividing the community is shown clearly in this excerpt from the minutes of February 15, 1778:

When this town views the overbearing conduct of the last council in settling Mr. Perley here, contrary to the sense of the town, & against much greater opposition than the same men so lately in council, before, said would obstruct his usefulness & so disserve the Interest of Religion here.

The Town cannot impute it to any other reason than that of being without the fear of God before their eyes, or a view to promote the interest of Christs Kingdom: or else how could men of their sacred order and profession dare to perform that under the name of serving religion, when they must be sensible it would greatly injure and disserve the same.

Removal of Perley hardly resolved the issue. Town records indicate that he sought to force an equitable settlement through negotiations with Colonel Moulton, chairman of the proprietors.

A dissident group was not content to see Perley forced out and they sought, at two February town meetings, to retain him in the pulpit. Every vote taken on the issue saw the Perley faction go down to defeat. The town finally settled with Perley in October 1781 when the freeholders voted to have the selectmen levy a tax bill proportionally upon inhabitants.

Moultonboro called the Rev. Jeremiah Shaw to replace Perley in 1779; he served until his death in the early 1800s. Colonel Moulton, in a letter to Shaw offering him the position, summarized the controversy surrounding Perley, while attempting to reassure Shaw that all would be well if he accepted the call. In the letter precise terms regarding annual salary of fifty-five pounds for the first year, the cutting of thirty cords of wood for his use, and his rights to the minister's lot were carefully described.

Meeting its obligations proved a problem not only in religious matters, but in secular matters as well. Moultonboro, like Wolfeboro had difficulty in furnishing its quotas of recruits for the Continental Army. On February 22, 1781, the town voted that "the Selectmen make a return of the Soldiers heretofore Enlisted for different terms, who have since Enlisted in the Continental Army for three years, or during the War." Because of the difficulty, this list was designed to show that soldiers from town had been, and were still, serving in the army.

The general shortage of money during the Revolution is reflected in the fact that pay to town officers was in bushels of Indian corn. Part of the Reverend Shaw's annual stipend was likewise paid in kind. Even after ratification of the Constitution in 1788, Moultonboro continued to be plagued with financial problems. In 1793 and 1794 residents were refusing to pay their "Minister's Tax." As a result, the constables were authorized to collect the tax "immediately." A related problem was the difficulty in getting delinquent parishoners to pay for their pews in the meetinghouse.

John Wentworth (1737–1820) portrait by John Singleton Copley, 1769. Born into New Hampshire's leading family, John Wentworth became a proprietor of Wolfeborough as early as 1759. He succeeded his uncle Benning as governor of the province in 1767, and began building an elaborate country estate in Wolfeborough shortly thereafter. Courtesy of the Hood Museum of Art, Dartmouth College, Hanover. Gift of Esther Lowell Abbott in memory of her husband Gordon Abbott.

Education of children in town was likewise plagued by financial difficulties. In 1786 freeholders approved funds for keeping a school which was to be moved around to different parts of town. The appropriation was renewed in 1787 and 1788, but defeated the following year. Not until 1790 did voters approve the construction of schoolhouses in each district, "when called for."

Supporting evidence for this continual financial difficulty is found in three letters from Reverend Shaw written between January 1789 and March 1791. In the first he complained to the proprietors that he should have received the thirty-pound settlement which had been voted nine years before. Thirteen months later, little had changed, as a 1790 letter to the clerk of the proprietors indicates:

Living in a cold leaky house with little lights [window panes] & that mostly borrowed not being owner of so much whole glass as to make a single window of 15 squares. Being obliged for want of convenience to study amidst the noise & confusion of children & family business and interruptions of comers in not having concerns with me. And having much of my hay yearly hurt in my barn for want of shingling. I stand now as I have for years back in great need of what is due to me from the Proprietors of MBorough.

Finally on March 26, 1791, Shaw wrote a letter, which was really a petition, to the proprietors regarding his rights, as the first settled minister, to a lot in town and to the thirty pounds noted above. Shaw described his existing land as "one Mutilated Lot" which he did not believe met the terms of the town charter. The town records for 1792 imply that Shaw was threatening to leave town.

At a town meeting on June 8th voters abated all of Shaw's back taxes and called on delinquent taxpayers to pay their ministerial tax. Also, those present exempted Shaw from any taxes and voted him ten dollars in cash toward his annual salary of sixty-five pounds per year. Shaw, most likely because the town took decisive action, remained as the settled minister.

By comparison, mention in town records of the election of a delegate to the conventions in Exeter and Concord is cursory. The only references to official town action regarding the Federal Constitution are brief entries describing the election of an official delegate to represent Wolfeboro, Tuftonboro, Ossipee, and Moultonboro. Lieutenant Nathaniel Shannon of Moultonboro was chosen following two attempts in January and early February, 1788. According to the "Journal of the Convention [in Exeter and Concord]," Shannon attended every session, and voted for ratification in Concord on June 21, 1788. Nothing in the town files suggests that Shannon discussed the document with the voters or wished to have the town propose any amendments. In short, all surviving evidence indicates that the Federal Constitution did not make any great impact on voters and residents of Moultonboro.

When the convention to amend the State Constitution met in 1791 Moultonboro was represented by Col. Nathaniel Hoit who attended all but three days of the first session, but only twice at the September 1792 session, missing the last two days of the convention. In marked contrast to 1788, however, the drastically amended State Constitution of 1792 was discussed at an April meeting which voted to have two townsmen read the document. Town records are mute as to any official action, but the convention journal indicates that Moultonboro voted 16-0 in favor of the amendments.

The number of voters on the State Constitution was surprisingly small when compared to the 46 voters who had participated fourteen years earlier in the dispute centering on Samuel Perley. Moultonboro had increased in population since 1778: all the records contain references to issues that only a growing community would be debating and deciding. The census of 1800 lists

857 persons residing in the town. In this context the 16 votes cast in 1792 may suggest that town freeholders were apathetic about the State Constitution.

The religious harmony which seems to have prevailed in the 1780s—despite the unwillingness of the freeholders and proprietors to honor financial obligations to their minister—dissolved in the mid-1790s. Although town records contain much less detail than for the Perley controversy, one can read the implications of the warning to the voters posted on June 20, 1794: "to see what method the town will take to settle their ministerial disputes and put an end to law suits." The town meeting approved the raising of thirty pounds. No further mention of any suit appears.

The post-1800 history of Moultonboro is beyond the purview of this narrative, but records extant for the first decade of the new century indicate that the town had utilized much of its available land for settlement. The proprietors were still dividing land in 1806, but the land under consideration was located in a remote area along the border with Ossipee. By that date several taverns existed, including one operated by Nathaniel Shannon.

If Moultonboro was racked periodically by problems with its ministers, financial problems, and apathy regarding the state and federal constitutions, how did events in Wolfeboro compare? The towns shared remarkably parallel courses during these decades in contrast to their differences in the early years. Despite John Wentworth's association with the town, Wolfeboro supported the patriot cause from the commencement of the Revolution. Attendees of a public meeting on August 7, 1775, voted to send Moses Ham to represent the town in the state's Provincial Congress. At one point (probably between 1778 and 1780) the selectmen listed seven persons who had "gone in the Army."

Town records for the 1770s suggest that primary concerns of the voters centered on such matters as raising money for town expenses, choosing town officers, repairing roads, and, after 1775, some concern for "preaching during the summer." Like Moultonboro, Wolfeboro had difficulty getting adequate funds from its taxpayers in such troubled times. For example, in acting upon an article at the March 1776 town meeting, those present voted "That the Town agree that the Select Men take Samuel Mellourt[?] a poor child belonging to this Town and put it out to some suitable place to be provided with proper victuals and cloathing in the cheapest manner they can."

Inventories and records surviving from the Revolutionary years indicate that the town added population rather slowly, and that it manifested relatively few of the attributes associated with a prosperous agricultural community. The inventory for 1775 showed forty-four polls over eighteen years old and one slave. In 1776 the town census listed one hundred fourteen males and ninety four females, two "negros and slaves for life," and four persons "gone in the army." The town had no acreage in orchards—despite evidence that the

Wentworth estate had some before 1775. A total of 335 acres had been cleared for tillage, mowing, and pasture.

By 1778 seventy polls over 18 lived in town. All blacks had left—those listed earlier likely lived on the Wentworth or Livius estates. Cleared land for tillage, mowing, and pasture had increased to 1,128 acres. The rents collected on mills and the value of real estate had likewise risen a commensurate amount. However, the entry for orchard land remained at zero. The next extant inventory, for 1797, showed 159 polls, 1492 acres of cleared land, and 15 acres of orchard land.

The issue of hiring a minister for the town came before the voters in 1781. At a special meeting on November 13, the vote was 17-13 in favor of hiring Andrew Collins "to preach and keep school among us." After the meeting some voters from the northeast part of town claimed that "they were not sufficiently acquainted with the purposes of the last meeting" and "did not appear to act in the same." They presented a petition to the selectmen requesting another meeting on the matter, and the selectmen granted their request.

On November 29, 1781, another special meeting took place and this time the Reverend Collins was approved by a vote of 12 to 9. Town records indicate that he remained in Wolfeboro several years preaching and teaching school, probably at his home and at those of other residents in town. The divisiveness indicated by the second meeting was certainly less serious than that in Moultonboro. Controversy does not appear in the records on any sustained basis until the hiring of the Rev. Ebenezer Allen in 1792.

Unlike Moultonboro, which had a meetinghouse as early as 1777, Wolfeboro was unable to gather sufficient resources with which to construct one until 1789. In 1773 the grantors voted a donation of 30 pounds toward building a meetinghouse, but in 1774 the freeholders refused to appropriate any town funds for this purpose. Not until 1786 did the subject again come before town meeting. The condition of the economy under the Articles of Confederation then acted upon the proprietors to change their original offer of 30 pounds cash to one of building materials for the structure and "thirty gallons of West India Rum."

The building was apparently finished in 1791. Pews were sold to finance the pulpit and residents were taxed to pay for a canopy over it. The first established minister to use the new meetinghouse was the Rev. Ebenezer Allen who was called in September of 1792. The town set his salary at £45 (compared with 55 for the Reverend Shaw) to rise to £60 as "the ratable estate of the Town" should increase. Voters exempted Allen from taxation and gave him a lot which had originally been reserved for the first settled minister. Thus Wolfeboro residents resolved the issue of the ministerial lot far more rapidly than did their neighbors in Moultonboro.

But what met the letter of the law did not suit many non-Congregational residents. Baptists, who comprised an important minority, dissented from this action. They decided to call their own clergyman, the Rev. Isaac Townsend, rejecting Allen and any tax support for him. They even selected October 25, 1792, as their date of ordination—the same date set for the ordination of Allen. In his ordination sermon Allen outlined the duties of a minister and observed that "The gospel of Christ is not to be preached by a novice, nor by any men who are ignorant and unlearned. It is to be preached only by men of learning and such as are faithful, apt and able to be esteemed as the ambassadors of Christ."

Participating in the ordination ceremony was Reverend Shaw of Moultonboro, who gave the actual charge to Allen. Shaw must have had mixed emotions about the situation since he had come to Moultonboro in the midst of controversy surrounding Reverend Perley. Nevertheless, Allen survived the challenge of the Baptists. He never was the sole minister in Wolfeboro and he continually had to face the fact that the disgruntled Baptists resented paying a ministerial tax to support Congregational preaching.

The resentment increased to the point that the tax collector seized a cow from one Thomas Cotton for his refusal to pay the tax. Cotton filed a lawsuit against the town for the seizure, and, after several delays, the town capitulated in 1806. It abated the tax and paid Cotton $20 for the cow which had been sold at auction. This ended compulsory taxation for ministerial support.

Like Moultonboro, Wolfeboro seemed far more absorbed in the problems of town and community-building on the frontier than in the affairs of nation-building and statehood. Financial difficulties and religious quarrels permeate surviving records and seem to have led to a lack of interest in the world beyond. No individual of John Wentworth's stature appeared in Wolfeboro in the years after 1775. Although the freeholders did elect Nathaniel Shannon to represent them at the 1788 conventions in Exeter and Concord, they did not participate at all in the amending of the State Constitution in 1791–1792, nor did they even bother to vote on the amendments submitted to the people for ratification.

Lacking men of John Wentworth's grand vision, the sturdy farmer-frontiersmen and their families had to plunge ahead as best they could. Inevitably their primary concerns focused on survival and improving a marginal lifestyle, as well as on the status of their souls.

"A GREAT MANY GOOD THINGS"
Conway, New Hampshire, and the Adoption of the U. S. Constitution

Helene-Carol Brown

Mission Vigao, California

*E*nglish traders called the place Pigwacket. Beautiful and nearly inaccessible, the rock-strewn hills at the confluence of the Saco, Swift and Pequaket Rivers long remained unsettled. King George III changed that when he brought Pigwacket out of obscurity in 1765. The king granted 23,040 acres as a township to be named Conway, after Horace Walpole's friend, Henry Seymour Conway.

Conway's legitimate new proprietors met in Chester in December 1765 to plan settlement. John Dolloff, James Osgood, Ebenezer Burbank, Capt. Henry Brown and others elected Thomas Merrill town clerk. The charter required the grantees to settle their land within five years or forfeit the grant. By 1771, when several "old rights" had not been claimed, Andrew McMillan of Concord, with others petitioned the General Court asking permission to take over the unclaimed land. With legislative approval, McMillan took several claims and built a tavern and house; his business account book reads like a town diary.

Before the Revolution, Conway settlers concentrated on clearing land, raising livestock and grain, and organizing public affairs. Merrill was voted twenty dollars (Spanish) to "spot a road"—that is, survey a thoroughfare from Sandwich to Conway. Such a road was essential since most of Conway's trade was with Concord and Derry. The town frequently engaged in debates over ownership of land, especially the grazing land in the intervale. Captain Henry Brown and others were appointed to consider redistribution but they convinced the town that the original apportionment was accurate. The proprietors gave mill privileges along with a considerable estate to Dr. Thomas Chadbourn as encouragement to settle. In time he would serve as a justice of the peace, representative to the General Court, and selectman.

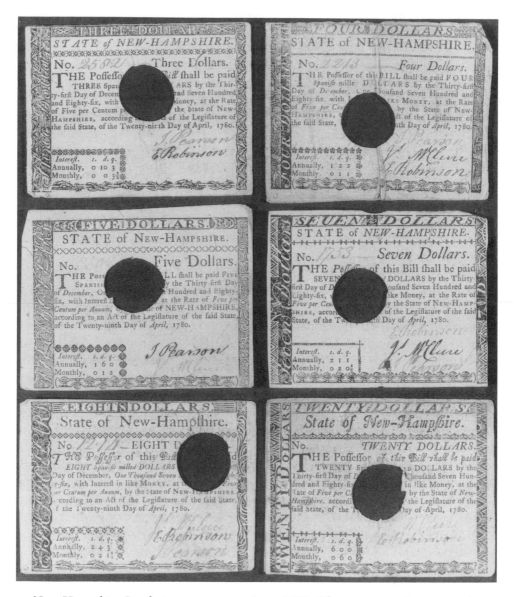

New Hampshire Revolutionary currency, issue 1780. The notes carry interest at the rate of five percent per year payable at maturity in 1786. The circular punch in each note prevented its reuse after payment. Courtesy of the N. H. Historical Society.

Still an infant community, Conway recorded 43 ratable polls (voting male citizens) in 1773. These had cleared 120 acres of arable land, 57 acres of mowing land, and showed 6 horses, 34 oxen, and 43 cows among the town's assets in the inventory reported to the legislature. Among their liabilities, they noted that produce was difficult to get to market and less valuable by the time it could be delivered. Every citizen had to turn his hand to several occupations for the community was too inaccessible to attract most itinerant craftsmen. Andrew McMillan's Ledger Book is replete with entries showing he could wear several hats:

1774	to my team to haul wood 1/2 Day	£0-12-0
1775	to putting a head in a barrel	£0-0-6
1778	to sowing 1/2 bushel flaxseed	£0-12-0
	to 2 days mowing	£0-6-0
	to serving a dinner [to travellers]	£0-5-0
	to making ten pairs of shoos and teaching John how to mend	£4-16-3

If craftsmen rarely ventured so far north, neither did clergymen. The primary purpose of a meetinghouse in a Congregationalist community was to provide a place for religious services. In September 1773 the town voted one hundred dollars to build a parsonage for a "setled preacher" and his family, but none arrived. The town paid a Mr. Chaplin for preaching one Sabbath, but apparently he never returned. In July 1774 Conway began negotiations with the Rev. Moses Adams. The town went to considerable trouble for him, voting him a dwelling house and five acres. But Adams proved a shrewd bargainer. He wanted £50 a year salary with a raise of 5 per year. To allow for inflation and to offset the dearth of hard money, Adams wanted to be paid half his annual salary in Indian corn, wheat, rye, or peas at the first of each year according to the market price. McMillan's ledger book quoted wheat at six shillings per bushel in 1774.

Deliberations continued as to design of the meetinghouse. Should it be 36 feet long and 30 feet wide and 12 feet high or 46 feet by 40 feet and two stories high? Or, should the settlers build two meetinghouses—one on each side of the river which half the town would forever have to cross? This was a significant issue for all, including the Reverend Adams. He had accepted the town's offer, but had refused to come. It appears from the town records that his parsonage and the meetinghouse were going to be on opposite sides of the river. The town voted Adams a "good Carage road" and "proper boats" but he remained unswayed. In desperation, on September 26, 1774, Conway voted Adams "sheds and a Proper house by the Meating house." Adams answered that he and the town "must say farewell forever."

At the outbreak of the Revolution Conway had other needs. Guards had to be posted on the northern frontier to watch for Indians and British troops. At its annual meeting in 1775 the town directed officers to raise £15 for building the meetinghouse, £30 for road repair, and £30 for schools. Joshua Heath, innkeeper, was put in charge of the town militia as Conway bolstered its courage to "Presearve our Selves, and Liberties" in the face of British chastisement. In March of 1776 citizens chose a committee of safety and military officers. Captain David Page, a leader in local affairs, was voted chairman of the committee which included Heath, McMillan, and Burbank. The Revolution spurred the collection of highway taxes. Isolated from other towns, Conway needed paths for local protection and for communication with the rest of the state. Fearing entrapment of its northern citizens, the town, in 1778, appropriated funds for Jeremiah Ferrington to build a bridge over the mill brook.

On July 7, 1778, Conway petitioned the General Court to be transferred from Grafton County to Strafford County. The town lamented that it was fifty miles from the nearest town in Grafton County, and even further to a shire town, which in winter was exceedingly inconvenient. The General Court granted the petition on November 10, 1780.

At its March 1778 meeting the town decided yet again to begin building its much discussed meetinghouse. In that year, the Rev. Nathaniel Porter accepted Conway's call, five years after efforts to settle a minister began. The town voted to build him a house and to pay him a salary of £65. Later in the year his salary was revised downward to £55, half to be paid in produce at the beginning of the year owing to strained town finances. Porter served Conway long and well; his last entry in the church record book was for January 18, 1821.

In the 1780s we can conclude that Conway emerged from an obscure mountain settlement to become a busy highland township, the first truly "White Mountain town." From town meeting records it is apparent that a dozen or so men controlled Conway. These men seem to have played a sort of political musical chairs, holding various offices such as selectman, representative to the General Court, justice of the peace, or tax assessor.

After 1780, these leaders faced several difficulties in guiding the town through war, debt, and inflation. The selectmen called a meeting that August of 1780 to discuss how to provide the town's share of beef for the Continental Army. Conway could ill afford to give its food supply away, since winters in so remote an area made bringing in foodstuffs difficult. Yet the alternative to supplying the beef was raising money to pay a fine for which the town lacked hard currency. David Page, moderator, agreed to let everyone think over the issue. They returned in September but the records do not show their decision. The heavy debts which the town incurred later suggest that the vote was to pay the fine with money borrowed from the state.

In 1781, wages and prices proved to be serious problems for Conway.

Selectmen suggested that everyone must literally put in a day's labor on the much needed highway upkeep, for labor was now so expensive that the town could not afford to hire out the work. Citizens voted to raise forty bushels of wheat—or the value thereof—in order to pay town expenses. A year earlier, the "expenses" had cost $900 [Continental], but money had become even less valuable than before, specie was nowhere to be found, and the town resorted to barter, like many other communities, in order to keep itself going. Financial desperation drove Conway to pay even the bounty for wolves in bushels of wheat.

Other town problems included clearing a space for a ford across Black Cat River and getting a ferry across the Swift River. Town records included three pages of carefully measured road surveys, as well, for if the town was to have any success in selling its crops and getting specie, it could only do so by trade. And for that, communications had to remain open. The school would be supported from the sale of one hundred bushels of wheat as there was no hard money.

Summer in 1781 brought confrontation from the Continental Army. Congress had notified Conway that it must raise its quota of soldiers for three-month enlistments, or suffer the penalties of sanctions and fines. Conway thereupon re-voted three soldiers and their salaries. Colonel Joseph Whipple came from Exeter to collect Conway's required thirty—not three—men for Continental service. After three days of recruiting through the surrounding forest, Whipple returned to Conway amazed and disheartened to find that no potential recruits were in evidence. Town leaders told Whipple that it took all available men just to watch the frontiers, leaving none for Continental duty. Indeed, the town suggested that Whipple ask Congress to send thirty men up north to protect Conway.

In June 1782 the town met to hear the "undertakers" of the meeting-house—Heath, Merrill and McMillan—announce that they had gone as far as they would until the town found more funds. The three had so far paid expenses out of their own pockets. They warned that if the proprietors could not come forth with at least half the money from the sale of pews in the meetinghouse, the building would remain in its uncompleted state with timbers up and some planking but with no windows. Alarmed, the townsmen agreed to raise half the pew money by December if the three committeemen would finish the building. But what did "finish" mean? A debate ensued over what exactly was meant by "finish." Once again the town resorted to orderly agreement: "When the frame shall be covered, shingled, clapboarded, and all the ground Part shall be glazed, the floor laid, and the outer Doore Hung, it shall be called Half-Done." Selectmen noted that anyone could void his claim to a pew: the town would buy and re-sell the claim.

In March 1783 Conway accepted the meetinghouse as it stood and sold the pews to raise money to finish it. At the same meeting the voters chose

George Atkinson as president of the State by a margin of 48 to 3. Because of his opposition to hard money, Atkinson's opponent, Portsmouth merchant John Langdon, found no favor with Conway citizens. Of all the issues which Conway faced after the war the ones which occupied most of their attention were local expenses, road building, and getting the meetinghouse completed.

The struggle for economic stability was further complicated by the on-going struggle with nature. In autumn of 1786 torrential rains fell, and the town suffered its worst natural disaster ever. The "Great Freshet," as it was known ever after in Conway, nearly destroyed all the hard work of twenty years which the good townspeople had put into their community. Conway petitioned the General Court of New Hampshire for financial help. The rains washed away houses and barns, drowned cattle, and carried produce and furnishings from the homes of the settlers. The town had not the wherewithal to pay its apportioned taxes and implored the General Court to have these abated.

Andrew McMillan listed the damage for the petition:

327 acres	totally spoiled
2 barns with hay	carried away
7 dwelling houses	totally destroyed
4 barns	totally destroyed

10 oxen	
12 cowes	
80 sheep }	all drowned
2 horses	
25 swine	

nearly all the corn, cut and in the fields, washed away
all the fences
1 saw mill
1 grist mill
and every bridge (costing £100 each)   washed away
1 1/2 tons of potash, carefully collected, swept downstream

The normally beautiful rivers, all three of them, had gone on a rampage through the settlements built alongside. Selectmen first thought to abate the taxes of Conway citizens, then reneged, realizing that the town needed every contribution which could be had.

In 1787 the General Court declared that towns should elect representatives to go to a convention "to be holden at Exeter" in February 1788 for the "purpose of the full and free investigation, discussion, and decision upon the Federal

Constitution transmitted to the General Court of this state through the medium of Congress." This announcement is the first evidence that Conway had begun deliberations on the coming federal form of government. The town was of Jeffersonian persuasion, as were many frontier towns, but the minister, Nathaniel Porter, was an ardent Federalist.

In January 1788 Conway selected David Page to attend the Exeter convention. Richard Kimball and Charles Hill were chosen to write the town's instructions for Page to follow at the convention. After a "full and free investigation," Conway decided that while the new plan proposed some good ideas, on the whole they opposed it: "As we find a great many good things in the proposed Constitution blended with what we cannot approve, and as there is not to be any alterations to be made in said Constitution, we Desire you [David Page] to do all in your power to hinder the Establishment thereof."

As the townspeople understood the document, it would not have a bill of rights and it could not be amended. This was a source of mistrust. They felt they already had one layer of bureaucracy over their local decisions—state government—which would be doubled with a set of federal officials. As Jere R. Daniell notes in *Experiment in Republicanism*, debates about accepting a federal governmental system prompted ambivalent feelings in the hills of New Hampshire.

The research of another scholar, Lynn Turner, confirms this feeling by New Hampshire settlers, and Conway townsmen in particular. Agitation among "poor, isolated, suspicious farmers" ran high. They were afraid of the "great men"—that is, the big merchants. Backwoods people thought that paper money would solve their trade and tax problems, and the aversion to issuing paper money which Langdon, Sullivan and others evinced only made frontiersmen the more dubious of their being in control. In addition, Turner notes, settlers, north of Rochester certainly, identified more with Maine than with fellow New Hampshirites.

David Page duly voted as his town instructed him. At its annual meeting that March, the town returned to its preoccupation with local affairs. The subject of the Constitution is never recorded again. Yet, since New Hampshire delegates reconvened in Concord, the townspeople had news of the Exeter deliberations and knew of the controversy throughout the state over the ratification. But Conway had had its say, and it evidently chose not to reconsider.

Conway conducted meetings in the final years of the 1700s with traditional concern for schools, roads, ferries, bridges, and payment for local officials. In 1789 debates about schools made it clear that two schoolhouses could not provide for all the children. A third was needed, on the main road near Maj. Joshua Heath's place. A fourth would best be placed near Thomas Russell's house, and a fifth should be near Abiathar Eastman's farm. A sixth school would serve children who lived out by Moses Kendall's homestead. One of the things this set of school placements indicates is that the settled areas in the town were

STATE OF NEW-HAMPSHIRE.

The Government and People of said State.

To the Selectmen of *Conway* in said State.   Greeting.

YOU are hereby required to notify the legal Inhabitants paying Taxes in the *Town of Conway & Locations* (giving them fifteen Days Notice) to meet at some convenient Place in your Town, on or before the tenth Day of December next, to elect *one* Person (having a real Estate of the Value of Two Hundred Pounds, Lawful Money, in this State) to represent them in the General Assembly to be holden at Exeter in said State, on the third Wednesday in December next, at three o'Clock in the Afternoon, and to empower such Representative for the Term of one Year, from their first Meeting, to transact such Business, and pursue such Measures as they may judge necessary for the public Good, and particularly to impower such Representative to vote in the Choice of Delegates for the Continental Congress. And the Person who shall be elected you are to notify to attend at Time and Place above-mentioned.

And at said Meeting each Voter, as aforesaid, on one Paper is to bring in Votes for *Two* Person being reputable Freeholders and Inhabitants in your County, (having a real Estate of Two Hundred Pounds) to serve as Members of the Council for the Year ensuing. And the Clerk of your Town is hereby directed to seal up all such Votes under Cover, and send them to *Rochester* in your County, by the second Wednesday in December next, directed to *Joseph Badger, James Knowles & Joshua Wingate*, a Committee appointed to receive them.

AND IT IS RESOLVED, That no Person be allowed a Seat in the Council or Assembly, who shall by himself, or any Person for him, before said Choice, treat with Liquor, &c. any Electors with an apparent View of gaining their Votes, or afterwards on that Account.

And make Return of this Writ, with your Doings thereon, into the Secretary's-Office at Exeter, by the third Wednesday in December next.

Exeter, August 29th, 1781.   *M Weare* President.

                                    John Langdon Speaker.

By order of Council and Assembly,
E Thompson   Secretary.

Order from the state government to the selectmen of Conway for taxpayers to vote for a representative to the General Court to convene in December 1781. Courtesy of the State Archives.

at considerable distance from each other. No single schoolhouse could serve such disparate settlements. In 1793, the Reverend Porter expressed concern about the quality of education, noting that the schools were not progressing beyond dame school status. Trained schoolmasters with professional qualifications were not yet come to the far north. Porter lobbied ardently for the hiring of better qualified teachers, foresightedly, but the tiny budget which the town could provide each annual meeting allowed for no such extravagance.

Without doubt the primary concern of Conway for the 1790s was the recurrent question of the construction of its meetinghouse. By July 1793 the church congregation was prepared to resolve the question of the meetinghouse by dividing the town into two parishes with a meetinghouse in each one. Those with houses at the north end would become the parish of North Conway while those in the south would constitute Conway proper. Both parishes retained Nathaniel Porter as their minister. They liked Porter for his gentle, peaceable temperament. Further, he was regarded as preeminent in his calling for he ordained a number of other ministers during his career in Conway. By May 1794 the town had laid out the road for the meetinghouse of the new parish and surveyors had checked several locations to put a bridge across the Swift River.

The only challenge to the religious harmony of the town came with the withdrawal of several younger members of the congregation to join the Baptist Society in Sandwich. Only in the opening years of the nineteenth century, however, did polarization begin to show in Conway. The Baptists began to agitate for a church of their own in the community. Going all the way to Sandwich to sing hymns and listen to sermons was less palatable than it had been. The numbers of Baptists in the area began to exercise some voice at the town meetings in resistance to paying for a building and an organization which they did not find to their liking. But all this was some years hence.

While local concerns dominated in the 1790s, the town did vote on proposed revisions to the State Constitution. Conway favored most of the amendments. It disliked, however, the times when the legislature proposed to meet, fearing that spring planting would just be underway when representatives would be called from their local areas to meet in the capital. This was good for those in trade or shipping, but bad for farmers. Besides this objection, there were unanimous votes against changes in voter qualifications and property requirements for office holders.

The outermost areas of Conway "plantation" were known from the days of the royal charter as "locations." Two of these, Archibald Stark's and Andrew McMillan's, officially joined North Conway in 1796. McMillan owned 2000 acres of this outerland, as well as 300 acres of the southern parish. He was quick to see that he would be a controlling factor of the new town as he was of the older. In fact, he moved to the northern village and remained there until his death in 1800.

The annual meeting of 1797 was the first in which the entire budget was recorded in dollars, not pounds. Indeed, the most systematic change in the management of Conway in these last years of the century was the organized, recorded, and strictly enforced collection of taxes. Too often the town had cheerfully voted an amount of money for some project, only to find that when the enthusiasm of the moment wore off collecting the money proved a more difficult matter.

The end of the eighteenth century found that Pigwacket had grown from an obscure "location" at the foothills of the White Mountains to a brace of towns named Conway. In thirty-five years the community had become the home of 705 souls. Several prominent families had guided its fortunes, shared in its prosperity and its hard times with less well-known folk, and a few patient and stable men had led the town to energetic accomplishments. War had left the settlement relatively unscathed, and the new Federal Constitution had brought them—seemingly against their own will—a measure of long-awaited commercial benefit.

Of all the factors in Conway's growth, however, the citizens were fortunate in their selection of Nathaniel Parker as minister. Politics aside, the people respected and liked their minister, and he in turn shepherded them through their hardest years of development with a particular concern for unity of spirit.

Conway had succeeded against all odds in conquering its environment and had emerged a burgeoning collection of bountiful farms. What had begun as an outpost for fish and furs had become a clutch of settled villages with verdant fields, stout dwelling houses, and finished meetinghouses. A "great many good things" had indeed come to the settlers along the Saco.

JOSHUA MORSE,
DELEGATE FROM HOPKINTON

Stephen D. Thomas

Hopkinton, New Hampshire

*W*hether he went by sleigh, or on horseback, or afoot, and what passable town roads he followed in a day before the first turnpikes had been built, we do not know. In February 1788 the journey of sixty miles or more, from Hopkinton to Exeter, would have given Joshua Morse the opportunity to mull over the issue of a Federal Constitution.

On the one hand, he had his orders; he knew what he must do. One month earlier, at a town meeting on January 14th, his fellow citizens had chosen him as their delegate to the convention in Exeter, called to ratify or reject the proposed Constitution for the United States, and they had instructed him to vote "no." Perhaps he himself had urged them to this conclusion.

In spite of the Hopkinton mandate, he was likely a man willing to hear the opposition. Down a string of roads toward Exeter, through a bleak winter landscape, he could anticipate those arguments. More than one hundred other delegates were also en route to the opening session on Wednesday, February 13. Some were from towns larger and richer than Hopkinton; some from barely settled areas where all energies still went toward subsistence.

Morse was, however, not unlike many of the delegates he was about to meet. As boys, they had been British subjects in provincial towns or on the edge of dark and endless forests. As young men, they had first fought with the British army against the French and then watched provincial ties with the mother country deteriorate. Mature, they had faced the same "world turned upside down" in the colonial revolt against the king's government. Together they now turned toward the uncertain aftermath.

Joshua Morse was born on July 3, 1742, in Newbury, Massachusetts, the son of Joshua and Prudence Morse. Shortly before his seventeenth birthday, he was one of Capt. William Davenport's company under the command of Gen. James Wolfe in the expedition to take Quebec. The company was engaged in

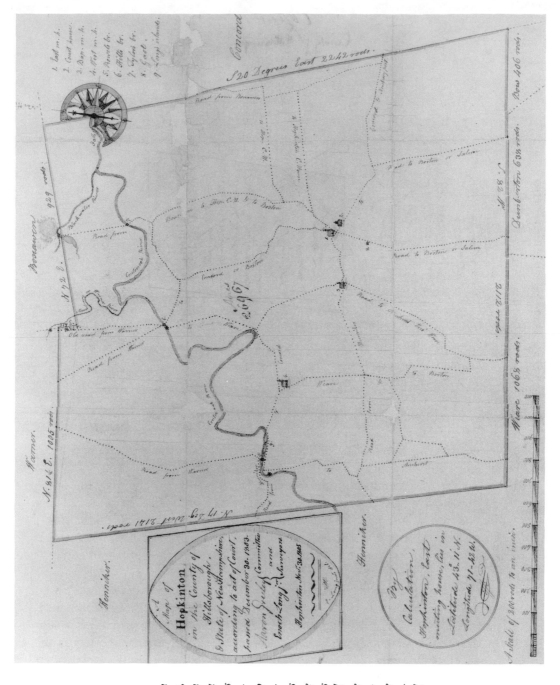

Map of Hopkinton by Enoch Long, Jr. 1805. Drawn to comply with a survey of towns ordered by the legislature, the map locates several major landmarks including the three meetinghouses (East, West, and Baptist) and the courthouse. Courtesy of the State Archives. Photograph by Bill Finney.

battle on the Plains of Abraham on the day Generals Wolfe and Montcalm were killed, and was present at the surrender of Quebec on September 30, 1759.

A joiner by trade, Morse married Rebecca Patten who was born in Newbury on January 14, 1740. Their first child, Joshua, was born in Newbury on December 14, 1766, and died there before he was three months old. A daughter, Rebecca, was born in 1768, and a second daughter, Prudence, in 1770. Records show that this third child died at the age of one week. Another daughter named Prudence, born July 31, 1772, died at the age of five months. Daughter Rebecca was still living after 1781 when the Hopkinton town clerk listed the Morses' children in the town records.

In 1772, Morse had purchased two forty-acre lots in Hopkinton from William Eastman for £300. The property was located at the crest of what would later be known as Dimond Hill, on the south side of the "Grate Road" from Hopkinton to Concord. With a quarter-mile of frontage, the two contiguous parcels stretched a half mile southward from the road. Looking over his property prior to purchase, Morse undoubtedly met Deacon William Peters whose land abutted his on the west. An original grantee of the town and the first settler on Dimond Hill, Peters could have sketched its history for Morse.

"New Hopkinton" had been granted by the Province of Massachusetts Bay to a group of Hopkinton, Massachusetts men in 1735. Twenty pounds had been allotted by the proprietors in 1737 to clear the road from Rumford (now Concord) to the center of the town, and by 1738 settlement was underway. In 1757 the town had settled its first minister, the Rev. James Scales, and two years later William Peters had been elected its first deacon.

The fact that their charter was from the Massachusetts Bay government, however, created problems for the proprietors and early settlers. Both the Bay Colony General Court and the royal government at Portsmouth were simultaneously granting towns in the area to the west of the Merrimack River. The New Hampshire grant to the proprietors of Bow overlapped the Bay Colony's town of Rumford (1727) and a portion of New Hopkinton, including the Dimond Hill area.

Twenty years after the establishment of the Massachusetts–New Hampshire boundary in 1741, the citizens of New Hopkinton applied to the Portsmouth government in 1762 and were again granted the original territory, renamed "Hopkinton, New Hampshire." On December 13, 1763, just eight years prior to Morse's purchase, the New Hampshire government had formally annexed that portion of Bow lying within Hopkinton to the latter town.

Across the road from the land of Morse and Peters lay the property of Hezekiah Foster, consisting of eighty acres, and to the west of Foster, the one-hundred acre tract of Moses Sawyer. In 1772, two weeks after Morse's purchase, Foster sold his land to Jonathan Chase of Concord. The two families would be neighbors for the remainder of Morse's life. Both Joshua and Rebecca witnessed the two deeds of sale to Chase. Today, their houses remain on Dimond Hill, the Morses' a small cape on the south side, and the houses of Charles and Daniel Chase, sons of Jonathan, large four-square colonials on the north side.

The Hopkinton which the Morses had come to had a population of nine hundred people, settling their second minister, the Rev. Elijah Fletcher, of Westford, Massachusetts in 1773. Joshua and Rebecca Morse brought their fifth child, Joshua, to the new minister for baptism shortly after his birth in November 1773. As pastor of the Church of Christ, Fletcher, was by virtue of his position, part of the religious controversy which plagued the town for many years. The problem had its roots in the terms of charter granted by both the Massachusetts Bay Colony and the Province of New Hampshire. The charters called for the construction of a meetinghouse and the settlement of a minister, all "at the Cost and Charge of the Grantees and their associates."

Every citizen of the town was expected to pay the tax for the support of the "orthodox" church, but the formation of a Baptist society in 1771, as well as the presence of itinerant Baptist preachers before that time, allowed the townspeople some choice. Every citizen was furthermore expected to attend the established church, yet Fletcher and his faithful were forced to meet frequently to consider those members who were "absenting themselves from lecture and communion." Now one brother, and now another, including Morse, was charged to call upon wayward members.

There were more mundane matters to attend to. On December 9, 1775, Morse registered his earmark with the town "for his creatures…a slit in the end of the left ear and a Slit A crost the upper Sid of same." By dint of hard work, the Morse homestead would eventually be a successful small farm including up to two acres of orchard, four of tillage, fifteen of mowing land, and twenty-four of pasture. Tax inventories for the Morse property show one horse, two oxen, and eleven cattle under his care. The purchase of twenty acres in Hopkinton from Ephraim Fisk in 1795 increased the estate to one hundred acres.

Charles C. Lord, gathering information for a town history more than a century later undoubtedly asked Morse's great-granddaughter, Helen Morse Goodspeed, or his great-great-grandson, Professor Arthur J. Goodspeed, for stories about their ancestor. Lord writes what family tradition had handed down: "Joshua Morse was…at Ticonderoga with Ethan Allen; and three years in all in the Revolutionary army, being at Yorktown and White Plains. At the latter place, he received from General Washington a walnut stick, which he brought home and made into a cane, which is in the possession of his descendants to this day." Whether Morse was at home on August 16, 1775, for the birth of Aaron, his second son, or at Ticonderoga, the church record does not say.

Along with neighbors Chase and Peters, Morse was one of 161 Hopkinton men to sign the oath of allegiance to the American cause in the spring of 1776 in response to an order by the New Hampshire Committee of Safety. Rebecca gave birth on May 28, 1777, to a third son, Samuel, who was baptised by the Reverend Fletcher on June 1st. Samuel's birth meant that Rebecca would have had three little boys, ages 5, 3, and 1 to care for, with the assistance of ten-year-old Rebecca, in addition to assuming responsibility for the running of the farm, when Joshua enlisted as a private in Capt. Joshua Bailey's company of General Whipple's brigade on August 7, 1778. Thereafter he left for twenty-three days of service in Rhode Island under General John Sullivan. Perhaps neighbor Chase lent a hand in that haying season as Morse might have done for Chase previously.

In 1778, Morse began nearly thirty years of civic and religious service to Hopkinton. On March 2, at the twelfth annual town meeting, the 35-year-old Morse was elected a selectman, and was also chosen one of the surveyors of highways. This latter position required not only the ability to balance the needs of the town with the rights of property owners but a cool head as well, for the laying out of a road could be a hotly contested issue. Morse's family increased with the birth of Jane on September 10, 1779, and Judith, born on July 27, 1781. In November 1782 Joshua and Rebecca became members of the Hopkinton Congregational Church.

Morse's involvement in politics continued with his selection as one of nine members of a "Committee of Examination" on November 18, 1782 to consider how the town would instruct its delegate to vote on the proposed New Hampshire Constitution. Hopkinton had rejected two previous proposals, but evidently the committee returned a favorable verdict as the town voted its acceptance, with proposed amendments, on December 23, 1782.

A census of Hopkinton in 1783 showed a population of 1,488, and from this population it was the responsibility of Constable Morse to collect £341.18.11 in taxes, one-half to be paid by August 1 and the other half by December 30. He was charged also with paying the Reverend Fletcher £34 by the last day of February 1784 as well as with collecting £91.10.3 1/2 in War Rates for that year. At town meeting in 1784 he was again voted surveyor of highways and charged with examination of the selectmen's accounts. Church records for the same period indicate that he was chosen one of two collectors for the church "for the time being."

The financial strain of the Revolution as well as its indirect effect upon properties—essential tasks not completed or done in a cursory manner—shows up in tax inventories for the town during the 1780s. The value of real estate owned by residents, recorded as £7,380 in 1782, dropped to £7,347 in 1788, fluctuating between the two amounts in the intervening years. Decreases in the amount of arable land, orchard acres, and mowing acres also suggest the residual effect of the war years.

As a collector of taxes, Joshua Morse encountered hardship cases, not to

*Credentials of Lt. Joshua Morss [sic] as "a Delegate to Represent this Town of Hopkinton"
at the convention. Courtesy of the State Archives. Photograph by Bill Finney.*

mention instances of difficulty for those even of moderate means. In his history,
Charles Lord cites an example of the escalating inflation, stating that in 1779
the price of a man's labor for highway work was $5 per day, but that by 1781 it
had soared to $30. So unstable were monetary values that on June 4, 1787, the
town voted to dispose of all its paper money. Chosen to serve as selectman in
March 1786 and as moderator in 1787, Morse would have known first-hand the
close straits of running a town government in the most adverse of times.

It was during this unstable period that on April 8, 1786, the Rev. Elijah
Fletcher died, leaving the town without the moral, and often political, guidance
that he had provided. For three years a succession of ministers supplied the pulpit. A settled minister might have shaped the attitudes of the Hopkinton
community about a constitution. As it was, the citizens were left to whatever
informal discussion at tavern or mill might do to urge a voter this way or that.
Hopkinton residents, whose news often came from their attendance at the'
county courthouse in Amherst—often complaining about the distance they had
to go to transact county business—voted on November 30, 1787, that "our
Representative should use his influence in the General Court that if theare is
anything Dun Relitive to the Court House being removed from Amherst that it
should stand as near the Senter of the County as is Convenant."

Prevailing word from Amherst as to the Federal Constitution would doubt-less have included discussion of the Anti-Federalist views held by Joshua Atherton, a prominent lawyer who lived there. He was one of the new govern-ment's most vocal opponents, and any Hopkinton resident who visited Amherst during the fall and early winter of 1787–1788 would probably have become aware of his sentiments in opposition to the proposed Constitution.

On January 14, 1788, Lieutenant Morse was chosen as delegate to the con-vention to consider the Federal Constitution which was to gather on February 13 at Exeter. Morse was instructed to oppose the new government.

It is interesting to speculate as to his own feelings, which he was later allowed to consult in determining how to vote. Which of his life experiences had most shaped his thinking, his sense of the way of the world? Against what practi-cal realities would he have weighed the arguments for a strong central government? He had known the difficulties of starting from scratch, surely; of having to devise while in motion. As a joiner he would have appreciated the value of a sound plan.

Perhaps he was one of the eleven men calculated by the New Hampshire Federalist leaders believed as individually supportive of the Constitution's approval but bound by their instructions to oppose it. As things turned out, he did not have the opportunity to cast that negative vote after attending each ses-sion of the ten-day convention.

Within two weeks of the February adjournment, Morse was elected modera-tor of the 1788 Hopkinton town meeting. If officially he must preside as neutral, he was nevertheless unofficially in a position to be heard. We may only guess at the role he played in bringing about the results of a June 14 town meeting vote which instructed him to "act in convention as he shall think best for the Public Good."

The town of 1,600 people could not or would not bring itself to affirm the proposed Constitution, nor could its voters find reason to reject it. Perhaps the voters had heard enough, had come to believe that as far as the business of plant-ing and building, and getting a good harvest was concerned, a federal government, hundreds of miles away, was hardly of importance to their lives. Whatever deter-mined their mood and their vote, they were nonetheless certain of one thing: Joshua Morse, whom they respected and trusted, could well speak for them.

Four days later, on Wednesday, June 18, the convention reopened at Concord, and adjourned on Saturday, June 21. Lieutenant Morse cast his vote: an "aye" for ratification. Having thought "best for the public good," Morse had been able to envision for his fellow townsmen that strength—deep in the social and political foundation far below daily awareness—which the United States Constitution would provide.

Whether Morse realized how momentous a slice of history he had taken part in, no surviving letters or diaries say. He returned to yet another twenty

State of New Hampshire } To the Honble the Senate and House of Representatives for Said State to be Con=veaned at Portsmouth the fourth Wednesday of December A^d 1789 ————————

Humbly Shews the Subscribers Inhabitants of the Town of Hopkinton in the County of Hillsborough and State aforesaid that it is Rational to Suppose and favoured by the Constitution of Said State that no person ought to be Com=pelled to pay Taxes for the Support of a Minister of the Gospel whose Sentiments in Religion are Different from his — that in February last the Rev^d. Jacob Cram was Ordained in said Hopkinton Previous to which Many of us by ourselves and Agents Objected against his being Ordained thinking his Sentiments not agreable to ours — Notwithstanding he was Ordained and we are Taxed toward his Support We think it Cruel that we Should in a Day when a Spirit of Liberality in Religious Sentiments Pervades the Continent and not a single Constitution in the United States compells a Man to pay where he cannot Conscientiously hear & be Compelled to pay this Man; We wish to Support the Preaching of the Gospel at the Same Time wish for a Man of our own Choosing We therefore Beg that we may either have a Poll Parrish in Said Town or that the Same may be divided in Such manner as the Honble Court Shall think best And as in duty bound Shall ever Pray

Thaddeus Ladd   Stephen Harriman
Moses Jones   Ezekiel Hadley

Petition to the General Court from some inhabitants of Hopkinton objecting to paying taxes for the support of the Rev. Jacob Cram. Courtesy of the State Archives. Photograph by Bill Finney.

years of public service as many another delegate perhaps did also. Morse now entered the most active period of his service to the town, including over the next sixteen years, five one-year terms as selectman and twelve as moderator. He was also drawn into the nagging problems arising from the ill-defined relationship between church and town.

The town had voted to call the Rev. Jacob Cram as its minister on November 10, 1788. Between his acceptance and his installation on February 25, 1789, the meetinghouse was destroyed by fire, an act of arson. While a new meetinghouse was built, with Morse serving on the committee charged with planning it, enormous controversy ensued owing to contention by many over Cram's installation and payment of his salary through taxes, a practice which the Federal Constitution prohibited. In the midst of this complexity, Joshua Morse—pro-Constitution, town officer, and active member of the the "orthodox" church—must have scratched his head more than once.

As controversy continued to swirl, the town voted to assemble a council to review the "pastoral relation," and on January 6, 1792, by mutual agreement, the Reverend Cram ended his pastorate in Hopkinton. Support for a minister continued to plague the town for a number of years. Morse served on a committee in 1805 to "consider and report" on the difficulty of collecting ministerial taxes. The group reported taxes due for the past several years of $141.07 and deemed $83.30 of it legal and collectible. By 1811, the town had withdrawn from the process of raising money for the Congregational minister. In 1819 the General Court put an end to civil support of any religion. The Federal Constitution had actually pointed this way all along. As for religious matters, its eloquent silence had said, this civil government will neither debate nor legislate.

While public service engaged Morse during these years of controversy, there were private griefs to be borne. On May 9, 1790, his 15-year-old son, Aaron, died. The cause of his death is nowhere recorded, nor can a marker be found in the Hopkinton cemetery. He also lost a daughter, Judith, aged 23, in 1804.

Two weeks later Morse moderated a town meeting for the last time. In July of 1804 the Morses became grandparents for the first time with the birth of a son, Joshua, to their eldest son, also Joshua, a joiner and landowner in Boscawen.

By 1800 Hopkinton was enjoying steady growth and a satisfying prosperity. A population of 1,537 in 1785 had increased to 1,715 in 1790, and to 2,015 in 1800, on the way to more than 2,200 people by 1810. Half-sessions of the county court were convened in its bustling center. Morse himself was one of the committee chosen to work out details for the improvement of the townhouse in preparation for further sessions of the legislature which would gather there in 1801, 1806, and 1807. The year 1812 would see the completion of the Londonderry Branch Turnpike in Hopkinton as a growing system of highways throughout the state made travel easier.

In 1810 Joshua exchanged deeds to property with his sons, settling Samuel in Boscawen and deeding the old Hopkinton farm to Joshua and his family. The presence of his young family would certainly have been of great comfort to Morse at the time of Rebecca's death on February 21, 1812, at the age of 71. She was buried in the Morse lot in the Hopkinton Village Cemetery, where a handsome slate stone, still in fine condition, marks her grave.

Morse continued to watch town affairs, an elder statesman with a keen constitutional sense. The War of 1812 brought an order from President Madison for the raising of military manpower, ready to move at a moment's notice. At a meeting on July 6, characterized by patriotic ardor, the town voted to pay seven dollars a month to soldiers raised in Hopkinton for this force. In a lengthy letter to the selectmen Morse objected to this taxation:

> it is amoung my objections to the afore-said vote that they will not answer to the purposes discribed in them, and that they must fail of making to the draft that compensation which they deserve; becaiuse I believe the whole of said votes to be illegal, and not constitutionally binding on the inhabitants of this Town. The powers which Towns possess of Assessing taxes on the inhabitants, is limited by the same laws which creates it. The constitution and laws of the State of New Hampshire, in my opinion give no power to Towns to tax their citizens to such purposes as are mentioned in the afore-said votes.

His objection was overridden.

In October of 1814 he married Lydia Farnum of Concord, the wedding performed by the Rev. Asa McFarland of the Congregational Church there.

One of Morse's last public acts made a fitting close to the controversy of religious taxation with which he had had to contend for so much of his time in Hopkinton. As the General Court prepared to pass the "Toleration Act," separating the functions of church and town, the members of the Hopkinton church entered a covenant to establish the First Congregational Society, a governing body for the institution. Morse was handed the pen to sign first, no doubt well satisfied by this final resolution to a long story.

On June 4, 1823, Joshua Morse died in Hopkinton at the age of eighty-one. He was buried in the Village Cemetery beside his first wife, Rebecca. Three years later, on July 4, 1826, Thomas Jefferson and John Adams were also to die, giants of a generation passing from a world whose human politics, shaped by both the great and small of that generation, would never be the same.

CONCORD AFTER THE REVOLUTION, 1780–1800

Frank C. Mevers

New Hampshire State Archives

*I*n 1780, as the war for independence from Great Britain continued, Concord found itself on the fringes of the contest. The town served as a nucleus for surrounding communities on either side of the Merrimack River and for some distance north and south. Its population of approximately 1,600 equaled that of its western neighbor Hopkinton while it exceeded that of the other communities. Concord was contributing men and materiel to the war effort but like the rest of New Hampshire had escaped military havoc. A close neighbor, Canterbury, would soon contribute the talents of a leading citizen, Abiel Foster, to the Continental Congress and, later, to the first federal Congress.

First settled in the 1720s, Concord was granted by the Massachusetts General Court to Ebenezer Eastman and others as Penacook Plantation and in 1733 was incorporated by Massachusetts as Rumford. A 1727 grant by the New Hampshire government to the proprietors of Bow, overlapping land in Rumford, resulted in a dispute which lasted until 1765 when, following a decision of the king in council, the New Hampshire legislature incorporated Rumford as a parish and changed its name to Concord.

The same topographical and geographical features that would later lead to its growth were those responsible for its settlement. A plain with good soil located at a calm stretch between sets of falls on a major river and in the geographical center of the province attracted Eastman and his followers.

In 1780 a stable group of leaders held sway over town affairs, the same two dozen or so names appearing repeatedly in the town records as holders of various offices. Not holding a civil office but commanding the universal respect of Concord's citizenry was her one ordained minister, Timothy Walker, Jr., who looms above all as the town's counsellor. In a time when church and state were synonymous, Walker led the community for half a century after his ordination in 1730.

House of the Rev. Timothy Walker, built in the 1730s and later enlarged, as it appeared in an 1853 woodcut (above). House of the Rev. Timothy Walker, c. 1960 (below). Courtesy of the N. H. Historical Society.

In assessing the status of Concord and its surrounding communities in the late 18th century too much emphasis cannot be given to the influence of Timothy Walker. He inspired the community as much by his manner as by his doctrine. Born in Woburn, Massachusetts, in July 1705, he was descended directly from that town's first settlers. Walker received his A.B. from Harvard, held several teaching assignments, and returned for his M.A. in 1728, arguing that one may be certain of one's fate. In 1730 Walker accepted the call to Rumford, married in Woburn, and came north. In 1734 the Walkers began work on a house that is frequently described as the first two-story dwelling between Haverhill, Massachusetts, and Montreal, still a Concord landmark.

In other practical undertakings, Walker established Concord's first dairy herd, planted its first English grass, and created a working farm which served as a model for others. By 1780 he owned three Negro slaves to help work the farm. He quickly gained, and retained, the respect of his parishoners and of surrounding Indian leaders.

Walker kept his congregation on a steady course through the religious upheavals of the "Great Awakening" and was, in 1780, in as strong a leadership position as ever as he continued to fill the only pulpit in town. He allowed his people to study the Bible and form their own opinions. His liberality generally extended to other ministers of the Gospel, but he drew the line against allowing Baptist preacher Hezekiah Smith to sermonize in the town because Smith and his fellows were perceived as destroying the peace and unity of the church.

Much of his popularity derived from his active leadership in settling the controversy between Rumford and Bow resulting in Concord's incorporation in 1765. Between 1753 and 1765 much of Walker's energy went toward gaining independence for Concord from Bow. Walker actually went to London in 1753 and again in 1762 where he argued with apparent effect for Rumford's position in the debate, that is, for its right to property that the provincial authorities had included in their grant to Bow.

Politically, Walker agreed with the Whigs but his decision to support the colonists against British arms was painful for him. His son, Timothy, and two of his sons-in-law fought in the Revolution, but another son-in-law, Benjamin Thompson, who later took the courtesy title Count Rumford, left in deference to the British cause.

Walker's guidance carried the town into the 1780s: replacing him proved to be no easy task. It was well into the 1780s before the Rev. Israel Evans, one of several ministers found by the search committee, agreed to accept the call and was ordained in 1789. Evans had difficulty filling Walker's pulpit and resigned in July 1797. Later that year the town welcomed the Rev. Asa McFarland who remained for a long tenure. Diversity and dissension increased. By the turn of the century other religious forces had spread throughout the state and within

Leather pocketbook of the Rev. Timothy Walker, dated 1741. Courtesy of the N. H. Historical Society.

only a few years several denominations had established themselves in Concord.

It was not through Timothy Walker's leadership alone that Concord attained its eminence but by the steady direction of a group of about two dozen citizens with family names of Walker, Stickney, Abbott, Kimball, Carter, Green, and Emery. They swapped public offices including those of selectman, clerk, moderator, sealer of leather, fence viewer, and constable, and it was these men who along with Walker's son Timothy collectively filled the void left by the death of the Reverend Walker.

Despite the postwar recession in the state, Concord was growing, and it was assuring a central meeting place for state government. Between 1778 and 1783 four conventions met in the city, at the direction of the General Court, specifically to write a constitution for the state. Beginning in 1782 the legislature met with increasing frequency in Concord.

Society had moved westward or inland from the coast where Portsmouth and its neighbor Exeter had ruled as capitals of the colony, province, and state since

1680. In the decades before and after 1800 Concord vied with Exeter, Hopkinton, and other towns to become the permanent capital. By 1807 the site was fixed and construction of the state house was begun in 1816. Thus, between 1780 and 1800 Concord did much to ensure that it would become the political and civil center, just as it was already at the geographical center, of New Hampshire.

Of course one of the most important meetings to take place in Concord was the second convention to consider the proposed Federal Constitution, which gathered in Concord in June of 1788. At that meeting, to the surprise of some nineteenth century historians, the Concord delegate voted no.

Concord town meeting minutes note simply that Capt. Benjamin Emery was selected as a delegate to the convention that was to consider ratification of the Federal Constitution in 1788. The record states that "At a legal meeting of the Freeholders & other Inhabitants of the Town of Concord on Wednesday the second Day of January AD 1788 past the following Votes: Chose Captn Benjn Emery to set in Convention at Exeter on the second Wednesday of February next to take under Consideration the proceedings of the late Federal Convention." There is no indication of any instruction given to Emery.

Emery took an extremely active role in Concord government, holding nearly every office at one time or another. He was in the lumber business and his residence was located near the meetinghouse. Research has turned up precious little about his personal life or character. Tradition holds that he was a big, bluff, commanding person. Whether he was a native of Concord, or even of New Hampshire, we cannot be sure. Town records and town histories steadfastly refer to him as "Captain" Emery, a title he probably picked up as commander of a company in the Revolutionary War regiment of Colonel Nathan Baldwin.

His service in the military ended in February 1776, and his name appears in the town records consistently thereafter for the next quarter century. He was a selectman in 1775 and 1782 and held other positions over the years. Emery was one of the town's larger taxpayers: in 1796 he paid $70.39 to collector Timothy Bradley, one of the greater amounts on that particular list. We can conjecture that because he took such a prominent role in the community during this period, and that because Concord appears to have been such a stable and normally developing town, Emery saw no need for such radical change in government as the new constitution proposed.

We might also consider Concord's decision on the State Constitution debates between 1779 and 1783. In 1779 Concord approved the proposal but only by a vote of 26 to 25. In January 1782 the town rejected the second proposal, 48-0, suggesting that the governor not have a privy council and that the people at large appoint their militia officers. Again, on December 16, 1782, Concord rejected a constitution, 52-0. Finally, the town favored the fourth proposal by a vote of 20-10 on September 29, 1783. This last was ratified by

[No. *19.*]

THIS certifies, That *Nathaniel Whitmore* of *Pembroke* in the county of *Rockingham* is the Proprietor of Share number *Nineteen* in Concord Bridge ; which Share is transferable, by making an assignment on this Certificate, and causing the same to be entered in a book, kept by the Clerk for that purpose.

 In testimony whereof, the Seal of the Incorporation is hereunto affixed, the *Sixteenth* day of *November* in the year of our Lord, one thousand seven hundred and ninety *six*

    Tim.º Walker — Director.
Attest,
    Charles Walker Proprietors Clerk.

 THE within named *Nathaniel Whittemore* in consideration of *One hundred & thirty dollars* paid me by *William Duncan Esq.ʳ of Concord* the receipt whereof I do hereby acknowledge, do hereby assign the within mentioned share, number *Nineteen* and all the rights and privileges to the same appertaining, to *him* the said *William Duncan Esquire* to have and to hold the same to *him* and *his* heirs and assigns, to *his* and their sole use and behoof forever.

 Witness my hand and seal, this *first* *day of* *December* *in the year of our Lord, one thousand seven hundred and ninety* *six.*

Signed, sealed, and delivered,
in presence of
Nath.ª Clough
David Kimball

     Nath.ᵈ Whitmore (Seal)

Rockingham ss ǁ *Concord December 1. 1796*

THEN personally appeared the above named *Nath.ᵈ Whittemore* and acknowledged the foregoing instrument to be his deed, before me,

    Richard Bartlett Just. Peace.

CONCORD-BRIDGE·1795·CONCORD-BRIDGE·1795·CONCORD-BRIDGE·1795·CONCORD

Certificate for a share of stock in the Concord Bridge issued to Nathaniel Whittemore of Pembroke in 1796 and subsequently endorsed over to William Duncan of Concord. Courtesy of the State Archives. Photograph by Bill Finney.

enough towns to take effect in June 1784. These votes suggest vigorous debates regarding questions of authority. Given Concord's hesitancy in regard to the State Constitution and its rejection of article VIII of the Articles of Confederation (agreeing to pay prorated charges of the war), its vote on the federal plan is not surprising.

When Emery's fellow delegates came to Concord for the convention in June of 1788, they approached the meetinghouse by walking, riding, or driving down Main Street. In 1788 Main Street was icy, muddy, or dusty, depending on the season and the weather. Passersby still had to put up with livestock roaming the street, then only a wide swatch of dirt with buildings randomly placed on either side. Some improvements ensued in 1790 when the town built a new town house to accomodate the General Court. In 1791 and 1792 the convention called to revise the 1784 state constitution utilized this building on North Main Street. The convention, led by William Plumer of Epping, devised a revision which was adopted in 1792 and took effect in June 1793. Not until 1795 was Main Street officially "layed out" by a committee of which Benjamin Emery was a member.

By the end of 1796 the ferries over the Merrimack at both the north and south ends of Main Street (Merrill's and Butters', respectively) had been replaced by bridges. Concord Bridge stood at the south end of town, while the Federal Bridge provided access to the north end. There was some trouble with the access roads to the Concord Bridge, possibly stemming from proprietors of the Federal Bridge who attempted to monopolize the river crossing trade. The Concord Bridge was completed by the fall of 1795 at a cost of $13,000, some $3,000 over budget, and it was only several months later that a group of prominent citizens of the north end applied as proprietors to build the northern or Federal Bridge leading into Main Street. It was through such projects that Concord secured its place as a commercial and governmental center.

A traveler from Portsmouth would approach the town via the turnpike from Durham, cross the Federal Bridge, and make his way south on Main Street passing the Walker House on his left. To stay in town he could lodge at one of several taverns including Osgood's or Butters'. The traveler would pass by a number of businesses including the printing shop of George Hough.

Hough established his press, the first in town, in January 1790. His first issue of *The Concord Herald,* and *New Hampshire Intelligencer,* published January 6, 1790, contained news from Congress and foreign capitals, an editorial, quips, and advertisements. It ran for many years, in folio size, usually four pages long, and printed on rag paper. Advertisements included rewards for indentured servants such as Moses Garvin, 17 years old, belonging to John Mann of Pembroke. John Burbank of Hopkinton offered 18 pence reward for Samuel Savery Hardy, 16-year-old indentured servant, but John Harris of Canaan offered 3 pence for Mary Birts, a servant girl. Cash in any form was offered for rags, salt, tea, nails,

Engraving of Concord's North meetinghouse, completed in 1784 and later enlarged, in which New Hampshire's ratification of the Constitution took place. Following its abandonment by the church in the mid-1800s, it housed a theological seminary and was later converted to a boarding house prior to its destruction by fire in 1870. The Walker School now stands on the lot. Courtesy of the State Archives.

butter, fresh eggs, flax, coffee, sugar, and other commodities.

The newspaper reveals that, well after the Revolution, Concord society continued to deal not only in English pounds, shillings, and pence, but also in dollars, coppers, and pistareens. The changing value of money had posed a serious problem throughout the American states in the 1780s, and the situation had reached a crucial point in New Hampshire when a mob in Exeter in 1786 virtually locked the legislature in its chambers until the governing body assured the citizens that rectifying measures would be taken. Only settlement into a federal currency as prescribed by the new constitution provided relief, but it took several years to put into practice.

The printing office of George Hough served also as a post office and loan office. Post riders delivered mail between states and towns, but not to individual houses. Hough advertised mail that sat waiting to be picked up. As the combined post office and printing press, Hough's establishment seemed a logical place for Continental Loan Office certificates and state notes of New Hampshire and Massachusetts.

The traveler, on the right day and in the right place, might have seen a body of men exercising as the town's militia. Looking across the meetinghouse yard he would have spied the town cemetery, then a small but increasing plot. He might well have noticed a school for the town's citizenry was acutely aware of the benefits of educating its youth and was making headway towards establishing a formal system of education. During the 1780s Concord established the position of school keeper and converted the pest house, set up in 1776, to a schoolhouse.

New Hampshire law had fostered public schooling since the seventeenth century. Governors and legislators since then have verbally supported education. Historian Lynn Turner noted that New Hampshire's "constitution-makers paid lip service at the shrine of learning in 1783 when they enjoined future legislatures to cherish the interests of seminaries and public schools and to encourage all other means and expression of knowledge."

In 1792 Governor Josiah Bartlett said in his address to the General Court that "every regulation that will have a tendency to diffuse knowledge and information, and to encourage virtue, morality and patriotism among the people, especially among the Youth and rising generation, cannot fail at being abundantly useful and beneficial to the state, as it is a maxim well-established 'that no Republic can be lasting and happy unless accompanied with Knowledge and public virtue at large.'" Writing at the same time, Jeremy Belknap in his history of New Hampshire recognized the usefulness of education but the lack of consistency in making it available to citizens around the state.

Concord influenced the founding of the New Hampshire Medical Society. The organization was officially begun at a meeting in Exeter on May 4, 1791, led by Portsmouth's Dr. Hall Jackson and Kingston's Dr. Josiah Bartlett, with the latter becoming the Society's first president. Elected to the first board of directors were Concord doctors Philip Carrigain and Peter Green. In Concord, at Gale's Anchor Tavern at the corner of Main and Warren streets, seven men, including Moses Sweatt and Benjamin Gale of Concord, met to consecrate the Blazing Star Lodge of the Order of Free-Masonry on May 6, 1799.

In perspective one must conclude that Concord entered the federal union and the 19th century as a vibrant, growing society.

THE FIRST NEW HAMPSHIRE CONVENTION TO RATIFY THE CONSTITUTION,
February 1788, and the Toscan Report

John B. Archer

Contoocook, New Hampshire

New Hampshire delegates to the state convention, called to debate the proposed new constitution of the United States, met at Exeter, Wednesday, February 13, 1788. The convention was adjourned nine days later when it was evident that the majority opposed ratification. Some of the opposition delegates had been won over, but felt morally bound by previous instructions to reject the constitution if it came to a vote. A second meeting was set for the following June in Concord. More time was needed to overcome the fears of the people that their liberties would be jeopardized under the new constitution. The Federalists, who favored ratification, hoped that the intervening four months would be sufficient time to enable them to rally support throughout the state.

Such was the situation when the French vice-consul in Portsmouth, Jean Toscan, wrote the date, February 29, 1788, at the head of what was to be a report, in French, of the proceedings of the convention, addressed to "Monseigneur." Monseigneur, in this case, was probably the Count de Moustier, who had recently been installed as the new Minister Plenipotentiary of France to the United States. It was part of Toscan's assignment to keep his government informed of any political events of importance in his area, which comprised the state of New Hampshire. His principal duties, as a consular official, were mainly commercial, but the Revolution had brought to a standstill what little commercial activity there had been with France in New Hampshire's only port, and there was little for a vice-consul to do.

Toscan occupied himself in part by translating, as he said, "whatever there is of interest in the newspapers." By newspapers, he seems to have had in mind principally the *New Hampshire Spy* and the *New Hampshire Gazette,* both printed in Portsmouth. For additional information, he could "drop in at the barber's where the newswriters assemble." Such may have been the main sources for his notes on the convention. His expense account for the month of February, 1788, does include a trip to Exeter, so that he may also have been among the spectators at the convention, although what he wrote, as will be seen, does not suggest direct reporting on his part.

George Washington, as president of the Convention that had framed the proposed constitution, had presented it to Congress the previous September (1787), and Congress had moved quickly to call upon the states to hold conventions for ratification. Whereas the Articles of Confederation had required unanimous consent by the states, Congress took a new step in saying that the consent of nine states would be sufficient to establish the new government. By early February of 1788, six states had ratified the proposed constitution, Massachusetts having been the most recent, on February 6th, only a week before the New Hampshire delegates met at Exeter.

The situation in the country was critical. With the War for Independence behind them, the states tended to turn back on themselves and relax their support of a central government. In spite of widespread distrust of a strong executive, thoughtful people were in agreement that something had to be done. Toscan noted that "the new constitution has been on everybody's mind for six months. The newspapers talk of nothing else and the citizens in their private correspondence have only one topic, the new government." Copies of the constitution had been on sale in Portsmouth during the time of which Toscan speaks.

The debates of the Massachusetts Convention had been made available to the public in some detail in Boston newspapers. The *New Hampshire Gazette,* borrowing from these accounts, began printing the proceedings in its issue of January 16, only a week after the Massachusetts delegates had first assembled in Boston. It continued its series of articles for the next ten weeks, when it suddenly dropped them, having covered only the first ten days of the debates. However, by the time the New Hampshire delegates, at their convention, began consideration of the first controversial article of the constitution—the question of annual versus biennial elections for the proposed House of Representatives—the leaders among them were already well versed in the arguments on this topic, pro and con, that had been presented in Boston.

In contrast to the extensive reporting that had taken place in Massachusetts, the New Hampshire newspapers were strangely remiss in their coverage of the Exeter convention. The only paper to succeed in presenting even a small part of the debates was the *New Hampshire Spy.* The editor made excuses in several instances, speaking of "The very short time allowed us to prepare the above"; and later saying, "We have not been able to procure any debates further

French Vice-Consul Jean Toscan boarded with the widow Catherine Moffatt Whipple in the Moffatt-Ladd House, Market Street, Portsmouth from 1787 until 1789. The house was built in 1763 by Capt. John Moffatt for his son Samuel; it is now maintained as a house museum by the National Society of Colonial Dames. Photograph by Douglas Armsden.

than those published in our last." Other papers only echoed what the *Spy* had already printed. This is even true of Exeter's own paper, *The Freeman's Oracle,* which reported on the convention getting under way, and later on its conclusion, and followed the *Spy* in saying, "We should have been happy in (furnishing) our readers the debates on the several paragraphs in dispute, (but we) have not been able to procure them."

The New Hampshire delegates, with some not yet present, assembled in Exeter on February 13th. After a brief meeting, they adjourned to the next morning when officers were elected and the first debates began. On Friday the 15th, the usual semi-weekly edition of the *Spy* came out in Portsmouth. After an account of the convention preliminaries, the *Spy* did mention the opening debate on biennial elections; but of the arguments of the main opposition speaker, Mr. Atherton (of Amherst), the *Spy* said only that "he had many weighty objections to the paragraph in debate, and (that he) proceeded to enumerate them." No further details were given except for a brief exchange between Atherton and the Rev. Mr. Benjamin Thursten on whether state legislatures should have the right to recall representatives in Congress.

On Friday the 22nd, after announcing that the convention had "finished debating upon the new Constitution by paragraphs," the *Spy* again excused itself by saying, "Our situation not allowing us to be present at all the debates, prevents us from laying before our readers a summary of the whole." It did go on to name the principal speakers against adopting the new constitution, as well as those in favor of it, and mentioned that the opposition was particularly fearful of entrusting Congress with too much power. For further proceedings, the reader was referred to "*The New-Hampshire Spy, (Extraordinary).*"

The "Extraordinary" was a special edition published the following day, Saturday, February 23, 1788. It is of particular interest because it contains the only detailed account of some of the speeches that were made, pertaining, in this case, to the Judiciary and the Religious Test. There was opposition to the establishment of federal courts and to the fact that no avowal of religious belief was to be required of government officials. These same speeches were to be published again in the *Massachusetts Gazette* of February 29 and March 4, in the *American Herald* (Boston) of March 3, and finally in the Exeter newspaper of March 7 (1788).

What the *New Hampshire Spy* had been first to print remained the only significant source material in the public domain until 1827. On July 7th of that year, the *New Hampshire Statesman and Concord Register* printed a speech which it introduced as follows: "It is greatly to be deplored that no records of the debates of the convention of New Hampshire which adopted the Federal Constitution of the United States have been preserved. They would be of inestimable importance to the present and future inquirers into the origin and establishment of our political institutions. We do not recollect that a single speech on the adoption of any one section of the Constitution was ever published. By accident we lately found the following abstract of one made by the Honorable JOSHUA ATHERTON, delegate from Amherst, on that section relating to the Importation of Slaves, in the following words...." Then followed the purported speech.

C. P. Whittemore, in his biography of John Sullivan, noted that, "Atherton's speech against slavery was probably written out long after the event." The same speech appeared again in 1836 in Jonathan Elliott's *Debates of the State Conventions on the Federal Constitution 1787–1788*, this time introduced as follows: "A friend has favoured the Editor with the following fragment, being the only speech known to be preserved in the New Hampshire Convention, on adopting the federal Constitution of the United States." George Barstow, in his *History of New Hampshire*, published in 1842, reprinted Atherton's speech, saying, "Mr. Atherton opposed this clause with great warmth; and the following extracts from his remarks are believed to be the only relict of the debates of the convention, which has descended to the present time." Joseph B. Walker wrote a *History of the New Hampshire Convention*, published in Boston in 1888. Speaking of the February convention at Exeter, he says nothing more about the actual debates than to name the first topic discussed, Annual versus Biennial Elections, and then to add that "The examination of the proposed Constitution thus commenced was continued from day to day." In the same year, 1888, the *Granite Monthly* carried an article by William F. Witcher on "New Hampshire and the Federal Constitution." He wrote as follows: "Very little is known concerning the detailed proceedings of the convention, since its journal gives but the most meager account of its work, and its deliberations and debates were unfortunately never reported." He does go on to say, "The opponents of the constitution reproduced the objections which had just been urged in Massachusetts; they complained of the absence of a religious test; they denounced the twenty years sufferance of the foreign slave trade...," adding a brief quote from Atherton's speech.

None of these men, writing in the 19th century, seem to have had knowledge of the accounts in the *New Hampshire Spy*, and particularly of the special edition of the *Spy* of February 23, 1788. With this background in mind, we turn now to the text that Toscan was preparing by way of a report on this first New Hampshire convention. Although, as we have said, Toscan's February trip to Exeter leaves open the possibility that he may have been a spectator at at least part of the debates, what he wrote, apart from some summarizing and editing on his part, appears to be translated from English texts. This is suggested further by certain stylistic corrections that he made in his draft, substituting, as an afterthought, in some instances, a more idiomatic French turn of phrase.

In the following presentation, sections of Toscan's draft report are followed by quotations from possible sources. The quotes from the *New Hampshire Spy*, as indicated, all relate to the Exeter convention, whereas those from the *New Hampshire Gazette* are of the previous Massachusetts convention. Although Toscan's report is dated February 29, it definitely includes material that appeared in the March 5th issue of the *Gazette*. In making the comparison between Toscan's text and the newspaper quotations, it should be noted that the English translation of Toscan's French was done before the translator had any knowledge of the accounts in the New Hampshire newspapers, which makes the closeness of certain passages all the more striking.

Mgr   Portsmouth
                                                                                        February 29, 1788
     The New Hampshire Convention to accept or reject the new Constitution met at Exeter the 13th of this month and after long and violent debates by the

parties for and against the new Constitution the meeting was finally adjourned to Concord the third Wednesday of June.

It is with much regret that I have the honor of announcing to you that (at) the Convention of this State meeting at Exeter on the 13th of this month after a nine day session in which the new Constitution was debated paragraph by paragraph the majority was for rejection and the members who were for accepting it proposed that the Convention be adjourned to Concord the third Wednesday of June hoping that before that time the example of the other States will show New Hampshire its error and folly in opposing the only means likely to save America from the anarchy into which she will most surely fall if the new Constitution is not accepted. In the following account I treat the subject of the debates in some detail.

The members of the Convention of New Hampshire meeting at the town hall at Exeter February 13th chose for their president his Excellency John Sullivan and the honorable judge Calfe as their secretary. The new proposed constitution was read.

The honorable judge Livermore rose and moved that the new constitution be considered and debated by paragraphs.

[*The New-Hampshire Spy.* Friday, February 15, 1788]
Proceedings of the New-Hampshire State Convention
A majority of the members elect assembled at the Court-House in Exeter on Wednesday afternoon last, and having made the necessary arrangements, and settled the contested elections (there being but two) adjourned.
Thursday, A.M. February 14, 1788
The Convention met agreeable to adjournment, and proceeded to the choice of a President, when his Excellency JOHN SULLIVAN, Esq. was chosen.

The Convention then made choice of the Hon. Judge CALFE, for their Secretary, and proceeded to business, when, the proposed Constitution being read, the Hon. Judge Livermore rose, and after a short speech, introduced a motion "that the Convention do now proceed to the consideration of the proposed Constitution by paragraphs."

[Toscan] An objection to this motion was made by the honorable Mr. Pickering who thought that it was more expedient for the Convention to review the old constitution to show its faults and weaknesses and the necessity of adopting a new one. He was seconded in this motion by the honorable judge Batletet [*sic*].

[*N. H. Spy*] This motion was objected to by the hon. Mr. Pickering, who thought it most expedient for the Convention to take a review of the old Constitution, point out its defects—and the necessity of having a new one

Toscan designed and built this "bungalow" in Greenland about 1800 on land which his wife had inherited. Notable for its unusual architecture, it was destroyed by fire in the 1970s. Courtesy of the N. H. Historical Society.

adopted—preparatory to any other proceeding. He was seconded by the Hon. Judge Bartlet—who was of the same opinion.

[Toscan] The honorable judge Livermore replied to the honorable Mr. Pickering that the defects of the old constitution would show up as they debated the new one and it was decided by the majority to discuss the new constitution by paragraphs.

[*N. H. Spy*] Hon. Judge Livermore, in answer to the Hon. Mr. Pickering, said, he tho't the defects of the old Constitution would naturally be made to appear as the Convention debated upon the new—that it was the most consistent way of proceeding, and he wished the question might be put.

The question was then put, whether the Convention would proceed to the consideration of the proposed Constitution by paragraphs—when it passed in the affirmative.

[Toscan] The Convention began by considering biennial elections.

Mr. Atherton got up and said that he had strong objections to make against the paragraph in question and began by saying that annual elections have been the practice of these States since their inception, that there has never been any objection to this mode of election which has been considered the safeguard of the people's liberty, that to wipe it off the books would open the door to tyranny, and that it is well known that tyranny has introduced itself into nations by prolonging the period of their parliament or legislative body, and that the safety of the liberty of the people lies in frequent elections and that making a change can lead to elections for life, that the doctrine of frequent elections is sanctified by antiquity and by recent experiences and the general way of thinking. They must be very precious to us, etc., etc..

[*N. H. Spy*] The Convention then proceeded to the consideration of Biennial Elections—when Mr. Atherton (from Amherst) rose, and informed the Convention, that he had many weighty objections to the paragraph in debate, and proceeded to enumerate them. [These objections, we are informed, were much the same as those mentioned by the opposition in the Massachusetts Convention.]

[*N. H. Gazette,* Jan. 23, 1788, reporting the proceedings of the Massachusetts Convention of Monday, January 14, 1788]
       "(Dr. Taylor)—it has indeed, sir, been considered as the safeguard of the liberties of the people; and the annihilation of it, the avenue through which tyranny will enter."
       Ibid., "It had been mentioned by some gentlemen, that the introduction of tyranny into several nations had been by lengthening the duration of their parliaments or legislative bodies...."
       "(Mr. Ames) ...I am sensible, sir, that the doctrine of frequent elections, has been sanctioned by antiquity; and is still more endeared to us by our recent experience, and uniform habits of thinking."

[Toscan] Messers Langdon, Livermore, Pickering and the Reverend Doctor Thirston replied to Mr. Atherton and each one in favor of the paragraphs as it exists for it does not follow that because annual elections are safe, biennial elections have to be dangerous.

[*N. H. Spy*] He was answered by Judge Livermore, Mr. Langdon, Mr. Pickering, Rev. Dr. Langdon, and the Rev. Mr. Thirston;—who severally spoke in favour of the paragraph as it stood.

[*N. H. Gazette*] "(Mr. Ames) ...it does not follow, because annual elections are safe, that biennial are dangerous: for both may be good."

[Toscan] They can both be good but biennial elections are preferable because of the size of the country.

[*N. H. Gazette*] "... we ought to prefer...biennial elections to annual...(because of) the extent of the country to be governed...."

[Toscan] (A newly elected member of Congress coming) from the frontiers of Penobscot or from the strait, if he is elected for only one year, loses half of his time on route.

[*N. H. Gazette*] "(Mr. Ames) ...It seems obvious, that men who are to collect in Congress from this great territory, perhaps from the bay of Fundy, or from the banks of the Ohio, and the shore of Lake Superior, ought to have a longer term in office, than the delegates of a single state, in their own legislature."

[Toscan] It is not possible that in so short a time in the Congress he can get to know the true interests of the Union, and two years are not too long to enable a man to form sound judgments about a State he has never seen.

[*N. H. Gazette*] "It is not by riding post to and from Congress, that a man can acquire a just knowledge of the true interests of the union."

[Toscan] A man elected for two years will feel the independence of his position, and the people will be attentive to the merit of the candidate, and two years will enable him to deserve well of his constituents.

[*N. H. Gazette*] "...the member chosen for two years will fee some independence in his seat.... The people will be proportionably attentive to the merits of a candidate. Two years will afford opportunity to the member to deserve well of them, and they will require evidence that he has done it."

[Toscan] It has been asked why annual elections are not preferable to biennial. A sound reply to that is to say that if annual elections are good, biennial elections are even better.

[*N. H. Gazette*] "...and as it has been demanded, why annual elections were not preferable to biennial, permit me to retort the question, and to enquire in my turn, what reason can be given, why, if annual elections are good, biennial elections are not better?"

[Toscan] Powers accorded to Congress

These powers produced violent debates. The opposition party saw with the greatest regret Congress given the power to raise taxes and dispose of the money, to raise an army, to create a navy, to construct forts, magazines, arsenals. Congress can thus perpetuate its existence in obtaining for itself the resources of war and money, and the people will remain helpless to defend their liberty.

[*N. H. Spy*, Feb. 22, 1788] The dangerous tendency...of trusting Congress with too much power—of their holding the purse and the sword—of their laying direct taxes, &c. &c. &c., was properly noticed by the opposition.

[*N. H. Gazette*, Wednesday March 5, 1788] "(Major Kingsley).... I will examine what powers we have given to our masters—They have power to lay and collect all taxes, duties, imposts and excises—raise armies—fit out navies—to establish themselves in a federal town of ten miles square, equal to four middling townships, erect forts, magazines, arsenals, &c. Therefore, should the Congress be chosen of designing and interested men, they can perpetuate their existence, secure the resources of war, and the people will have nothing left to defend themselves with."

[Toscan] A glance at Ancient History will show that the Romans after a long war thought that the government would be safe in the hands of the decemvirs, who were given all powers and elected for three years only, but they managed to arrange a second election. The manner in which they exercised their power not leaving them the hope of a third election, they declared themselves masters of Rome, spent the funds of the city and stripped the people of their rights.

[*N. H. Gazette*] "...Let us look at ancient history. The Romans, after a war, thought themselves safe in a government of ten men, called the Decemviri—these ten men were invested with all powers, and were chosen for three years:—by their arts and designs they secured their second election; but finding, from the manner in which they had exercised their power, they were not able to secure their third election, they declared themselves masters of Rome—impoverished the city—and deprived the people of their rights."

[Toscan] Who can prevent Congress from establishing an arbitrary government after it has fortified itself in a federal city, when it will have the power of issuing currency, of maintaining an army and will have all our money? The people will have no resource to maintain their rights. They will become miserable under the burden of taxes, and Congress like a despot having the government's revenues enitrely in its hands can use it to crush and annihilate all the noble sentiments which quicken the republican spirit and with which we have always been nourished. We will find no advantage in having exchanged a British tyrant for several American tyrants.

[*N. H. Gazette*] "…after we have given them all our money, established them in a federal town, given them the power of coining money and raising a standing army; and to establish their arbitrary government; what resources have the people left? I cannot see any."

[*N. H. Spy (Extraordinary)*, Feb. 23, 1788] Col. Stone observed our situation would not be much happier by changing one set of tyrants for another—British for American tyrants.

[Toscan] The reply to these objections was that the members of Congress were (to be) chosen by the people of the various States, who would take great care to elect only people whose integrity and abilities would be well known, that these members would take great care not to give their sanction to any oppressive law of which they themselves would have to bear the consequences when they returned to private life.

[*N. H. Gazette*, March 12, 1788] "(Honorable Mr. Bowdoin)… As then the individulas in Congress will all share in the burdens they impose, and be personally affected by the good or bad laws they make for the union, they will be under the strongest motives of interest to lay the lightest burthens possible."

[*N. H. Gazette*, March 26, 1788] "(Mr. Sedgwick)…the representatives and people, he said, are equally subject to the laws, and can therefore have but one and the same interest—that they would never lay unnecessary burthens, when they themselves must bear a part of them…."

[Toscan] that the weakness of the old Confederation, the poor administration since the peace caused by the lack of authority and power in Congress, showed clearly that it was necessary that this body have all the powers which have been announced in the new constitution not only for domestic affairs but also for concluding alliances with foreign nations, treaties of commerce and executing them; that Congress whose duty is to watch over the health and defense of the United States needed the power to raise taxes to maintain an army and to build a navy; that the lack of respect and consideration which the various States have shown regarding obligations contracted in time of war, (plus) all the regulations made since the peace, in fact (regarding) everything that has emanated from Congress, has put an almost irreparable blemish on the national character; finally that it is impossible for the new Government, composed as it is of three branches controlling each other and elected by the people, not to work for the general welfare.

Toscan's report does not end here. The text continues with a final section on the Religious Test. This is not included here, since it is a verbatim translation of the account of that debate in the *New Hampshire Spy (Extraordinary)* of February 23, the original English text of which is available. The *Spy* begins this account by saying, "As the following was commited to paper without taking notes at the time, and barely from memory, the Editor must beg pardon of those gentlemen whose arguments are weakened, or (even) debased, by an attempt to gratify the public." Toscan paraphrased this, at the end of his translation, to say, "At the New Hampshire Convention there was no one present able to take down in shorthand the various debates and the above extract was given by memory only." It appears that adequate reporting remained an unsolved problem for the local press.

It should be noted that Toscan did not translate the debates on the federal judiciary, which compose the first part of the account in the *Spy Extraordinary*. His summaries, then, as given on the preceding pages, treat only the two topics of Biennial Elections and the Powers of Congress, the basic material for which appeared only in the *New Hampshire Gazette's* account of the Massachusetts debates, copied from Boston newspapers. If we assume that what Toscan wrote reflects with any accuracy what was said at the New Hampshire convention, one is, of course, struck by how closely it parallels, even to the very language, the arguments presented by the Massachusetts delegates. This was noted by contemporary observers. William Plumer, "an observer and lobbyist at the Exeter Convention," wrote that Atherton's "arguments were but a recital of objections which had been so often repeated in the journals of the day that they had become stale." *The New Hampshire Spy* of February 15, after stating that Mr. Atherton had many objections to biennial elections, went on to say that "These objections, we are informed, were much the same as those mentioned by the opposition in the Massachusetts Convention."

Furthermore, New Hampshire delegates were not limited to newspapers as a channel for ideas. One writer tells us that "Besides the efforts of local Antifederalists, partisans in Massachusetts sent aid to their beleaguered brethren (in New Hampshire) through Dr. James Kilham of Newburyport, who took his young friend John Qunicy Adams along as an observer. Kilham brought a bundle of pamphlets, which he turned over to Atherton." And again: "In the corridors there were visitors from Massachusetts alongside General Nathaniel Peabody, who were busy buttonholing delegates."

There is no record of what these "visitors" may have said, and Kilham's pamphlets have apparently not turned up for any researchers on the subject. We are left with the fact that Toscan had access to sources we have not been able to trace. As one example, we quote again the following sentence: "...Congress like a despot having the government's revenue entirely in its hands can use it to crush and annihilate all the noble sentiments which quicken the republican spirit and with which we have always been nourished." This had the ring of oratory of the times, of an authentic fragment of a speech, in spite of its having passed through two translations to come back into English. We have no evidence that Toscan's draft was ever put into finished form and submitted to "Monseigneur." But brief and inconclusive as it is, it is still a document to be taken into account in any bibliography of that first New Hampshire Convention of February 1788.

———

This article was originally published with footnotes in *Historical New Hampshire*, XXXVI, No. 1 (Spring 1981), 38–57. It is reprinted by permission of the author. John B. Archer is the former head of the Modern Languages Department at St. Paul's School. He has translated the Toscan Papers at the New Hampshire Historical Society. See also John B. Archer, "Jean Toscan, 1752–1805," *Historical New Hampshire*, XXXIV, Nos. 3 & 4 (Fall/Winter 1979): 179–201.

William Plumer (1759–1850) portrait by C. B. J. F. de Saint-Memin, c. 1805. Plumer devoted most of his life to public service as a member of both houses of the state legislature, as a U.S. senator, and as governor. A prolific chronicler of men and events, Plumer attended sessions of the convention at Exeter as an observer, having failed in his attempt to be chosen as a delegate from Epping. Courtesy of the N. H. Historical Society.

COUNTING NOSES
Delegate Sentiment in
New Hampshire's Ratifying Convention

Jere R. Daniell

Dartmouth College

$\mathcal{T}$here was strong opposition in New Hampshire to the proposed federal Constitution. A majority of town delegates elected to the ratifying convention—held at Exeter in February, 1788—arrived expecting to vote negatively. At Exeter, however, some among the initial "anti-Federalist" majority began to rethink their position and expressed a willingness to postpone action on the plan of union until a later date. The pro-Constitution or Federalist minority readily accepted the offer. On the 22nd the convention, by a narrow margin, voted to adjourn until June at Concord. The Concord session ratified the Constitution by a vote of 57-47.

Over the years I have accumulated material which makes it possible to describe with a good deal of precision how the pro-Constitution forces snatched victory from apparent defeat. Most of the story has been told in two published narratives of the ratification process. The purpose of this article is to supplement these narratives by making available three unpublished documents concerning ratification, by showing how these documents fit with previously available evidence, and by using both the new and the old to reconstruct the two key votes at the convention sessions.

I

Two of the documents are tabulation lists of delegate sentiment drawn up between the Exeter and Concord sessions. The third is a letter by one of the delegates who described the final vote taken at Concord. All three documents were the work of strongly pro-ratification men.

William Plumer of Epping and a future governor of New Hampshire made the first tabulation. Plumer had campaigned unsuccessfully to become a convention delegate but attended parts of the Exeter session out of curiosity. The last day of the convention the local newspaper, the *Freeman's Oracle,* printed a list of attending members. Sometime soon thereafter Plumer sat down with his copy of the *Oracle* and marked 58 of the delegates either "Y," "N," or "D." The first two letters stood for expected "yes" and "no" votes; the "D" probably meant "doubtful."

New Hampshire's state postmaster, Jeremiah Libbey of Portsmouth, made the second and more elaborate set of predictions. Libbey was a close friend of Jeremy Belknap, the former minister in Dover who had moved to Boston and was still deeply involved in writing his *History of New Hampshire.* Libbey promised soon after adjournment to send Belknap a listing of how delegates stood. On May 12th he made good on the promise. "I now inclose you the list of our members as they stood about three weeks past," he wrote, adding optimistically that "several of which since that time are said to be quite altered from Antifederal to Federal." Libbey used essentially the same list of convention members as Plumer, identified delegates as "Fed," "Anti," or "uncertain" (his D's stand for "ditto") and labeled all but one of the 107 members listed. The specific predictions of both Plumer and Libbey are contained in the table presented in part II.

Both Plumer and Libbey did reasonably well with their estimates. The future governor hit 47 right out of 48 among those men for whom he made firm predictions and who also voted on the main motion. Only one of his doubtfuls became a Federalist, while five answered "Nay" at Concord. Libbey chanced more and therefore made more mistakes. His score was 76 right and 9 wrong among his "Feds" and "Antis"; his "uncertains" went three for and ten against ratification. Neither man, of course, could predict that five elected delegates would be no-shows at Concord and that four in attendance would refuse to vote.

The third document is a letter from Portsmouth delegate Pierce Long written July 7, 1788, to his friend Paine Wingate, a New Hampshire delegate to the Continental Congress. The bulk of the letter describes the June convention session which, according to Long, degenerated into "dry arguments gone over again until both sides were quite tried out." Bored with the proceedings, the Federalists "determined to take the question—when we saw a probability of obtaining it—if by a majority of one only." Long then described the decision to move the main motion. "Accordingly though we could count but upon that number we took it, and to our surprise had a majority of eleven, three of the opposition were excused from voting and one left the house—and three or four whom we did not expect voted in favor." Long reported the final vote to have been 57-46.

What an exciting find! For one thing it puts to rest the recurring and now clearly apocryphal story of Timothy Walker enticing the four non-voting convention members with a sumptuous noon-time repast to prevent them from voting. Just one of the non-voters physically left the convention building, and only at the last minute. Secondly, the letter makes clear just how close the struggle remained until the end. Federalist tabulators apparently thought there were 107 delegates present of whom only 54 were committed to vote "Yea." (Actually there were 108 present, the final margin was ten not eleven, and the 54 would not have been a majority without the surprise "three or four" votes and the abstainers.) Finally, in conjunction with other evidence, including the Plumer and Libbey tabulations, Long's letter makes it possible for us to know who provided the swing votes at Concord. In fact, these three documents also allow us to make accurate estimates about who helped save the day at Exeter.

II

The following table has a double function—to integrate the information in the three documents with other known information about delegate behavior, and to provide readers with a condensed profile of what role each individual delegate probably played in the ratification process.

Most columns are self-explanatory. The first describes the town or towns each delegate represented (where appropriate I have added the modern town name); the second lists the delegates themselves. The fourth and eighth columns (At Ex? and At Co?) note whether individuals actually attended the convention sessions. Columns six and seven list how Plumer and Libbey labeled each man; I have changed Plumer's Y's to F's and N's to A's. The last, or tenth, column records how the delegate actually voted, again with F standing for Federalist or a yes vote. The NV in this column indicates that the delegate was recorded in attendance but chose not to vote.

Column three requires some explanation. Formal instructions to delegates from the towns played a key role in the battle over the Constitution. More than a century ago town meeting minutes on matters having to do with ratification were collected in what were known as the Goodwin Town Papers; these are now in the State Archives under the label "State Convention, Federal Constitution, Election of Delegates." Some town meetings voted directly on the Constitution, other appointed committees to instruct their delegates. Delegates took both votes and committee instructions very seriously. The total number of instructed convention members was at least thirty, and although some with negative instructions managed to avoid voting, none of the eighteen men whose specific instructions we know cast a ballot in violation of town wishes. I have assumed that in those cases where we know the delegate was instructed by committee but don't know what the instructions were, the final vote was consistent with those instructions. In column three I use A and F as elsewhere in the table. "A(c)" therefore means negative instruction by committee. "F(v)" means the town meeting voted for ratification. In some towns there was both a vote and a committee.

Ebenezer Webster (1739–1806) anonymous portrait, c. 1790. Among the first settlers in Salisbury in 1760 and father of Daniel, Webster held many town and state offices. In choosing him as a delegate to the ratifying convention, the town meeting also designated a committee to "Consult the Constitution and to advise with sd Delegate," an action which no doubt influenced his decision to abstain when the final vote on ratification was taken. Courtesy of the N. H. Historical Society.

A word on numbers. The highest contemporary estimate of instructed delegates was forty, made by Belknap in Boston. It would not be surprising, given the nature of rumors, that what he heard was exaggerated. My own count of thirty certain and one maybe (marked "?") could be low, although I did check directly a number of town meeting records when I suspected the gatherer of the Goodwin Papers might have missed something. No additional information ever turned up. The Goodwin Papers, incidentally, confirm what all contemporaries said—that the overwhelming majority of instructions were to vote against ratification. I have it twenty-six to four.

The two columns not yet described are the fifth ("VAdj") and the ninth ("FTPL"). VAdj stands for probable vote on adjournment where "F" means for and "A" against. Most F's, of course, were also Federalist, which makes the notation consistent with notations elsewhere in the table. FTPL stands for Federalist tabulators prediction list. Those labeled "F" were among the certain yes votes when the motion to ratify was made in June. Section III of this article will explain how in the absence of specific documentation I was able to determine the entries in these columns.

Readers should now be ready to get a quick profile on their favorite delegate. For example, Gilman of Exeter was not instructed, did attend at Exeter, voted for adjournment, was labeled a Federalist by both Plumer and Libbey, went to the Concord session, was expected to vote for the Constitution and did so. Runnels of Londonderry was instructed by a town committee to vote against ratification and did so, attended both sessions, voted against adjournment, and was labeled anti-Federalist by both predictors. Smith of Meredith and New Hampton, who played a key role in the convention, was instructed by both town vote and committee to oppose ratification, went to Exeter, and voted for adjournment. Plumer considered him doubtful and Libbey uncertain. He was present at Concord but did not vote on the main motion. The case of Taylor of Merrimack is among the most complex in the table. Taylor received negative instructions from a town committee, at Exeter probably but not certainly—thus the question mark—voted against adjournment, was considered doubtful by Plumer but a Federalist by Libbey, and voted against the Constitution. The "3" above the "F" in column seven directs you to a table footnote, as do other raised numbers.

Town(s)	Delegate	Inst?	At Ex?	VAdj	Pl	Li	At Co?	FTDL	V
Rockingham County									
Portsmouth	John Langdon, Esq.	no	yes	F	F	F	yes	F	F
	John Pickering, Esq.	no	yes	F	F	F	yes	F	F
	Pierce Long, Esq.	no	yes	F	F	F	yes	F	F
Exeter	John Taylor Gilman, Esq.	no	yes	F	F	F	yes	F	F
Londonderry	Col. Daniel Runnels	A(c)	yes	A	A	A	yes		A
	Archibald McMurphy, Esq.	A(c)	yes	A	A	A	yes		A
Chester	Mr. Joseph Blanchard	no	yes	F	F	F	yes	F	F
Newington	Benjamin Adams, Esq.	no	yes	F	F	F	yes	F	F
Greenland	Dr. Ichabod Weeks	no	yes			F	yes	F	F
Rye	Mr. Nathan Gross	no	yes	F		F	yes	F	F
New Castle	Henry Prescott, Esq.	no	yes	F	F	F	yes	F	F
North Hampton	Rev. Benjamin Thurston	no	yes	F	F	F	yes	F	F
Hampton	Christopher Toppan, Esq.	no	yes	F	F	F	yes	F	F
Hampton Falls Seabrook	Rev. Samuel Langdon	no	yes	F	F	F	yes	F	F

Town(s)	Delegate	Inst?	At Ex?	VAdj	Pl	Li	At Co?	FTDL	V
Stratham	Mr. Jonathan Wiggin	no	yes	F	F	F	yes	F	F
Kensington	Jeremiah Fogg, Esq.	no	yes	F	F	F	yes	F	F
South Hampton East Kingston	Mr. Benjamin Clough	no	yes	A			yes		A
Kingstown	Hon. Josiah Bartlett, Esq.	no	yes	F	F	A^1	yes	F	F
Brentwood	Dr. Thomas Stow Ranney	no	yes	F	F	F	yes	F	F
Epping	Mr. Nathaniel Ladd	no	yes				no		
New Market	Nathaniel Rogers, Esq.	F(v)	yes	F	F	F	yes	F	F
Nottingham	Thomas Bartlett, Esq.	no	yes	F	F	F	yes	F	F
Deerfield	Dr. Edmond Chadwick	no	yes	F	F	F	yes	F	F
Northwood Epsom Allenstown	Maj. James Gray	no	yes	F	F	F	yes	F	F
Chichester Pittsfield	Benjamin Sias, Esq.	A(c)	yes	A?	D	U	yes		A
Canterbury	Col. Jeremiah Clough	no	yes	A	D	A	yes		A
Northfield	Mr. Charles Glidden	no	yes	F	F	F	yes	F	F
Loudon	Mr. Jonathan Smith	A(c)	yes	A		A	yes		A
Concord	Capt. Benjamin Emery	no	yes	A	A	A	yes		A
Pembroke	Samuel Daniels, Esq.	no	yes	A	A	A	yes		NV
Candia	Mr. Stephen Fifield	A(c)	yes	F?		U	yes		A
Raymond Poplin (Fremont)	Mr. Thomas Chase	no	yes	A	D	U	yes		A
Hawke (Danville) Sandown	Mr. Nehemiah Sleeper	no	yes	A		A	yes		A

Town(s)	Delegate	Inst?	At Ex?	VAdj	Pl	Li	At Co?	FTDL	V
Hampstead	John Calfe, Esq.	no	yes	F	F	F	yes	F	F
Atkinson Plaistow	Col. Benjamin Stone	A(c)	yes	A	A	A	yes		A
Salem	Lt. Thomas Dow	no	yes	A	A	A	yes		A
Newtown	Capt. Robert Steward	no	yes	A		U	yes		A
Wyndham	James Bettan, Esq.	F(c)	yes	F	F	F	yes	F	F
Pelham	Rev. Amos Moody	no	yes	F		F	yes	F	F
Strafford County									
Dover	Dr. Ezra Green	no	yes	F	F	F	yes	F	F
Durham	Excy. John Sullivan, Esq.	no	yes	F	F	F	yes	F	F
Somersworth	Moses Carr, Esq.	no	yes	F	F	F	yes	F	F
Rochester	Mr. Barnabas Palmer	no	yes	A		A	yes		A
Barrington	Maj. Samuel Hale	no	yes	F	F	F	yes	F	F
Sanborntown	William Harper, Esq.	no	yes	A	A	A	yes		A
Gilmantown	Hon. Joseph Badger	no	yes	A	A	A	yes		A
Lee	Capt. Reuben Hill	no	yes	A		A	no		
Madbury	Rev. William Hooper	no	yes	A	A	U	yes		A
Meredith New Hampton	Col. Ebenezer Smith	A(v,c)	yes	F	D	U	yes		NV
Sandwich Tamworth	Daniel Beede, Esq.	no	yes	F	F	F	yes	F	F
Moultonboro Tuftonboro Wolfboro Ossipee	Mr. Nathaniel Shannon	no	yes	F	F	F	yes	F	F

Town(s)	Delegate	Inst?	At Ex?	VAdj	Pl	Li	At Co?	FTDL	V
Barnstead New Durham New D. Gore (Alton)	Mr. Jonathan Chesley	no	yes	F?		U	yes	F	F
Wakefield Middletown Effingham	Nr. Nicholas Austin	no	yes	A	A	A	yes		A
Conway Eaton Burton (Albany) Locations	David Page, Esq.	A(v,c)	yes	A		A	yes		A

Hillsborough County

Town(s)	Delegate	Inst?	At Ex?	VAdj	Pl	Li	At Co?	FTDL	V
Nottingham West (Hudson)	Mr. Ebenezer Cummings	no	yes	A		A	yes		A
Litchfield	Mr. Daniel Bixby	A(c)	yes	A		A	yes		A
Derryfield (Manchester)	Lt. John Hall	no	no				yes	F^2	F
Dunstable (Nashua)	Deac. William Hunt	A(v,c)	yes	A?		F^3	yes		A
Merrimack	Timothy Taylor, Esq.	A(c)	yes	A?	D	F^3	yes		A
Bedford	Mr. Stephen Dole	no	yes	A?		F^3	yes		A
Goffstown	Mr. William Page	A(c)	yes	A		A	yes	A	A
Hollis	Capt. Daniel Kindrick	A(v)	yes	A		A	yes		A
Amherst	Joshua Atherton, Esq.	A(v,c)	yes	A	A	A	yes		A
Raby (Brookline) Mason	Deac. Amos Dakin	no	yes	F?		U	yes	F	F
New Ipswich	Capt. Charles Barrett	no	yes	A		A	yes		A
Francistown	Mr. Thomas Bixby	A(v)	yes	A		A	yes		A
Wilton	Mr. William Abbott	no	yes	F		F	yes	F	F

Town(s)	Delegate	Inst?	At Ex?	VAdj	Pl	Li	At Co?	FTDL	V
Lyndeborough	Dr. Benjamin Jones	A(v)	yes	F?		U	yes		A
Temple Peterboro Slip (Sharon)	Deac. John Cragin	A(v)	yes	A		A	yes		A
Peterboro Society Land	Maj. Nathan Dix	A(v)	yes	F	D	U	no		
Hancock Antrim Deering	Mr. Evan Dow	no	yes	A		A	no		
Henniker Hillsborough	Mr. Robert B. Wilkins	no	yes	F	F	F	yes	F	F
New Boston	John Cochran, Esq.	no	yes	A?		F[3]	yes		A
Weare	Mr. Jonathan Dow	no	yes	A		A	yes		A
Hopkinton	Mr. Joshua Morss	A(v)[4]	yes	F		A	yes	F[4]	F
Dunbarton Bow	Mr. Jacob Gerrish	no	yes	A	D	U	yes		A
Salisbury	Col. Ebenezer Webster	A(c)	yes	F	D	U	yes		NV
Boscawen	Col. Joseph Gerrish	no	yes	F?		U	yes	F[5]	F
Fisherfield (Newbury) Sutton Warner	Nathaniel Bean, Esq.	A(v)	yes	F?		U	yes		A

Cheshire County

Town(s)	Delegate	Inst?	At Ex?	VAdj	Pl	Li	At Co?	FTDL	V
Charlestown	Benjamin West, Esq.	no	yes	F	F	F	yes	F	F
Alstead	Capt. Oliver Shepherd	no	yes	F		F	yes	F	F
Keene	Rev. Aaron Hall	no	yes	F		F	yes	F	F
Swanzey	Maj. Elisha Whitcomb	no	yes	F		F	yes	F	F
Richmond	Mr. Jonathan Gaskill	no	yes	A	A	A	yes		A

Town(s)	Delegate	Inst?	At Ex?	VAdj	Pl	Li	At Co?	FTDL	V
Jaffrey	Mr. Abel Parker	no	yes	A	A	A	yes		A
Winchester	Capt. Moses Chamberlain	no	yes	A		A	yes		F
Westmorland	Mr. Archelaus Temple	no	yes	A		A	yes		F
Chesterfield	Dr. Solomon Harvey	no	yes	A		A	yes		A
Rindge	Capt. Othniel Thomas	A(v,c)	yes	A		A	yes		A
Walpole[6]	Mr. Aaron Allen Genl. Jonathan Chase	A(v)	yes	A		A			
Claremont	Deac. Matthias Stone	A(c)	yes	F?		U	yes		A
Cornish Grantham	Genl. Jonathan Chase	no	yes	F	F	F	yes	F	F
Newport Croydon	Mr. John Remmele	no	no				yes		A
Acworth Lempster Marlow	Daniel Grout, Esq.	no	yes	A		A	yes		A
Wendell (Sunapee) Unity	Mr. Moses True	no	no				yes		A
Surry Gilsum	Col. Jonathan Smith	no	yes	A		A	yes		NV
Stoddard Washington	Thomas Pinneman, Esq.	no	yes	A		U	yes		A
Dublin Packersfield (Nelson)	Samuel Griffin, Esq.	no	yes	F		F	yes	F	F
Marlborough	Mr. Jedediah Tainter	A(v)	yes	A		A	yes		A
Fitzwilliam	Lt. Caleb Winch	A(v,c)	yes	A		A	yes		A
Plainfield	Maj. Joseph Kimball	no	yes	F		F	yes	F	F

Town(s)	Delegate	Inst?	At Ex?	VAdj	Pl	Li	At Co?	FTDL	V
Hinsdale	Mr. Uriel Evans	no	yes	F		F	no		

Grafton County

Town(s)	Delegate	Inst?	At Ex?	VAdj	Pl	Li	At Co?	FTDL	V
Holderness Campton Thornton	Hon. Samuel Livermore	F(v)	yes	F	F	F	yes	F	F
Plymouth Rumney Wentworth	Francis Worcester, Esq.	no	yes	F	F	F	yes	F	F
New Chester (Hill) Alexandria Cockermouth (Groton)	Mr. Thomas Crawford	no	yes	F		F	yes	F	F
Enfield Canaan Cardigan (Orange) Dorchester Grafton	Jesse Johnson, Esq.	no	yes	A?	D	F	yes	F	F
Hanover	Jonathan Freeman, Esq.	no	yes	F	F	F	yes	F	F
Lebanon	Col. Elisha Payne	?[7]	no			F	yes	F	F
Lyme Orford	William Simpson, Esq.	F(v)	yes	F	F	F	yes	F	F
Haverhill Piermont Warner Coventry (Benton)	Col. Joseph Hutchins	no	no				yes		A
Lincoln Franconia	Capt. Isaac Patterson	no	no				yes	F[8]	F
Bath Lyman Landaff	Maj. Samuel Young	no	yes	A	A	A	yes		F

Town(s)	Delegate	Inst?	At Ex?	VAdj	Pl	Li	At Co?	FTDL	V
Littleton									
Dalton									
Lancaster	Capt. John Weeks	no	yes	F	F	F	yes	F	F
Northumberland									
Stratford									
Dartmouth									
(Jefferson)									
Piercy									
(Stark)									
Cockburn									
(Columbia)									
Coleburn									
(Colebrook)									

III

By far the two most important votes taken at New Hampshire's ratifying convention were on the February 22 motion to adjourn, and on the motion to ratify unconditionally four months later. Had the adjournment motion failed, the anti-Federalists would have forced some kind of action rejecting the Constitution. Such rejection would certainly have blunted Federalist momentum elsewhere in the country, and might have altered the dynamics of the ratification process enough to prevent eventual approval. Be that as it may, adjournment allowed the Federalists in New Hampshire sufficient time to scrape up additional support and win on June 21. That vote, although of immense importance in New Hampshire, made less difference in a national context. Virginia ratified four days later, thus providing nine anyway.

Evidence now available makes possible a detailed reconstruction of these two votes. I'm reasonably certain which delegates voted for adjournment and which ones were on Long's list of 54 solid supporters in June. These tabulations, in turn, allow us to identify the handful of delegates who at Exeter voted for adjournment in spite of negative instructions from their constituents. The tabulations also make it possible to pinpoint the surprise "yea" votes Long mentions in his letter.

First, the adjournment. The formal records of the convention say simply that the motion passed. The absence of a recorded vote is consistent with a convention rule adopted earlier prohibiting recorded votes except on the main question. However, someone was tabulating delegate sentiment carefully. The *New Hampshire Spy* on February 23 reported that the margin of victory had been 56-51, and Libbey wrote to Belknap that Portsmouth delegate John Pickering—who may well have been in charge of Federalist nose counting—told

Jonathan Chase (1732–1800) portrait attributed to Joseph Steward, c. 1790. Chase was one of Cornish's original settlers in 1765; he soon became a leading citizen, operating saw and grist mills, a store, and a tavern. He was chosen to represent Cornish and Grantham at the convention, and voted to ratify the Constitution. Courtesy of the N. H. Historical Society.

him the 56 were composed of 45 solid pro-ratification delegates and 11 bound by negative instructions but willing to postpone action. Attendance figures recorded by the secretary indicate that 105, not 107, delegates were present, and in the absence of a voting list we don't know which figure is accurate.

To reconstruct the adjournment vote I first tried to identify the 45 hard-core Federalists. The obvious starting point was Plumer's 35 "Y's" ("F's" in table). Libbey agreed with Plumer on all 35, with the mysterious exception of his designating Josiah Bartlett an "anti." Next I combed the table for delegates who (a) were present on February 22, (b) had not been negatively instructed, (c) were Federalist on Libbey's list, (d) were neither "A's" nor "D's" in Plumer's predictions, and (e) either voted for the Constitution or were absent June 21. Ten individuals met these rigid criteria, which added to Plumer's 35 comes out precisely to the 45 solid votes cited by Pickering and Libbey. All 45 are labeled "F" in column five.

I then went through the list of negatively instructed delegates for evidence of softness, i.e., uncertainty about their personal opposition to ratification.

Exactly eleven men seemed suspect. Smith (Meredith), Webster (Salisbury and, yes, Daniel Webster's father), and Dix (Peterboro class) all fall into Plumer's and Libbey's middle categories and all avoided voting on the main motion. Morss (Hopkinton) managed to get his instructions voided between sessions and ended up voting for ratification. Since there can be little doubt about all four having supported adjournment, I've also labeled them "F." The other seven all ended up voting nay in June, so I'm less certain about their adjournment vote. They are among the "?'s" in the VAdj column.

The 45 + 11 equals 56 figuring, however, is a bit too neat. The discrepancy of two between official attendance records and newspaper reports makes certainty about the exact number of votes impossible. A few delegates might have opposed adjournment simply because they didn't want to waste time on a second session. I wouldn't be surprised if some of Pickering's eleven compromisers came from among the uninstructed; the six other delegates labeled "?" in column five are the most likely adjournment supporters if the eleven did include uninstructed members. That increases the pool ("F's" and "?'s") from which the yea votes came to a total of 62, and leaves 43 delegates (labeled "A") clearly against adjournment.

The last step I took in attempting to reconstruct the adjournment vote was to differentiate among the thirteen "?" delegates. The ones who probably voted for are labeled "F?" and against, "A?." My reasoning in individual cases varied but rested mainly on two conjectures. One of these is explained in footnote 3 to the table: it seems very likely that Libbey was the victim of both false rumor and his own optimism in thinking Hunt (Dunstable), Taylor (Merrimack), Dole (Bedford), and Cochran (New Boston) would support ratification. I've labeled all of these men "A?," as I have the men Plumer gave "D's." Plumer undoubtedly attended the February 22 session, observed who voted how, and considered a negative vote evidence of anti-Federalist leanings. The total of "F's" and "F?'s" comes out to 56, and of "A's" and "A?'s" to 49, not much different from the 56-51 report.

As a final observation on the adjournment note, if my reconstruction is reasonably accurate, eight men can be said, from a Federalist perspective, to have saved the day at Exeter. These were the delegates instructed to vote negatively but who despite these instructions supported postponement of a decision on the main motion. They were Fifield (Candia), Smith (Meredith class), Jones (Lyndeborough), Dix (Peterboro class), Morss (Hopkinton), Bean (Fisherfield class), Webster (Salisbury), and Stone (Claremont). Add them to the long list of unsung heroes in the process of nation building.

Reconstruction of Federalist calculations before the final vote requires less explanation. Pickering, Long, and whoever else helped keep count had only two lists to maintain. They needed to know how many accredited delegates were present and therefore likely to vote, and how many certain Federalists were among this total. As long as the second figure was more than half the first and there were no surprise last-minute defections, ratification was assured.

At Concord things proceeded smoothly. The convention gathered on Wednesday, June 18. Since the legislature had been meeting in town for the past two weeks and about forty men, including both Pickering and Long, served in both groups, it had been possible to gather concrete information about current delegate sentiment. On the first day the convention decided two contested elections (Walpole and Boscawen) in favor of the Federalist candidates, in part because their credentials were more convincing, in part because the credential committee members all were Federalists, and in part because more than a dozen men expected to vote against ratification had as yet failed to arrive. Some Federalists probably regretted there had not been time to push the main question to a final vote.

Thursday the nose-counting must have begun in earnest. Of the 113 elected delegates, all but six were there. The convention members spent the entire day debating the merits of the Constitution while Federalist tabulators checked their lists. They thought they were in good shape—winning the contested elections certainly had helped—but they may have been confused about the total number present, and in any case needed an additional vote or two. Everything, however, was in place by Friday. Major Joseph Kimball of Plainfield, a committed Federalist, arrived. He provided the majority of one Pierse Long reported later in his letter to Paine Wingate. Since four of the still absent five delegates were expected to vote against ratification, the Federalists moved as fast as possible. No new delegates appeared on Saturday. The 57-47 vote of approval was completed by one o'clock that afternoon.

Who were the solid Federalist delegates? Long said there were "three or four" surprise votes in a total of 57, which means the list of sure votes was 53 or 54. Long's total figures add up to 107 present (of the 108 actually there), so 54 is the most likely total: 53 wouldn't have been a majority. To simplify the discussion I'll assume the tabulators did count 54 sure votes, and got three, not four, additional.

Column nine (FTPL) identifies positively all 54 solid Federalists. These calculations were relatively simple. I started with the positive 45 obtained in the adjournment vote reconstruction and subtracted the one man, Evans (Hinsdale), who missed the Concord session. Ten additional names were needed. Eight can be easily accounted for. Weeks (Greenland) was by every account Federalist, but for unexplained reasons left the Exeter session February 21, the day before the adjournment vote. Gerrish and Bellows, the victorious candidates in the contested elections, makes three. Double that figure because three Federalists not present at Exeter showed at Concord: Hall (Derryfield) and Payne (Lebanon) were elected before the February session and Patterson (Lincoln class) between sessions. The seventh is Johnson (Enfield class), whom Plumer thought doubtful but Libbey, six weeks later, considered Federalist. Morss (Hopkinton) could be counted on once the town withdrew its instructions. The most likely candidates for the remaining two sure votes are Chesley (Barnstead class) and Dakin (Raby class). Neither had instructions, Libbey rated both uncertain, and both, of course, voted "yes" on June 21.

By this process of elimination there are only three candidates for the three surprise votes. They are Chamberlain (Winchester), Temple (Westmoreland), and Young (Bath class). Libbey predicted that all would vote anti-Federalist and Plumer did the same for Young. What made them switch at the last minute is anyone's guess.

Twenty years ago, when I first wrote about ratification in New Hampshire, I never in my wildest dreams could have imagined understanding the process as richly as I do now. Accidental discovery of new evidence, personal maturing as a historian, and celebration of the bicentennial all have helped stimulate my renewed interest in the subject. "Counting Noses" is one product of the resulting desire to share what I've learned with fellow students of state history. Let's hope at least a few readers find the contents of the article as entertaining and its conclusions as plausible as I do.

Table Notes

T1. A fascinating prediction, since all historians have assumed that Bartlett was strongly committed to the Constitution from the start. There is no other evidence that he questioned the wisdom of ratification, even temporarily, so Libbey may simply have been misinformed. If one wanted to make a case for Bartlett having wavered between sessions, one could cite his long political association with leading anti-Federalist Nathaniel Peabody, and the fact that although he served as chairman of the ratification convention the first day in Exeter, he was not chosen convention president. Governor Sullivan won in a secret ballot which probably was prearranged. By Concord Bartlett certainly was in the Federalist camp. He seconded the motion for adoption. Daniell, "Ideology,"; Daniell, *Experiment*, 191, n 17, 212, 216; *NHSP*, X, 18.

T2. Local records make Hall's commitment to the Constitution clear even though neither predictor knew he would be attending. On February 6 the Derryfield town meeting first voted against ratification, then elected James Thompson as a delegate. The arrival of more townsmen altered the balance of power, and Hall, a Federalist, was elected to replace Thompson. Although the records for the February meeting are unclear as to the impact of Hall's election on the town vote against ratification, the town voted on

May 20 not to instruct Hall. Documents relevant to the Derryfield and other local disputes are collected in the Goodwin Town Papers.

T3. Of the fifty-two men Libbey predicted would certainly vote for ratification, four voted "nay." They were from the contiguous towns of Dunstable, Merrimack, Bedford, and New Boston, all in the center of the most strongly anti-Federalist part of the state. Since two of the four had negative instructions and no corroborating evidence for their supposedly Federalist sentiment exists, it seems likely that Libbey, an incurable optimist, was the victim of false rumor. I have kept Libbey's labels. However, by the start of the Concord session, Federalist tabulators knew the four men would vote negatively.

T4. Morss was instructed to vote against ratification, but the instructions were removed at a town meeting held May 31, well after Libbey drew up his list.

T5. Gerrish's election had been challenged between sessions. A rump town meeting chose another man, but the credentials committee sat Gerrish. Surviving documents from that dispute make clear that Gerrish would vote for ratification.

T6. The details of what happened in Walpole are not entirely clear. Initially Bellows was chosen. Perhaps because he refused to accept negative instructions he was replaced by Allen early in February. Allen attended the Exeter session and also served as Walpole's legislative representative in June. Both Bellows and Allen presented credentials at the Concord ratification session. Bellows was seated.

T7. Initially Lebanon elected Capt. David Hough and appointed the committee to instruct him. The town subsequently replaced Hough with Payne and in the process left things uncertain about instructions. Although Payne, a state senator, never made it to Exeter, his pro-Constitution sentiments were known. He was the only delegate absent at the first session for whom Libbey made any prediction.

T8. There could be no doubt about how Patterson would vote. He was there only because Federalist leaders felt the need for additional votes. He neither lived in nor was elected by either of the towns he supposedly represented. The story of how Patterson became a convention member is too complicated to tell here. I plan, however, to spell out the details in a subsequent article explaining Grafton County's all but unanimous Federalist sentiment.

John Langdon portrait by U. D. Tenny based on the original by John Trumbull, now in the State House in Concord. Courtesy of the State of New Hampshire. Photograph by Bill Finney.

JOHN LANGDON AND JOHN SULLIVAN
A Biographical Essay

Richard F. Upton

*J*ohn Sullivan and John Langdon stand out as leaders in the successful move-ment to secure the ratification of the Constitution of the United States by New Hampshire, the ninth state to do so. While their lives present a study in con-trasts, each in his own way played a major role in "placing the Key Stone in the great arch" as Langdon described the process in his letter of June 21, 1788, to Gen. George Washington. A study of their respective backgrounds is useful in determining why they supported the new Constitution.

Both men were born in the Province of New Hampshire, Langdon at Portsmouth on June 26, 1741, and Sullivan at Somersworth on February 18, 1740, making Sullivan the elder by sixteen months.

Langdon was the younger of two sons in a family of six children. There had been Langdons in the province dating back to 1660. Langdon's father, John, Sr., was a respected farmer, who served by election as a town selectman. The Langdon farm, where the Langdon children spent their early years, was in the Sagamore Creek area about two miles from the center of Portsmouth.

Sullivan, also, was one of six children. His father, Master John, had emi-grated from Limerick, Ireland, about 1731 and eventually was employed by the Parish of Somersworth as its schoolmaster. A man of considerable education, the father had spent some of his formative years in France, during the political exile there of his father, Maj. Philip O'Sullivan, learning French and other languages. In 1747 Master Sullivan moved his family across the river to Berwick in the District of Maine (then part of Massachusetts) where he continued as a school-master and also supervised the upbringing and education of his children, two of whom, John and his younger brother, James, were destined to go far in life.

It is likely that Master Sullivan began life as a Roman Catholic, but it is also likely that he drifted away upon leaving his native Ireland. It is recorded that two of his children owned pews in the North Parish Church of Berwick. His son John, the subject of this essay, expressed open hostility to Roman Catholicism at the time of the adoption of the Quebec Act by Parliament in 1774.

While the Sullivan children learned from their father, the two Langdon sons, John and his older brother, Woodbury, attended the Latin grammar school on King Street in Portsmouth, presided over by Maj. Samuel Hale, a Harvard graduate, who taught there "with great zeal and ability for nearly forty years."

The handwriting and composition of John Langdon's letters over a lifetime show that he was a man of better than average education and understanding. The papers of John Sullivan, published in three volumes by the New Hampshire Historical Society in the 1930s, illustrate similar intellect and capacity.

In 1760, at barely eighteen years of age, John Langdon left the farm to enter the employment of Daniel Rindge, a prominent merchant and member of the Wentworth family. Langdon worked at first in the counting room, lived in the Rindge home, and sat in their pew at church. Eventually he captained several of Rindge's ships trading with the West Indies and Nova Scotia. Later, John commanded ships owned by a partnership composed of his brother, Woodbury, and Henry Sherburne on longer voyages to London. By 1767, he had become a shipowner, sailing as master of his own vessels. Shortly after 1770, he ceased going to sea and became a Portsmouth merchant in his own right. He attended the North Church (Congregational) but did not became a member until many years later.

In contrast to Langdon, John Sullivan chose the law as his profession. He studied law from 1758 to 1760 in the office of Samuel Livermore, perhaps the most able and respected lawyer in the province, whose office was then in Londonderry. Law teachers often make a lasting impression on their students and Livermore had the background and character calculated to impress. A graduate of Nassau Hall (now Princeton), he served by appointment of Gov. John Wentworth both as King's Attorney General and as Advocate of the Court of Admiralty until the downfall of royal government in 1775, and was elected attorney general of the new state by the legislature in 1776. His independence and integrity made him immune to suspicion of Toryism. Thirty years later when Livermore was chief justice of the state and resided in Holderness, he joined forces with John Sullivan and John Langdon in support of ratification of the Federal Constitution by New Hampshire.

John Sullivan began to practice law at Berwick, Maine, but shortly moved to Durham, which became his permanent home. He was financially successful as a practicing attorney and acquired property including several mills.

Thus on the eve of the American Revolution, our two subjects were well established and successful, Sullivan as an active lawyer in Durham and Langdon as a prosperous merchant in Portsmouth. Each had much at stake as the War of Independence approached. However, it is not the purpose of this essay to relate in detail the part that each played in that struggle. Each was an ardent supporter both of the move toward independence and of the resistance to the various measures

John Langdon House, Portsmouth, photograph c. 1875. Courtesy of the Society for the Preservation of New England Antiquities.

adopted by the British government to collect revenue from the American provinces.

One of these measures was a royal order-in-council, October 19, 1774, prohibiting the export of powder and arms to the provinces. At the same time, a secret order was issued from London warning all provincial governors to provide security for powder and arms at various government arsenals, one of which was Fort William and Mary at Portsmouth Harbor. Forewarned by Paul Revere, the resistance in New Hampshire, led by Langdon and Sullivan, took steps to gain possession of the powder and arms at the fort.

In the first raid on December 14, 1774, a group of about four hundred men from Portsmouth and vicinity, with Langdon in the fore, surrounded the fort in the daytime while Langdon and Capt. Robert White were admitted by the fort commander. In a parley, Langdon stated that the men had come to take away the powder in the magazine, inferring that they were acting on behalf of the province. The fort commander asked for a written order of the governor, whereupon Langdon replied that they had forgotten to bring any written order, but were determined to take the powder at all events. The commandant refused, and ordered Langdon to leave. Subsequently the waiting mob charged the fort, forcibly overpowered the small garrison, broke open the magazine, and carried away upwards of one hundred barrels of gunpowder.

John Sullivan portrait by U. D. Tenny based on original by John Trumbull, now in the State House in Concord. Courtesy of the State of New Hampshire. Photograph by Bill Finney.

In the meantime, Sullivan at Durham, informed of events, led a force of volunteers to Portsmouth the next day to remove cannon and munitions from the fort. Governor Wentworth sought to dissuade Sullivan who, appearing to agree, withdrew his men. The unit returned that same night and carried away sixteen cannon plus various small arms and munitions.

In all this, Governor Wentworth was powerless to apprehend and punish the offenders, so great was their popular support. "No jail will hold them long and no jury will find them guilty" he wrote to England. Their crime was treason, then punishable by death, as all concerned well knew, in the event the subsequent revolution had failed. Langdon and Sullivan as the most conspicuous leaders were in a particularly vulnerable position. Their status as true patriots was thus established beyond any question. The Fort William and Mary raids were the first violent revolt against British authority in the struggle for American independence.

The year 1775 saw hostilities at Concord and Lexington and fierce combat at Bunker Hill, the assumption of powers of government by the Continental Congress and the organization of a Continental Army under Washington. Governor Wentworth fled the province in the fall of 1775, never to return, thus ending royal authority in New Hampshire. Acting on advice of the Continental Congress, a popularly elected provincial congress of town delegates adopted a rudimentary state constitution in January of 1776, the first of the new states to do so. The Declaration of Independence followed in July and the ensuing war, both on land and at sea, continued for seven long years.

During the critical years Langdon and Sullivan took different paths in supporting the American cause.

Sullivan, while a delegate to the Continental Congress, was commissioned a brigadier general by the Congress on June 22, 1775. Except for commanding and drilling a contingent of local militia, he had no military education or experience. He was given command of New Hampshire's three regiments of the Continental line and promptly resigned his seat in Congress. His zeal and energy in legislative matters had impressed Congress that he was fit for command. He shortly joined Washington's army then beseiging Boston from headquarters at Winter Hill. In March of 1776 the British army evacuated Boston by sea and military activity shifted to New York City and vicinity.

New Hampshire's John Stark and Nathaniel Folsom, both of whom had fought in the colonial wars preceding the Revolution, felt that they should have received the appointment given to Sullivan by reason of their greater experience and were quick to voice their criticism of Sullivan. The resulting friction, which was perhaps to be expected, was a handicap to Sullivan's ability to command that he keenly resented.

Following the evacuation of Boston, Sullivan was given command of an expedition to Canada to relieve Montgomery's ill-fated army. The American forces failed in this effort, were out-maneuvered at Three Rivers and forced to retreat to Crown Point. Sullivan was replaced by General Gates and rejoined Washington in New York. He was promoted to major general in August of 1776. At the Battle for Long Island the Americans suffered defeat, and Sullivan was taken prisoner but was soon exchanged. He next participated in the New Jersey campaign, in which the American forces won engagements at Trenton and Princeton. In 1777 he displayed his bravery in the battles at Brandywine and Germantown. In 1778 he commanded forces in the descent on Rhode Island, and in 1779 he headed the devastating expedition against the Six Nations of Indians in western New York. Impaired health led him to resign his commission on November 30, 1779, and retire to New Hampshire. In spite of Sullivan's personal failings and extreme sensitivity, Washington considered him a brave and loyal commander and sought unsuccessfully to dissuade him from resigning, believing that complete success in the field had eluded him more from bad luck than from incompetence. Sullivan left the army with unresolved and bitter grievances with the Congress over delays in payment for his military services and expenses.

Langdon's considerable contributions to the American cause were principally on the home front, aside from brief field service as commander of a volunteer Portsmouth infantry company, at Saratoga in 1777, and in Rhode Island with Sullivan in 1779. In early 1776 he was commissioned by the Continental government to build a ship of war at Portsmouth. The *Raleigh* was launched in sixty days but was delayed from service for nearly a year for lack of cannon to complete her armament. He later supervised the construction of the fourteen-gun frigate, the *America,* completed in 1782.

Langdon sought and obtained appointment as Continental Agent for New Hampshire in May of 1776, although his commission was held up by the Continental Congress until he agreed to resign as a New Hampshire delegate. As agent he was to take charge of all captured vessels brought into the state by warships of the Continental Navy or by privateers holding commissions from the Continental Congress. He was to libel these before the New Hampshire Court of Admiralty, and after the prizes had been condemned he was empowered to sell them and to distribute the net proceeds according to regulations established by Congress. He was also to assist the Continental Navy in purchasing, refitting, provisioning and manning naval vessels and to take care of other miscellaneous Continental business in New Hampshire. One such duty was to supervise the distribution of arms being secretly imported from France through Portsmouth.

Privateering competed with the Continental Navy for manpower and funds. Privateers were privately-owned warships converted from merchant vessels and commissioned either by Congress or the state to prey on enemy commerce at sea. The net proceeds from the sale of prizes were divided between the owners and the crew. Privateers provided a means of damaging enemy commerce at sea, were quickly available, and were not subject to the cost or the time required to build publicly-owned warships. Langdon, too, engaged in privateering, owning three such vessels outright and three others in partnerships. His biographer, Lawrence Shaw Mayo, states that Langdon "emerged from the American Revolution a rich man." For this he suffered considerable public criticism, as was to be expected.

Yet he also devoted considerable time to the civilian side of state govern-ment, serving as speaker of the House of Representatives from 1776 to 1782. At the critical time of Burgoyne's 1777 campaign, he advanced large sums of money from his own funds to finance Col. John Stark's expedition of New Hampshire forces to Bennington, Vermont, the success of which was to contribute substan-tially to the decisive American victory at Saratoga, a turning point in the war.

Langdon's brother, Woodbury, became a source of embarrassment to him in the later years of the war. Like John, he was a successful Portsmouth merchant but inclined to waver in his support of the Revolution and was in England col-lecting monies owed him by his British correspondents at the outbreak of hostilities. He remained in England awaiting a good opportunity to return to New Hampshire, which required that he obtain permission to come through the British lines in America. He returned in December 1777 and was for a time viewed suspiciously as "a closet Tory." Some of this ill will fell on John Langdon as well, because he vigorously defended his brother. Yet Gov. William Plumer of Epping, a keen observer of human character, also defended Woodbury in later years, writing that "in point of talents few men, if any, in the state exceeded him."

Sullivan's younger brother, James, was far from a burden. James had stud-ied law in John's office at Durham and had opened his practice at Biddeford, Maine. He supplemented his professional income by trading as an agent of the influential John Hancock, who introduced him to public service. During the war James served in the Massachusetts legislature and as a justice on the Massachusetts Supreme Court. After the war he was a delegate to the Continental Congress, later a probate judge, and for seventeen years attorney general of Massachusetts. In 1786 he married Martha Langdon of Portsmouth, sister of John. He was elected governor of Massachusetts in 1807 and reelected shortly before his death in 1809. His *History of the District of Maine* published in 1795 was an attempt to follow the example set by Belknap's history of New Hampshire. In politics his idol was Thomas Jefferson and he became a Jeffersonian Republican.

Upon his return in December of 1779 from four years of military service, John Sullivan resumed law practice and restarted his mills. The legislature pre-vailed on him to accept a term as delegate to the Continental Congress. While there he acted to protect New Hampshire's position in the dispute with New York over the status of the New Hampshire Grants (Vermont) and served as chairman of a committee to reorganize government finances. His claims for back pay for military service were still unresolved so that, being short of money, he accepted personal loans from the French Minister, the Chevalier de la Luzerne. For this Sullivan was criticized, but his claim that he repaid the loans was supported by one of his biographers, Dr. Randolph Adams. Along with a majority of the Congress, Sullivan supported many French claims then being negotiated for the peace treaty.

Sullivan accepted appointment as New Hampshire's attorney general in September of 1782 and served in that office until 1786. During that period, a group of New Hampshire towns in the Connecticut Valley sought to join Vermont for the second time since 1776. To thwart this move, the legislature voted to call out the militia if necessary and place it under Sullivan's command. George Washington wrote to Vermont leaders urging them to disclaim any jurisdiction over the New Hampshire towns. The Vermont legislature then renounced any jurisdiction east of the Connecticut River. Sullivan, riding circuit as attorney general, aided in reestablishing the authority of New Hampshire government in affected parts of Cheshire and Grafton Counties.

The Treaty of Paris in 1783 ended the war and confirmed the independence of the American states. New Hampshire had adopted a new state constitution effective at about the same time. By almost unanimous consent the first chief executive (president) chosen under the new constitution was the venerable Meshech Weare, the grand old man of New Hampshire. He retired in 1785. To succeed Weare, the candidates were John Langdon, John Sullivan and George Atkinson, Speaker of the House. In the popular vote, Atkinson had a plurality, Langdon was second, and Sullivan third. Since no candidate had a majority, the contest was decided by the Senate which chose Langdon. The House, however, elected Sullivan as its speaker, and both houses chose Sullivan as a member of the Executive Council.

In February of 1786, President Langdon nominated his brother Woodbury to be a justice of the Superior Court. Sullivan opposed confirmation, but on a day when he was absent, Langdon obtained confirmation from the remaining councilors. Sullivan, deeply offended, resigned as attorney general as well as commander of the state militia, and contested Langdon's bid for reelection as president. This time Sullivan won a clear majority. But Langdon had also been elected, as a representative from Portsmouth, and the House unanimously chose him as its speaker. The two men now became political rivals.

That September, while Sullivan was chief executive, an unruly crowd of paper money advocates surrounded the building in Exeter where the legislature was in session and sought to compel that body to meet their demands. Sullivan called out detachments of militia from neighboring towns and skillfully suppressed the insurgents. In 1787, Langdon and Sullivan again contested the election as chief executive. Langdon received a plurality but neither had a majority so the election was again thrown into the Senate, which this time chose Sullivan. Such was the situation as the convention to revise the Articles of Confederation met in Philadelphia in late spring of 1787.

The selection of Langdon and Nicholas Gilman of Exeter as New Hampshire's delegates, Langdon's personal advancement of funds for their attendance when the legislature failed to appropriate money for that purpose, their support of the proposed constitution, and its eventual adoption by the convention in September 1787 have been fully related elsewhere in this volume, as has the story of New Hampshire being the ninth state to ratify.

Sullivan served as president of the ratifying convention. Langdon was one of the principal floor leaders and strategists of the Federalist proponents, and engineered the crucial adjournment from February 22 to June 18, 1788. Chief Justice Livermore, Sullivan's law teacher, made the final motion to ratify, which carried by a vote of 57 to 47 on June 21, 1788. Throughout the process, Sullivan and Langdon cooperated fully, having laid aside their political rivalry.

Why did Langdon and Sullivan support ratification so strongly? In Sullivan's case, he had served in state government and knew its weaknesses at first hand. He desired an effective national government with strong military and financial powers. He was a "law and order" man and saw the powers of the national government as an antidote to internal insurrections such as had occurred in Massachusetts and New Hampshire. He had traveled about the country as an army officer and had seen conditions in the other states. The provision for a strong national judiciary appealed to him because it replaced the former appeals from the provincial courts to the Privy Council in England. Lastly, Washington's recommendation of the constitution was decisive, for Sullivan revered his former commander-in-chief.

In the case of Langdon, he was a merchant engaged in interstate and foreign trade. He, too, knew from state service that a single state was powerless to overcome trade barriers established by other states as well as to negotiate with foreign powers regarding trade and commerce. He favored the Federal Constitution because it vested full power over interstate and foreign commerce in the federal government. He also favored giving the federal government power to call out the state militia. Control of importation of slaves he foresaw must be vested in the central government rather than the states. Having served at the Philadelphia convention, he realized that the proposed constitution was "a good deal" for small states like New Hampshire. Finally, he realized, from his experience in handling money matters both as a merchant, as Continental agent, and as a state executive, that the strong powers over money and finance vested in the federal government were essential to bring about more stability in economic affairs in the new nation.

In the elections of 1788–89, New Hampshire chose five electors for President and Vice President and also two senators and three representatives in the Congress, under the Constitution. New York City served as the temporary capital. United States Senators were then elected by the state legislature, and New Hampshire chose John Langdon as one of its two senators. Langdon and his New Hampshire colleague, Paine Wingate, arrived in New York on March 4, 1789, the date set for the convening of Congress. There was no quorum present until April 6. On that date, John Langdon was elected president pro tempore of the Senate, and the members of the House of Representatives joined the Senate to count the electoral votes. The counting completed, Langdon announced from the chair that George Washington and John Adams had been elected, and dispatched a letter to Washington at Mount Vernon forthwith, transmitting "to your Excellency, the information of your unanimous election to the office of President of the United States of America." Washington came to New York on April 30, 1789, receiving a tumultuous welcome and prolonged cheers from the populace. He was sworn in by Robert R. Livingston, Chancellor of the State of New York, at Federal Hall (the former City Hall), then delivered his inaugural address, and began the first presidential administration under the Constitution.

Back in New Hampshire, Sullivan had been reelected president of the state. In the autumn of 1789, President Washington visited the northeast, including New Hampshire. Coming north from Boston through Newburyport and traveling on horseback and by "chariot" or coach, he arrived on the morning of October 31, 1789, at New Hampshire's southern boundary, where he was met by President Sullivan, Senators Langdon and Wingate, and other federal and state officials, together with a large detachment of mounted state militia in full uniform. Proceeding along the principal coastal highway through Seabrook, Hampton Falls, Hampton and Greenland, early in the afternoon the cavalcade clattered into Portsmouth, with Washington mounted on a "beautiful white horse."

Langdon had invited the President to remain at the Langdon mansion on Pleasant Street. Rather than stay in the home of any private citizens, the President selected accommodations at Brewster's Tavern on Court Street where he entertained at dinner that night many of those officials who had received him at the state line. The next day, Sunday, the President attended both the Episcopal and the Congregational services. On subsequent days, he toured Portsmouth harbor by boat, was entertained at a state dinner in the Assembly Room of the State House, and attended a tea at the Langdon mansion. On Wednesday, November 5, the President left Portsmouth traveling a route leading through Greenland, Stratham, Exeter, Kingston and Plaistow to the Massachusetts line. The President's visit to New Hampshire was a crowning point in the careers of John Sullivan and John Langdon, both of whom had labored so long in collaboration with Washington to establish a stable and effective national government.

In early October of 1789, not long before the visit to Portsmouth, President Washington had appointed Sullivan as the first federal judge for the District of New Hampshire. The court had few cases in its early years. Sullivan's health began to decline into premature senility. He died at his home in Durham on January 23, 1795, at the age of fifty-four, and was buried in a family plot on a knoll behind his home, overlooking the quiet Oyster River.

He suffered from distinct weaknesses of personality in that he was vain, boastful and unduly sensitive to supposed slights by others. He was a chronic complainer about money matters. Yet in the larger picture, he was a leader of people and a talented politician who served four difficult years in the Continental Army. After the war he entered vigorously into the public service of his native state. He realized early that government under the Articles of Confederation would hardly suffice. He stood for order and obedience to law, and loathed disorganization. He was an early supporter of New Hampshire's ratification of the Constitution, and was a major factor in the final vote of the 1788 convention. "A man of action, he recognized duty and met it unhesitantly," wrote his biographer, Charles P. Whittemore.

John Langdon outlived John Sullivan by twenty-four years. He remained in the United States Senate until 1801, having opted not to seek reelection in 1800. He frequently served as president pro tempore. He strongly supported the financial program of Alexander Hamilton including assumption of state debts and establishment of a national bank. During this period, he gradually changed parties drawing away from the Federalists and adhering to the Jeffersonian Republicans. When war between England and France erupted in 1793–94 he extended his sympathies to the French while the Federalists favored England, and he disapproved of Jay's Treaty with England. Langdon also disliked the aristocratic demeanor and political philosophy of many high-ranking Federalists. Many of his contemporaries believed that his change of parties was motivated by opportunism and ambition, and that he expected the eventual downfall of the Federalist Party.

From 1801 to 1805 Langdon was a member of the House in the state legislature and its speaker in 1804 and 1805. He declined President Jefferson's offer to serve as Secretary of the Navy in 1801. In 1805 he won the governorship, after four unsuccessful attempts, and was reelected annually, with but one year's interruption, until he retired from that office in 1812. That year the Republicans proposed his name as a candidate for vice president with James Madison, but he declined for reasons of health. On the 18th of September, 1819, he died at the age of seventy-nine and was buried in Portsmouth's North Cemetery.

He was generally ahead of his time in foreseeing the course of events, and this was true of his support of the United States Constitution, both in the drafting stage and in its ratification by his native state. While Sullivan was inclined to be direct and blunt, Langdon nearly always exhibited tact and diplomacy in public affairs. As a political strategist, he had few equals, and much is owed to his acumen in negotiating a three-months' recess in the New Hampshire ratifying convention while a favorable majority was being marshalled.

Governor William Plumer, a contemporary, wrote of him:

Few men in New Hampshire ever obtained so many offices, or held them for a longer period than he did. He owed his elections not to distinguished talents, but to his fascinating address, amenity of manners and his social habits of greeting every man he met, and to the spirit of party which existed at the time.

Samuel Penhallow's invoice dated November 4, 1788, for engrossing 2 copies of New Hampshire's ratification document on parchment. Courtesy of the State Archives. Photograph by Bill Finney.

TOASTING THE CONSTITUTION
New Hampshire's Celebrations of 1788

Richard G. Kalkhoff

The Center for the
Study of the American Constitution

On September 17, 1787, the Federal Convention, after nearly four months of hard work and lengthy debate, released its final creation: the United States Constitution. Following a brief debate in Congress, the new Constitution was submitted to the thirteen states with the requirement, stated in Article VII, that at least nine of them approve the document to make it operative. Nine months later, on June 21, 1788, New Hampshire became the ninth state to ratify the proposed frame of government and thus the new Constitution became the law of the land.

Although New Hampshire's long ratification struggle has inspired much research and writing, surprisingly little notice has been taken of the numerous public celebrations that blanketed the state in late June 1788. These patriotic celebrations culminated in a grand procession that flowed through the streets of Portsmouth after news from Concord announced that New Hampshire had at last ratified the Constitution and, more importantly, had erected the ninth and crucial pillar of the new federal edifice.

New Hampshire, like many other American states, had experienced its share of difficulties during the postwar years. A dispute over the method of town representation in the state legislature had been quite divisive. Moreover, the economic problems and interstate rivalries that plagued the nation during the Confederation years, coupled with Shays' Rebellion in nearby Massachusetts, had convinced many New Hampshirites that reforms were needed on the national, as well as the state, level. When the Federal Convention was called for the purpose of revising the existing frame of government, a Portsmouth newspaper predicted that the state's "difficulties will certainly be removed as soon as the States become united in ONE HEAD." Thus when the Federal Convention finally assembled in Philadelphia in May 1787, many New Hampshirites hoped for the best. *The*

New Hampshire Spy anxiously awaited "that glorious fabric which the united wisdom of our great MASTER-BUILDERS are about to erect."

The Constitution was printed for the first time in the state by the *New Hampshire Spy* on September 29. Three days later, the *Spy* printed the state's first original commentary on the Constitution:

> It is with real pleasure we announce, that the report of the Federal Convention meets with the greatest approbation in this metropolis. All ranks are highly animated with the pleasing hope, that this glorious structure, supported by thirteen pillars, will speedily be completed.

Indeed, many New Hampshirites looked forward to the ratification of the Constitution by their state.

The New Hampshire ratifying convention met at Exeter on February 13, 1788. It was widely assumed throughout the United States that New Hampshire would easily ratify the new Constitution, especially after Massachusetts' ratification on February 6. Everyone expected that New Hampshire would follow the lead of its influential neighbor. Indeed, news of Massachusetts' ratification was well received in New Hampshire but a South Carolina newspaper noted a decision to postpone celebration until New Hampshire too had added its name to the list of approving states:

> The general joy diffused through all ranks of people in this metropolis [Portsmouth], upon receiving intelligence of the adoption of the federal constitution by the Massachusetts convention, was really pleasing—a general rejoicing would have taken place...had not some of our patriots recommended a suspension of any public testimonials of joy until the grand question should be decided by the convention of this state.

However, much to everyone's surprise, the Federalists had underestimated their opponents' strength in the state convention; and thus, fearing defeat, the Federalists obtained an adjournment until June 18. The adjournment disappointed many New Hampshirites and plans for a celebration had to be postponed.

On April 28 Maryland became the seventh state to ratify the Constitution. Portsmouth residents expressed their joy upon hearing the news that another state had added its name to the lengthening federal roster. *The New Hampshire Spy* reported that a "number of patriotic citizens assembled at Brewster's Coffee House-Tavern and congratulated each other on the happy event" and drank thirteen "federal" toasts. It was noted that John Langdon, a delegate to both the Constitutional Convention at Philadelphia and the recently adjourned state convention at Exeter, defrayed the costs of the festivities—an act which proved "the greatness of his mind, and the joy he felt upon…so important an event." More importantly, the *Spy* intimated that based on the information collected, "little doubt may be had but that the proposed Constitution will be ratified by this State, at their next meeting—and that by a considerable majority."

Langdon and other Federalists worked hard between the adjournment at Exeter and the June meeting in Concord. They flooded the newspapers with articles espousing ratification, launched personal attacks on staunch Antifederalists, and tried to sway others who were undecided. They received a boost when news arrived that South Carolina had ratified the Constitution on May 23. Thus everyone realized the importance of New Hampshire's situation: the next state to ratify would be the ninth and deciding state—the Constitution would become the law of the land.

Besides New Hampshire, two other conventions were scheduled to sit in June—those of Virginia and New York. It was generally expected that one of these three states would put the new frame of government into operation. New Hampshire Federalists recognized their opportunity. In addition, they had one crucial advantage: public opinion. The day before the convention met at Concord the *New Hampshire Spy* anticipated "the general joy, which in all probability will diffuse itself through this metropolis, should the Federal constitution be ratified by the Convention of this state."

The New Hampshire convention came to order at Concord as expected on June 18. The scene was recreated by a Concord historian:

> The Convention excited an interest with which the proceedings of no other deliberative body in this State have ever been regarded. The galleries of the church where it assembled were thronged with spectators, and its members were surrounded, not only by large numbers of their own constituents, but by individuals from distant states engaged…in watching their deliberations.

All of New Hampshire, convention delegates and the general public alike, sensed the importance of what was happening. After only a few days of deliberation, the Concord convention, on June 21, 1788, ratified the Constitution by a vote of fifty-seven to forty-seven. Writing to his friend the New Hampshire historian Jeremy Belknap then living in Massachusetts, Portsmouth postmaster Jeremiah Libbey recognized the importance of the New Hampshire convention: "The Convention of this State on the 21st instant ratified the Constitution, and for anything we know of, have the honor to be the State that puts the corner or top stone to the Federal edifice." It was now time for New Hampshire to celebrate not only ratification, but its role as the ninth and decisive ratifying state.

Like other early Americans, the people of New Hampshire were accustomed to assembling publicly on special occasions. A public proclamation of the Declaration of Independence in Portsmouth in July 1776 brought three cheers from the townspeople and the local militia who had assembled in "peace and good order" on the occasion. Seven years later in the same town, the public pronouncement of the Treaty of Peace between the United States and Great Britain was celebrated with a peal of bells, the firing of cannon, displays of fireworks, and "lively demonstrations of joy." Local celebrations of the Fourth of July were traditionally marked by oratory, cannon fire and the drinking of thirteen toasts. The Constitution, and ratification of it by other states, offered similar opportunities for celebration.

Early in 1788, the people of Boston had introduced a new kind of celebration: the public procession. The citizens of New Hampshire were well aware of Boston's grand procession which followed Massachusetts' ratification in early February. The procession included public officials, men of learned professions, as well as tradesmen, who carried the tools of their trade and uniquely decorated banners and flags. The procession made a favorable impression on many New Hampshire folk. As a Massachusetts newspaper noted, the procession at Boston was "an exhibition to which America has never before witnessed an equal."

When news from Concord confirmed New Hampshire's ratification, the inhabitants of the state were ready to celebrate. The streets of Exeter blazed with bonfires on the evening of June 21. In a letter written to James A. Garfield on the eve of the Civil War, Lewis Cass recalled the night the bonfires burned in his hometown:

> When, at last, New Hampshire ratified the Constitution, it was a day of great rejoicing. My mother held me, a little boy of six years, in her arms at the window, and pointed me to the bonfires that were blazing in the streets of Exeter, and told me that the people were celebrating the adoption of the Constitution. So I saw the Constitution born.... I have loved the Union ever since the light of that bonfire greated my eyes.

The day after ratification, June 22, "mutual congratulations took place, and public thanks were returned in all churches." Because it was Sunday, no other celebrating took place, but much was planned for the following week.

On Monday afternoon, as John Langdon returned to Portsmouth from the convention at Concord, the city's bells rang out a "joyful" peal. He was escorted into town by "several corps of cavalry, infantry," and a number of other gentlemen "amidst the discharge of artillery and the shouts of his fellow citizens."

The citizens of Dover assembled in the afternoon of June 24 to express their joy and approbation of the new Constitution. The unique celebration began with the discharge of nine cannon, with an interval of nine minutes between each shot. The nine states that had ratified the Constitution were individually toasted, each shortly before a cannon shot, in the order of their ratifications. After the last shot was fired, nine cheers were raised by the crowd. Next, those present drank a toast to Dover's sole member of the New Hampshire convention, Doctor Ezra Green, a respected surgeon and the town's first postmaster.

The main event of the day, however, was a procession. The parade was led by a detachment of cavalry, followed by a band and a number of young boys "with hatchets lopping pine branches," as though clearing the way for the Union. They were followed by the ministers of the town and Ezra Green, "bearing the Constitution hand in hand." The main body of the parade consisted of farmers, traders, shipbuilders, sailors, tailors, and dozens of other trades, "each bearing implements and ensigns of their professions." Each hoped that the new Constitution would bring happiness and success to their respective trades.

After passing through the principal streets of Dover, the procession moved on to the town hall where all were refreshed with cold drink provided from nine "flowing" punch bowls. Four other bowls were left empty, symbolizing the states that had not yet ratified the Constitution. The day closed in harmony with the singing of nine songs.

It was noted that "many, who had been unfriendly to the Federal cause, joined in the hilarity of the day." Indeed, after losing their battle in the convention, Antifederalists in New Hampshire acquiesced, unlike their counterparts in a few other states. Moreover, it was also reported that many of the people who participated in the day's festivities were gathered in about two hours "which [served] to evince that their hearts [were] not less grateful or less animated…than the most dignified patriots of America."

All patriotic celebrations and expressions of joy culminated at Portsmouth on Thursday, June 26. *The Massachusetts Gazette* reported that "the joy which the ratification of the new Constitution by this State, has diffused through all states of citizens in the metropolis is hardly conceivable." A large number of patriots assembled near the state house on the Parade (Pleasant Street) for a procession, scheduled for that day. *The New Hampshire Gazette,* on June 26, printed an elaborate account of the procession and other festivities. At about eleven o'clock a.m. the ship *Union,* drawn by nine horses, arrived at the state house, signaling the start of the procession. The procession was led by a brass band which played "federal" music composed for the occasion. The band was followed by farmers and a plow drawn by nine oxen, symbolic of clearing the way. A number of reapers, mowers, and threshers tagged close behind carrying their implements. Next came the blacksmiths and nailers "with their forges, anvils and sledges, at work." They were followed by a group that made up a major portion of the parade: the men of the shipping industry.

Uniquely decorated for the occasion, the ship *Union* was next in line. The ship was described as completely rigged, armed and manned, under an easy sail, with colours flying, elevated on a carriage drawn by nine horses, a tenth, (emblematical of Virginia) completely harnessed, led, and ready to join the rest.

The printers were represented by a few pressmen and a printing press which was used during the procession to strike off a number of songs in celebration of New Hampshire's ratification, which were distributed to waiting spectators. One of the "federal" songs was "It Comes!":

> It Comes! It Comes! high raise the song!
> The bright procession moves along,
> From pole to pole resound the Nine,
> And distant worlds the chorus join.
> Tis done! the glorious fabric's rear'd!
> Still be New Hampshire's sons rever'd.
> Who fix'd its BASE in blood and fears,
> And stretched its Turrets to the Stars!

The printers also bore this motto:

> A government of freemen never knows
> A tyrant's shackles, on press t'impose.

The printers were followed by a number of different trades and professions including schoolmasters and their young scholars. A few young women who were students of geography designed a special globe which was carried in the procession. On the globe each state was distinguished, with "New Hampshire in the zenith and Rhode Island on the western horizon in mourning." The schoolmasters carried a flag bearing their motto:

> Where the bright beams of Federal freedom glow,
> The buds of science, in full beauty blow.

The schoolmasters were followed by judges, clerks, and lawyers who "supported the Federal Constitution." The president of the state (John Langdon), members of the late convention and of the legislature, and a number of the militia in uniform brought up the rear of the parade. It was noted that "every profession was distinguished by some insignia or badge peculiar to it" and that all trades and professions "intended to represent that in consequence of the Union, commerce, and all arts dependent on it, would revive and flourish."

New Hampshire's document ratifying the Federal Constitution, June 21, 1788, signed by John Sullivan, John Langdon, John Calfe as secretary of the convention, and Joseph Pearson as secretary of state. See transcription in appendix A. Courtesy of the State Archives. Photograph by Bill Finney.

The procession, after winding through the principal streets of Portsmouth, arrived at Union-hill where a cold collation stood prepared for all present. Nine patriotic toasts were drunk and each was accompanied by cannon fire. The federal songs, distributed by the printers to the multitude during the procession, were sung in order with the accompaniment of the band. The procession then re-formed and returned in the same order as it had come. Upon arrival at the state house, after a "federal" salute was fired from the ship *Union*, the grand procession dispersed.

In the evening the state house was "beautifully illuminated" with nine candles in each window and the band entertained a group of people from the balcony. Reporting on the day's events, the *New Hampshire Gazette* noted that "language is too poor to describe the universal joy that glowed in every countenance. Tis enough to say that the brilliance and festivity of the evening, were only equalled by the decorum and hilarity of the day."

The Portsmouth procession drew notice from New Hampshire's neighbor, Massachusetts. *The Massachusetts Spy* reported that "the adoption of the Federal Constitution by the Convention of New Hampshire was celebrated at Portsmouth...with great rejoicing; there was a grand Procession, similar to that exhibited some time since at Boston." *The Massachusetts Centinel* noted that a "GRAND PROCESSION, in a superior style, closed the rejoicing of the federalist citizens of our sister state."

There may even have been a feeling of competition between the inhabitants of Boston and those of Portsmouth. In relaying an account of the Portsmouth procession to Jeremy Belknap in Boston, Jeremiah Libbey proudly commented that "we have copied your State in having a procession; but a Boston gentleman who was present told me we really exceeded you."

In the shadow of Portsmouth's grand procession, the celebration at Keene at the end of the week was a kind of anticlimax. Keene's celebration began with a small procession consisting of the inhabitants of the town and the surrounding area, a band, and the militia. The procession marched to Federal Hill where a speech was given by Keene's delegate to the state ratifying convention, the Reverend Aaron Hall. Hall spoke of the reason for the happiness of the citizens of New Hampshire:

> When we consider the greatness of the prize we contended for, the doubtful nature of the contest in the late war, the favorable manner in which it has terminated, together with the establishment of a permanent energetic government, perfectly confident with the true liberties of the people, and this obtained in a time of peace, a thing not paralleled in history.... When we consider these things, we shall find the greatest possible reason for gratitude and rejoicing.

Hall's oration was followed by thirteen toasts, the last of which was to the "Antifederalists—may they read the Constitution without prejudice, have the wisdom to understand it, become good subjects, and enjoy the blessings of it."

At eight o'clock that evening, a forty-foot stage atop Federal Hill was set ablaze and followed by a fireworks display. In town, there was an elegant ball which many attended. Keene's newspaper, the *New Hampshire Recorder,* summarized the feelings of the townspeople: "A joyful spirit of Republicanism seemed to pervade every breast—the greatest order and good harmony was preserved—and the day was closed with hilarity."

With the new frame of government adopted, the Fourth of July celebrations in 1788 took on added meaning. Independence from Great Britain would be remembered, but Americans would now look forward to the rebirth of the nation. The Fourth of July celebration at Portsmouth provides a good example. *The New Hampshire Spy* reported that the day was celebrated "with all that joy which the sons of Freedom are capable of expressing upon so auspicious an occasion."

The celebration began with an oration by Jonathan Mitchell Sewall at the Rev. Samuel Haven's meetinghouse "before a very respectable and brilliant audience." In his eloquent address, Sewall, a respected Portsmouth lawyer who was known in local circles for his patriotic oratory, mentioned the ratification of the Constitution:

> At length Heaven has again graciously smiled upon us.... A Federal Constitution of government is now ratified by nine, which is, in effect, by all the United States. A Constitution which no earthly power short of our own, will ever be able to frustrate or violate!

At noon, a "federal" salute was fired from the castle by a company of artillery and all assembled drank "federal" punch. That evening many patriots dined at Newington where "joys sincere heightened the feast, and gave appetite new charms." After dinner John Langdon, recently elected president of the state, proposed thirteen toasts and the day closed with fireworks. *The New Hampshire Spy* summed up the feeling on the first anniversary of independence under the new Constitution:

> Long, very long, may the memory of this important day be engraven upon the hearts of the citizens of the United Columbia—and may it ever be celebrated in such a manner, as will best tend to inculcate the principles of order and good government; then shall we see the golden age returned, and Americans become independent indeed.

The celebrations in New Hampshire in the early summer of 1788 were an expression of public approbation for the new Constitution. The people of New Hampshire, like many other Americans, had anxiously anticipated the day when the proposed Constitution would become the law of the land. They believed that the new frame of government offered endless possibilities, and all looked forward to the prosperity and strength it would bring to their families, businesses, towns, state and ultimately, their country.

When New Hampshire became the ninth and "keystone" state responsible for the Constitution's approval, the patriotic inhabitants of New Hampshire celebrated, expressing their optimism and faith in the new government. These celebrations were special expressions of political joy which, in the words of Pennsylvania's Benjamin Rush, "is one of the strongest emotions of the human mind."

———

This essay, with footnotes, was published in *Historical New Hampshire* (Winter 1988), 291–303.

APPENDIX A
New Hampshire's Ratification Document: Transcription

STATE OF NEW-HAMPSHIRE

IN CONVENTION of the Delegates of the PEOPLE of the STATE OF NEW HAMPSHIRE June 21st. 1788

The Convention haveing impartially discussed & fully considered the Constitution for the UNITED STATES OF AMERICA, reported to Congress by the Convention of Delegates from the United States of America and submitted to us by a Resolution of the General Court of said State, passed the fourteenth Day of December last past & acknowledging with grateful Hearts the goodness of the Supreme ruler of the Universe in affording the People of the UNITED STATES in the course of his Providence an Opportunity deliberately & peaceably without fraud or Surprize of entering into an explicit & solemn compact with each other by assenting to and ratifying a new Constitution, in Order to form a more perfect union, establish Justice, insure domestick tranquility, provide for the common defence promote the general welfare and secure the blessings of Liberty to themselves & their Posterity. DO IN THE NAME, & behalf of the People of the STATE OF NEW HAMPSHIRE assent to & ratify the said Constitution for the UNITED STATES OF AMERICA & as it is the Opinion of this Convention that certain amendments & alterations in the said Constitution would remove the fears and Quiet the apprehensions of many of the good People of this State, and more effectually guard against an undue Administration of the federal Government. The Convention do therefore recommend that the following Alterations & provisions be introduced into the said Constitution.

FIRST THAT it be explicitly declared that all Powers not expressly and particularly delegated by the aforesaid Constitution are reserved to the several States to be by them exercised.

SECONDLY THAT there shall be one Representative to every Thirty Thousand Persons according to the Census mentioned in the Constitution untill the whole number of Representatives amounts to two hundred.

235

THIRDLY

THAT Congress do not Exercise the Powers vested in them by the fourth Section of the first Article, but in Cases when a State shall neglect or refuse to make the regulations therein mentioned or shall make regulations subversive of the rights of the People to a free & equal Representation in Congress, nor shall Congress in any case make regulations contrary to a free and equal Representation

FOURTHLY

THAT Congress do not lay direct Taxes but when the money arising from Impost, Excise & their other resources are insufficient for the Publick Exigencies; nor then untill Congress shall have first, made a requisition upon the STATES to assess Levy and pay their respective proportions of such requisition agreeably to the Census fixed in the said Constitution in such way and manner as the Legislature of the State shall neglect then Congress may assess & Levy such State's proportion together with the Interest from the Time of payment prescribed in such requisition

FIFTHLY

THAT Congress erect no Company of Merchants with exclusive advantages of Commerce.

SIXTHLY

THAT No Person shall be Tryed for any Crime by which he may incur an infamous punishment or loss of Life untill he be first indicted by a Grand Jury except in such Cases as may arise in the Government and regulation of the Land & Naval forces.

SEVENTHLY

ALL Common Law Cases between Citizens of different States, shall be commenced in the Common Law Courts of the respective STATES and no appeal shall be allowed to the federal Court in such Cases, unless the sum or value of the thing in controversy amount to Three Thousand Dollars.

EIGHTHLY

IN Civil Actions between Citizens of different States, every issue of fact arising in Actions at Common Law, shall be Tried by a Jury if the parties or either of them request it

NINTHLY

CONGRESS, shall at no time consent that any Person holding an Office of Trust or profit under the UNITED STATES shall accept a Title of Nobility or any other Title or Office from any King, Prince or foreign STATE.

TENTHLY	THAT no Standing Army shall be Kept up in Time of Peace, unless with the consent of three fourths of the Members of each branch of Congress nor shall Soldiers in Time of Peace be Quartered upon private Houses without the Consent of the Owners.
ELEVENTHLY	CONGRESS shall make no Laws touching Religion or to infringe the rights of Conscience
TWELFTHLY	CONGRESS shall never disarm any Citizen, unless such as are or have been in actual Rebellion.

AND THE CONVENTION DO, in the name & behalf of the People of this State enjoin it upon their REPRESENTATIVES in Congress at all Times untill the alterations & provisions aforesaid have been considered agreeably to the fifth Article of the said Constitution to exert all their influence & use all reasonable & legal methods to obtain a Ratification of the sd alterations & provisions in such manner as is provided in the said Article. And that the United States in Congress Assembled may have due notice of the assent & Ratification of the sd Constitution by this Convention. IT IS RESOLVED That the assent & Ratification aforesaid be engrossed on Parchment together with the recommendation & Injunction aforesaid & with this Resolution & that John Sullivan Esqr. President of Convention & John Langdon Esqr. President of the State Transmit the same Countersigned by the Secretary of Convention & the Secretary of the State under their hands & Seals to the United States in Congress Assembled.

s/ Jno Sullivan presidt of Convention
s/ John Langdon President of State
s/ John Calfe Secretary of Convention
s/ Joseph Pearson Secretary of State

———

One parchment original of this document is maintained by the Secretary of State at the Division of Records Management and Archives, Concord. A second original parchment, probably that sent to the Confederation Congress in New York, is maintained by the National Archives and Records Administration, Washington, DC.

News of New Hamshire's ratification of the U.S. Constitution and of Portsmouth's reaction to it was circulated by this June 26, 1788 edition of the New Hampshire Gazette and General Advertiser, *Courtesy of the N.H. Historical Society. Photograph by Bill Finney.*

APPENDIX B
In Celebration: Portsmouth's Parade

From the *New Hampshire Gazette and General Advertiser*
June 26, 1788

By a worthy member of the Convention, we are informed, the Constitution with the proposed amendments was unanimously agreed to;—the controversy arose chiefly upon the question—which was the most likely method to obtain the amendments? part were for adopting and risking them, others for adjourning, in order to try to obtain them first, had this been agreed to, there would not have been one dissenting voice.

Information being received that his Excellency, President LANGDON, was to arrive in town on Monday afternoon, Col. Wentworth's corps of Independent Horse, Capt Woodward's company of Artillery, and Col. Hill's company of foot, severally paraded, and, together with a very large number of gentlemen in carriages and on horseback, met his Excellency at Greenland, and escorted him into town, where he was received by a number of citizens, who complimented his return with several federal cheers. During the procession's moving into town, the bells were rung, and every testimony of joy exhibited, which a grateful people are capable of expressing, or a federal patriot worthy of receiving.

When his Excellency and suite arrived within a mile of the town, Capt. Woodward's company of artillery honored him with a federal salute.

What added greatly to the brilliancy of the scene was the appearance of a great number of ladies whose smiling countenances bespoke the congeniality of sentiment which ever ought to subsist between the sons and daughters of Adam.

Thursday being the day appointed to celebrate the RATIFICATION of the FEDERAL CONSTITUTION by the State of New-Hampshire, a numerous concourse of the inhabitants of Portsmouth, and the neighboring towns being assembled on the Parade, about 11 o'clock an armed ship was espied from the State-House, bearing down under full sail; being hailed on her approach, she proved to be the ship UNION, *Thomas Manning*, Esq. commander, from Concord, out five days, bound to the Federal city, all well and in good spirits. About a quarter past eleven, she dropt anchor, and having received a pilot on board, got under way and joined the procession, which moved in the following order.

A Band of musick in an open Coach and six horses decorated.

Husbandmen.

A Plough drawn by 9 yoke of oxen.

A man sowing.

A Harrow, Reapers, Threshers, Mowers, Hay-makers, each with their proper
    implements.

A man swinging flax.

A Cart for gathering in harvest.

Blacksmiths and Nailers with their Forges, Anvils and Sledges, at work.

Shipwrights with their tools.

Caulkers.

Rope-makers with a spinning-wheel and hemp round their waists, occupied.

Riggers.

Mast-makers.

Ship-joiners.

Block-makers.

Mathematical instrument-makers with an Azimuth compass.

Boat-builders at work on a boat nearly compleated.

Carvers.

Painters, Glaziers and Plummers.

Coopers trimming casks.

Cullers of fish.

Stowadores.

Pilots with Spy-Glasses and Charts.

The Ship UNION, compleatly rigged, armed & mann'd, under an easy sail with colours flying—elevated on a carriage, drawn by nine horses, a tenth (emblematical of Virginia) completely harnessed, led and ready to join the rest.

Ship Captains with their Quadrants.

Seamen.

Shoremen.

Truckmen.

Millers.

Bakers, preceded by a flag displaying the bakers arms.

Butchers.

Tanners and Curriers.

Cordwainers, with their lasts decorated.

Tallow-Chandlers.

Tailors.

Barbers.

Hatters.

House-wrights.

Masons.
Cabinet-makers and Wheelwrights.
Saddlers and Chaise-trimmers.
Upholsterers.
Goldsmiths, Jewellers & Silversmiths.
Clock and Watch-makers.
Coppersmiths.
Whitesmiths.
Brass-founders.
Tinmen, with nine pillars and stars on a pedestal.
Potters, with a table and wheel at work, nine pillars erected.
Brick-makers burning a kiln, others moulding bricks.
Leather-dressers.
Card-Makers with Cards.

Printers, preceded by two lads with open quires of printed paper, followed with Cases and Apparatus decorated. Compositors at work; Pressmen with M. Benjamin Dearborn's new invented Printing-Press (named the American Press) employ'd during the whole procession, in striking off and distributing among the surrounding multitude, songs in celebration of the ratification of the Federal Constitution by the State of New-Hampshire.

MOTTO
A Government of Freemen never knows
A Tyrant's shackles on the Press t'impose.

    Consuls.
    Merchants and Traders.
    The Boys of the different Schools with the insignia of their studies, decorated.
    The Terrestrial Globe, rectified for New-Hampshire, (and decorated by a company of young ladies, who are in the study of Geography.) carried by two lads in uniform. In the decorations each State was distinguish'd New-Hampshire in the zenith, and Rhode-Island on the western horizon, in mourning.
    The Masters of the Schools.

MOTTO
Where the bright beams of Fed'ral Freedom glow,
The buds of Science in full beauty blow.

    Clergy.
    Physicians and Surgeons.
    Sheriff preceded by his deputies.

Judges of Common Law and Admiralty Courts.
Clerks of Court.
Gentlemen of the Bar, supporting the Federal Constitution.
The President of the State and President of the Convention.
Secretaries of the State & Convention.
Members of the Convention.
Members of the Legislature.
Treasurer and Commissary General.
Militia Officers in uniform.

Every profession was distinguished by some insignia or badge, peculiar to it: The procession moved on thro' all the principal streets of the town, the band playing and singing the Federal Song. "It comes! It comes!" and after saluting the President of the State, & the President and Members of the Convention, at their respective lodgings with nine guns each, from the Ship, the procession moved on to Union-Hill, where a cold Collation was provided, the Band of Music playing during the repast, and the Ship lying to, with a man at masthead, sent to spy out the Ship VIRGINIA, which was hourly expected to join the rest of the fleet.

After dinner, the following toasts were given, the Artillery firing a salute between each, which was as often reply'd to with three cheers from the table,—

1.   The Convention of New-Hampshire.
2.   The confederated States.
3.   May every State in the old, participate in the blessings of the new Confederation.
4.   The friends and allies of America throughout the world.
5.   May America be as conspicuous for Justice, as she has been successful in her struggles for Liberty.
6.   May the flag of American commerce be displayed in every quarter of the globe.
7.   May the American landholders long experience the happy effects of the federal Constitution.
8.   May America become the nurse of manufactures, arts and sciences, and the asylum of the oppressed in every part of the world.
9.   Let peace liberty and safety be the birthright of every American.

Then fired a salute of nine guns, which was returned by three cheers, and immediately after the firing, the songs were sung, accompanied by the band—The Procession then formed and returned in the same order they came and on their return were saluted with thirteen guns from the artillery.

On their arrival at the State-House, a Federal Salute was fired from the Ship, return'd with three cheers; which ended the procession. The Ship proceeding on her destined voyage, again fired a Federal salute as she passed his Excellency's seat.

In the evening the State-House was beautifully illuminated with nine candles in each window, while a large company of ladies and gentlemen, formed in a semi-circle, were entertained by the Band from the Balcony.

Language is too poor to describe the universal joy that glowed in every countenance.—Tis enough to say that the brilliancy and festivity of the evening, were only equalled by the decorum and hilarity of the day.

*Plan of the town
of New Castle,
1806, drawn by
demand of the
General Court for
use by Secretary of
State Philip Car-
rigain to compile,
in 1815, the first
map of New
Hampshire show-
ing town boun-
daries. Courtesy of
the State Archives.
Photograph by
Bill Finney.*

APPENDIX C
A Guide to Research in the History of New Hampshire Towns, 1780–1800

By Karen Bowden with Quentin Blaine and Stephen Marini,

with special thanks to Frank Mevers

[This Guide was prepared for use of the site historians and researchers in the "After the Revolution" project. Its value as a research tool for New Hampshire history has led us to reproduce it as part of this volume in a shortened version—*Eds.*]

Introduction

This guide is intended for those who wish to participate in an effort to reassess and, in some cases, examine for the first time the local experience of the difficult years in which the new nation struggled with the consequences of the Revolution and the responsibility of self-government. It encourages research in primary sources—documents which were created during the years in question, 1780–1800. These include town warrants, tax records, deeds, wills, court, and church records, letters and diaries, newspapers and broadsides.

Researching the years after the Revolution can be a considerable challenge and requires a good deal of detective work. Records may be scattered over the state and beyond, and some may have been destroyed. A search for a particular kind of record may result in the discovery of the unexpected. This guide has been prepared to assist researchers in identifying and locating pertinent documents and in beginning to interpret them. We hope that use of the guide will result in new insight into the history of the crucial years after the Revolution and into the process of historical research itself.

Framing Questions

Although the focus of a study may shift in the review and interpretation of evidence, it is useful to start with a focus: a particular set or kind of evidence, an event or person to set in context, a delimited topic or question. This project, for example, is looking at several questions, but a new and part-time researcher might choose only one question or cluster of questions:

What is the history of the town prior to the dates of this study? When was it settled? Where did the patents originate? Where did settlers come from? Did they retain ties to their places of origin? What influence did these ties have on the life of the town?

How did citizens make their living?

How did the population, topography and townscape, economy, social structure, religious life, and political, life change in the period?

How did the town govern itself? Was debate characterized by consensus or division? What local, state, and national concerns occupied the town?

How did the town respond to ratification? Is there evidence of dissent? What can be learned about individuals or groups which took different positions in the debate?

Did the new Constitution have an effect on the town as reflected in its politics, economics, or culture?

Using Primary Sources

"After the Revolution" emphasizes research in primary and contemporary sources (i.e., written and other evidence from the period itself) to provide answers to these questions. In examining a document there are several factors and questions to keep in mind.

The document as artifact: Is the document hand-written or printed? Is it part of a set of documents? Was it intended to be part of a set or to stand alone? Is it plain or does it have any special markings? The researcher might also ask why this document still exists: was it written to be preserved? Is its existence today just a fortunate accident? If it is a copy, who made the copy and why?

Who wrote the document? Even the most apparently objective documents are subject to the perceptions, thoroughness and abilities of the recorder or author. What was his or her relation to the event? Did the author have an interest in the outcome? What does the language reveal about the recorder or author? To what degree is the language conventional (i.e., as in the conventions of wills, deeds, and parliamentary reporting?)?

When was the document written?

For whom was the document written? Who was the intended audience? one person? a group? the general public? history?

Why was the document written? Does it purport simply to record or describe? Was it meant to persuade?

Public Records

Town Records

Clerks' records include warrants and results of town meetings, agendas and minutes of selectmen's meetings, and correspondence. Sometimes the clerk kept vital statistics—records of births, marriages, and deaths. Not all towns have complete records for this period and rarely do such records include actual minutes of debate. A review of even spare records, however, can indicate issues of local conern during a given period. Voting results, examined over time, can suggest patterns of conflict and consensus.

Tax records were kept by the tax collector and usually list heads of household and their enumerated properties. They can serve as an indication of the comparative worth of property owners in the community, and of the gains and losses they suffered over time. Used in conjunction with wills, deeds, inventories (and even surviving buildings and artifacts), tax records can provide insight into the economy of families and communities. Again, for this period such records have not always survived or survived intact.

Proprietors' records are the often voluminous accounts of the sale and distribution of land by those who originally bought or were granted the land for the town. Given the project's focus on the period 1780–1800, these records will be of particular use for the study of towns established in the latter half of the eighteenth century. Kept by the proprietors and their representatives, these records can provide insight into the economic and social circumstances of settlement.

Other town records vary. Occasionally constable's records and early school records survive. Towns were required to establish schools under provincial and early state law; but many, as Jeremy Belknap complained, did so half-heartedly or not at all. Many town records include references to debates over compliance with school laws, and, although rare, records kept by schoolmasters are worth pursuing.

Finding Town Records: Town records for the period are sometimes found in the office of the town or city clerk. Occasionally early records have been sent for safe keeping to the public library or to the local historical society. Many early town records were microfilmed and indexed in the 1930s and are available on microfilm at the State Library. Some of the originals were then left with the State and are now at the State Archives. Proprietors' records are sometimes included in the records of the town; some are among the provincial records or the Masonian records at the State Archives; some are to be found among the private papers of the proprietors. The New Hampshire Historical Society has a large collection of private papers which includes proprietors' records.

County Records

Deeds establish ownership and describe property. They sometimes indicate the circumstances of property transfer, and they can occasionally provide clues to the topography and ownership patterns in a given neighborhood or district.

Probate records consist of wills and inventories. *Wills* reveal patterns of bequest and inheritance. Wills can suggest the kinds of possessions which individuals and families thought to be of significance and value and, along with inventories, indicate how wealth was held. Although some men of humble means and some women left wills, the majority were left by men of property.

By law, the widow of a man dying without a will received at least a third of household goods and a life estate in a third of the real estate until her remarriage or death. The property was otherwise divided among the children, if such distribution could be carried out "without division or spoiling." If the court determined that an estate should not be divided, it was offered to the eldest male, on the condition that siblings be paid for their shares. Wills sometimes reiterated these principles, but they were often written because the testator wanted a different disposition of his or her estate than the law provided. Wills sometimes provided a life interest in the whole estate for widows; and, throughout the eighteenth century, they reflect an interest in keeping the estate together. Such divergences from intestate law can suggest circumstances within families or communities which bear further examination.

Inventories are listings of the nature and value of real and personal property filed shortly after a person's death. They were required of all estates by law, but they were not always done. Inventories are more likely to have been completed for estates of the wealthy and are even more "biased" in this way than wills. Nonetheless they do reflect something of a socioeconomic range and do give a more detailed account than wills of property, goods, and chattels.

Court records. Both the statutes in question and the judgments rendered can suggest the prevailing understanding of law and morality and areas of conflict in families and communities. Many surviving court records are spare, listing only the plaintiff, the defendant, and the disposition of the case. Where fuller records—depositions, for example—exist, they can provide insight into individual events both ordinary and extraordinary.

Legal proceedings took place at several levels. Justices of the peace settled minor disputes at the local level. At the county level, the Inferior Court of Common Pleas adjudicated probate and civil cases, and the Court of General Quarter Sessions of the Peace heard criminal cases. The Superior Court of Judicature met twice a year in each county to consider appeals for all types of cases. The General Court and the Governor and Executive Council constituted the final courts of appeal.

Finding County Records: Deeds and probate records for the period 1623–1771 have been indexed and can be found at the State Archives and on microfilm at the New Hampshire Historical Society. Probate records are also abstracted in the New Hampshire Provincial and State Papers, volumes 31–40.

Since counties were established in 1769, land and probate records have been kept at the county level, indexed by name. Because county boundaries have changed over the years, researchers must first determine what county the town was in at the date in question. Belknap and Coos Counties, which have microfilm of deeds (but not of probate records) dating from the early 1770s.

Inferior and superior court records dating after 1772 are kept at the office of the county clerk of court, with the exception of Rockingham, Strafford, Hillsborough, Merrimack, and Sullivan County records, which are kept at the State Archives.

Militia records

Militia records include membership and muster rolls, regulations, lists of univorms, stores, and equipment for individual militia units around the state.

Finding Militia Records: Most extant militia records are at the State Archives while some are at the New Hampshire Historical Society.

State Records

Legislative Journals, kept by the clerks of the House and Senate, include records of attendance and remuneration, of issues debated, and of votes taken. They can provide an account of matters of local concern which were brought before the state government and indicate the role of individuals and communities in statewide debates.

Records of the President (or Governor) and Council can shed light on local questions in much the saw way that legisaltive records do.

Town Inventories were submitted to the state for tax purposes annually. They record the number of polls (voting and taxable citizens) and several different categories of property including: livestock; cultivates, pasture, and wild acreage; vehicles; and buildings. Studied comparatively and over time, town inventories can indicate seasonal cycles in agriculture and commerce and patterns of growth and decline within towns.

Petitions from towns, individuals, and groups to the General Court and/or the Governor and Council provide a variety of information about people, places, and events.

Maps. Two important collections of town maps can be found in the State Archives. Masonian maps were drawn between the mid-eighteenth century and the mid-nineteenth to establish town boundaries and, in some cases, the bounds of private holdings. They must be interpreted with care because they bear differing relations to actual ownership. Read in conjunction with other maps and other records, they can provide insight into patterns of town development.

Town plans, drawn by legislative direction and submitted to Secretary of State Philip Carrigain between 1802 and 1806, were used by Carrigain to compile his 1816 map of New Hampshire, the first to show the boundaries of each town. These "1805 Maps" vary in accuracy and detail but can be of value and interest if carefully checked against other records.

Finding State Records: Abstracts of the legislative journals and of the records of the Governor and Council are printed and indexed in *New Hampshire State and Provincial Papers* and some local petitions are included in the volumes devoted to town records. This forty-volume collection, also known as *Documents and Records Relating to New Hampshire,* was published between 1867 and 1942 and includes a range of public and private documents. The *Laws of New Hampshire, 1679–1835,* compiled between 1904 and 1922, are well indexed and record action on matters private as well as public.

Both the New Hampshire Historical Society and the Special Collections division of the Baker Library at Dartmouth College have significant collections of town plans and maps and of state maps which often contain revealing detail about town development.

Because of the incomplete nature of such printed material, however, research is best pursued in the collection of state records in the State Archives where originals of all materials noted here are kept. There is a printed Guide to the State Archives that should be widely available in the state. In seeking and using these and other primary source materials researchers should not be hesitant about asking assistance of staff personnel at the various repositories. Primary sources are seldom as readily catalogued or as easily accessible as secondary sources.

Church Records
by Stephen Marini

Before the Revolution, New Hampshire religion was dominated by Congregationalism, the faith of the colony's Puritan founders. Virtually every New Hampshire town contained at least one organized Congregationalist parish, its minister supported by public tax monies. Present in far fewer numbers were Quakers, Anglicans, and Presbyterians. The Society of Friends—as Quakers called themselves—organized a modest network of meetings in the Piscataqua and Connecticut Valleys. Anglicans—members of the Church of England—were concentrated in Portsmouth and other centers of royal power, while the Presbyterians were concentrated in the Scots-Irish settlements in the Londonderry area.

During and after the Revolution, revivals in the hill country produced new sects that soon challenged the dominance of the Congregationalists. Several of these were indigenous to New Hampshire: the Freewill Baptists were organized by Benjamin Randel at New Durham in 1780; the same year Caleb Rich founded a distinctive form of Universalism at Richmond; and in 1803 Elias Smith formed the first congregation of the Christian Connection at Portsmouth. The Shakers, though not native to New Hampshire, gathered substantial numbers of converts to their charismatic, celibate, and communitarian Societies at Canterbury and Enfield. Methodism did not arrive in New Hampshire until 1790, but John Wesley's movement grew steadily in the state thereafter. The largest dissenting community, however, was the Separate-Baptists, pioneered in New Hampshire during the Revolution by the itinerancy of Chaplain Hezekiah Smith of Haverhill and consolidated around the leadership of his highly successful convert, Dr. Samuel Shepherd of Brentwood. By 1800 the Separate-Baptists had organized several associations of churches in New Hampshire and approached institutional parity with the Congregationalists in the hill country.

All these communions kept records of widely variant quality and quantity. These records reflect not only the divergent social and cultural status of the different churches, but also their political attitudes and ideological orientations as well. The nature and availability of church records will differ from town to town, but some general guidelines for research can be drawn.

Congregationalist Church Records
Given the predominance of Congregationalism during the early period, the first records to seek are those of the Congregationalist parishes in town. These will likely be the most extensive records available on the religious life of the community. Congregationalist records typically contain several documents:

Church covenants state the beliefs and practices of the parish and were signed by all members in full standing. Some covenants are quite brief and simply constructed; others are lengthy and contain extensive doctrinal and moral stipulations. Where the latter circumstance exists, the parish can be more precisely classified as to its theological and cultural character.

Vital statistics were kept by the pastor, who, as the legally established minister, baptised infants born in the community and buried citizens who maintained membership in the parish.

Membership lists. When combined with tax, probate, and election records, church membership lists can establish correlations between religious belief, socioeconomic status, and political activity. Note especially that Congregationalist lists often distinguished between two levels of membership: "full covenant" and "halfway." The former were people who had made a public testimony of their religious experience and were admitted by vote of the other full covenant members to partake in communion; the latter were those who agreed only to abide by the doctrinal teachings and moral discipline of the church, but made no personal profession of faith. These "halfway" members were not admitted to communion, but their children could be baptized into parish membership. Normally, Congregationalist membership lists include only full covenant members; halfway members can be determined by examining vital statistics lists. Full members were normally congruent with the local political and cultural elite and therefore the full and halfway distinction is a valuable indicator for historians.

Pew rentals and economic records. Whenever a parish built a new meetinghouse or repaired an old one, funds were raised either by assissment or by rental of pews. Lists of these arrangements provide a picture of relative economic and social status in the town: the wealthiest families usually rented the most prominent and expensive pews; the rest of the community arranged itself according to income and religious commitment. Comparison with tax inventories will reveal the relative economic commitment to the parish of these renters.

Deliberations and decisions. The body of church records books contain votes of the parish on significant matters ranging from salary and support arrangements with ministers to the discipline of rebellious members to the construction and financing of the meetinghouse and parsonage. They therefore contain important economic, social, and even political information, since local religious disputes often correlated closely with local political or economic issues. The matter of ministerial support was especially sensitive, because salary settlements affected tax rates and often became the occasion for schismatic and dissenting citizens to press their political claim for religious toleration.

Records of the Dissenters

Records of the other denominations will also contain the same kinds of information, but with much less regularity and extensiveness. It is important, however, to obtain at least some documentation from these dissenting communions to gain a sense of the nature of religious division at the local level and its impact on important political questions of the day. Unfortunately, each denomination had its own form of organization and record-keeping. Presbyterians, for example, called their local governing body the Session (a board of elected Elders who made decisions for the parish), while Quakers termed the local authority the Monthly Meeting. All denominations, however, faced basically the same sorts of decisions at the local level as the Congregationalists (though Baptists and Quakers did not pay their ministers). The particular form of records is ultimately less important than the kind of information one can find in them; but in any case the researcher may have to clarify the language of the records in order to use them fully.

Ministerial Manuscripts and Imprints

Especially for Congregationalists, the theological persuasion of the local minister is an important key to understanding the ideological quality of the parish. Many Congregationalist ministers published sermons; virtually all of them wrote their sermons in notebooks. The most accurate biographical and bibliographical material on Congregationalist ministers is to be found in *Sibley's Graduates of Harvard College*, edited by Clifford Shipton; and Franklin Bowditch Dexter's *Biographical Sketches of the Graduates of Yale College*. For other denominations, consult William Buell Sprague, *Annals of the American Pulpit*, and the volumes of the *American Church History Series* (New York, 1885–1906). For manuscript sources, see section on "Private Papers" below.

Records of Denominational Organizations

Almost all local churches participated in some form of regional organization: Congregationalist ministerial associations, Separate-Baptist associations, Freewill Baptist Quarterly and Yearly Meetings, Quaker Quarterly and Yearly Meetings, Presbyterian Presbyteries and Synods, Methodist Conferences. In some cases, e.g. Separate-Baptist associations and Methodist conferences, deliberations, membership and ministerial lists, and policy decisions with social and political implications were published. In other cases these records remain in manuscript form. *The Early American Imprint* Series (see "Contemporary Printed Sources") is the best source of the former; denominational libraries and historical societies listed in "Useful Addresses" offer the best possibility for finding the latter.

Finding Church Records. This is often a matter of detective work, especially if the church has gone out of existence or combined with another. The first step is to check local and county histories to establish the religious history of the community. If the denomination still exists in the town, the current church is a likely source of manuscript records. It is quite common, however, for churches to deposit their early records with the local or state hisorical society or archives or with the denominational agencies listed in "Useful Addresses." Sometimes church records are mixed in with towns and will be found on microfilm in the State Library or the State Archives in original format. In any case do not assume that if there are no records on deposit locally they therefore do not exist at all. In religious documentation perhaps more than any other research area, resort to "outside sources" like denominational libraries is a standard procedure. Assume that some religious documentation exists and consult as many different sources of information as possible to find it.

Contemporary Printed Sources

During the period a number of presses were established around the state. By 1800 there were printers working in Portsmouth, Exeter, Walpole, Concord, Dover, Keene, and Hanover.

Newspapers

Newspapers are not always as revealing about state and local matters as we might like them to be but they do indicate the editors' and correspondents' concerns, in particular their political concerns. Like all of the other sources discussed here, newspapers are best interpreted in relation to each other and to other records. Consider not only the paper's coverage of news and opinion but its cultural pages, advertisements, and public announcements.

For towns without local papers try to determine what papers might have been available. Keep in mind that Massachusetts and even Connecticut papers may have had wider distribution in some parts of New Hampshire than papers published within the state. *The Essex Journal and New Hampshire Packet,* for example, was published in Massachusetts for distribution both there and in communities along the Merrimack. Listed below are some of the newspapers printed or circulated in New Hampshire in the period:

American Herald (Boston), 1787–1788.
Columbian Informer (Keene), 1793–1794.
Concord Herald, 1790–1794.
Courier of New Hampshire (Concord), 1794–1805.
Essex Journal and New Hampshire Packet (Newburyport), 1784–1794.
Exeter Chronicle, 1794.
Farmer's Journal [also *Museum*] (Walpole), 1794–1804.
Freeman's Oracle (Exeter), 1793–1794.
Mirrour (Concord), 1792–1799.
New Hampshire Gazette (Portsmouth), 1756–1795.
New Hampshire Gazeteer (Exeter), 1789–1793.
New Hampshire Journal (Walpole), 1793–1794.
New Hampshire Mercury (Portsmouth), 1784–1788.
New Hampshire Recorder (Keene), 1787–1791.
New Hampshire Spy (Portsmouth), 1786–1793.
Oracle of the Day (Portsmouth), 1789–1793.
Political And Sentimental Repository (Dover), 1790–1792.

Broadsides

Broadsides are announcements printed on one side and intended to be posted. State and local governments often used broadsides to announce laws, elections, meetings, and celebrations. They were also used by businesses to advertise merchandise or to announce relocation. Because they were posted, they had the potential of reaching a large number of people.

Other New Hampshire Imprints

Books and pamphlets printed in New Hampshire in the period can give a sense of the interests of printers and audiences in the state.

Finding Printed Sources: There are three major sources for printed materials: The New Hampshire Historical Society has significant collections of broadsides and some newspapers, books, and pamphlets; Special Collections at Dimond Library of the University of New Hampshire has a collection of New Hampshire imprints; and Baker Library at Dartmouth College has a large collection of printed material from the Hanover area and a significant collection of New Hampshire newspapers of the period.

Printed materials can also be found in the collections of libraries and historical societies around the state. In addition, a number of newspapers are available on Readex microprint and microfilm Early American Newspaper Series. The Dimond and Baker Libraries have some but not all New Hampshire newspapers in the series. Both also have the Early American Imprint Series, microfilms of a wide range of materials printed in America between 1643 and 1800 and indexed in Charles Evans' *American Bibliography*. The Bibliography lists printers by location in the appendix to each of its chronologically arranged volumes, but it is indexed only by author and title. A useful and manageable guide available at the New Hampshire Historical Society is *A Checklist of New Hampshire Imprints, 1756–1790* by Caroline Whittemore.

Private Papers

Letters

Although they must be read as subjective and must be compared with other records and accounts, letters provide valuable glimpses of public and private events.

Diaries

Diaries from the period are more often terse "account books" than detailed descriptions of private observations or feelings. Even the tersest, however, can reveal patterns of daily and seasonal activity, the workings of both cash and barter economies, and private and public events which warranted notice.

Business and Professional Records

In addition to diaries and letters which bear on life within particular occupations and professions, bills, accounts, and logs can reflect on the economy and on day-to-day patterns of activity.

Finding Private Papers: The New Hampshire Historical Society is a major depository for private papers and has indexed letters and diaries by name and letters by subject. The Baker Library at Dartmouth College has a large collection of materials pertaining to the College itself and to the Hanover area. Many libraries and historical societies around the state also have private materials, and occasionally they have been incorporated into town records. Some papers, of course, remain in private hands.

Useful Addresses

General

New Hampshire Historical Society, 30 Park Street, Concord, N.H. 03301

New Hampshire Division of Records Management and Archives, 71 South Fruit Street, Concord, N.H. 03301

New Hampshire Division of Historic Resources, 15 South Fruit Street, Concord, N.H. 03301

New Hampshire State Library, 20 Park Street, Concord, N.H. 03301

Special Collections, Baker Library, Dartmouth College, Hanover, N.H. 03755

Special Collections, Dimond Library, University of New Hampshire, Durham, N.H. 03824

American Antiquarian Society, 185 Salisbury Street, Worcester, MA 01609

Northeast Document Conservation Center, School Street, Andover, MA 01801

Denominational Libraries

Congregational Library, 14 Beacon Street, Boston, MA

New England Baptist Collection, Trask Library, Andover Newton Theological School, 210 Herrick Road, Newton, MA

New England Methodist Historical Collection, Boston University School of Theology

Unitarian Universalist Historical Society, Andover Harvard Theological Library, 45 Francis Avenue, Cambridge, MA

Friends Historical Society, Swarthmore College, Swarthmore, PA

Disciples Historical Society [Christian Connection], Nashville, TN

Presbyterian Historical Society, Philadelphia, PA

Shaker Village, Canterbury, NH

Episcopal Divinity School, 99 Brattle Street Cambridge, MA

Names of Towns and places Represented	Names of Delegates to Convention	No. of miles travel'd to N.H. from Exeter	Wednesday Feb 13	Thursday 14	Friday 15	Saturday 16	Sunday 17	Monday 18
Portsmouth	John Langdon Esqr	30	1	1	1	1	1	
	John Pickering Esqr	30	1	1	1	1	1	
	Pierce Long Esqr	30	1	1	1	1	1	
Exeter — 3	John Taylor Gilman Eqr	0	1	1	1	1	1	1
Londonderry — 4	Colo Daniel Runnels	44	1	1	1	1	1	
	Archibd McMurphey Esqr	50	.	1	1	1	1	
Chester — 5	Mr Joseph Blanchard	44	.	1	1	1	1	
Newington —	Benjamin Adams Esqr	30	1	1	.	.	.	
Greenland —	Doct Ichabod Weeks	18	1	1	1	1	1	
Rye —	Mr Nathan Goss	24	1	1	1	1	1	
New Castle —	Henry Prescutt Esq	36	.	1	1	1	1	
North Hampton — 6	Revd Benja Thurston	12	1	1	1	1		
Hampton —	Christopher Toppan Esqr	16	.	1	1	1	1	
Hampton falls & Seabrook	Revd Saml Langdon	10	1	1	1	1	1	
Stratham —	Mr Jona Wiggin —	8	1	1	1	1	1	1
	Jona Esqr	8	1	1	1	1		

Page from journal of 1788 convention showing names of some convention delegates. Courtesy of the State Archives. Photograph by Bill Finney.

APPENDIX D
Notes on Sources

In fairness it should be noted that several writers submitted footnotes with their essays, but that in the interest of continuity the editors decided to publish all in the same format. All the writers used primary sources as described in the "Research Guide" in Appendix C. The basic primary sources are given there and the editors refer researchers on New Hampshire in this period to the "Guide" as a beginning point for research. Nearly all the writers consulted the Goodwin Collection at the State Archives which contains the credentials given to the convention delegates by their towns. Printed primary sources used by nearly all include the *New Hampshire Provincial and State Papers*, edited by Nathaniel Bouton *et al.*, 40 volumes [Concord and Manchester: 1867–1940], and *Letters and Papers of Major-General John Sullivan*, edited by Otis G. Hammond, 3 volumes [Concord: New Hampshire Historical Society, 1930].

Secondary sources for this period abound, but the following warrant major consideration: Jeremy Belknap, *A History of New Hampshire*, 3 volumes [Boston and Philadelphia, 1784–1792]; Jere R. Daniell, *Experiment in Republicanism: New Hampshire Politics and the American Revolution, 1741–1794* [Cambridge, MA: Harvard University Press, 1970]; Lynn W. Turner, *The Ninth State: New Hampshire's Formative Years* [Chapel Hill: University of North Carolina Press, 1983]; and Richard F. Upton, *Revolutionary New Hampshire: An Account of the Social and Political Forces Underlying the Transition from Royal Province to American Commonwealth* [Hanover, NH: 1936; reissued Port Washington, NY: 1970].

An indispensable guide to all printed sources on New Hampshire is *New Hampshire: A Bibliography of Its History*, edited by John Haskell, Jr., and T. D. Seymour Bassett [Boston: G. K. Hall, 1979]. *Historical New Hampshire*, the quarterly publication of the New Hampshire Historical Society, often carries articles about this period. An index to the journal through 1970 is available from the Society. Published histories for many towns are available and should be consulted with care. A useful compilation of those for this period is *Towns Against Tyranny: Hillsborough County New Hampshire During the American Revolution, 1775–1783*, edited by William M. Gardner [Nashua: Hillsborough County Bicentennial Commission, 1976]. Historians of religion should consult Henry A. Hazen, *The Congregational and Presbyterian Ministry and Churches in New Hampshire* [Boston, 1875], and William Hurlin *et al.*, *The Baptists of New Hampshire* [Manchester, 1902].

In addition to the major secondary sources listed above each author relied on those specific to his or her topic.

William Gardner's essay about the current celebration should be studied in collaboration with volumes commemorating the centennial of New Hampshire's ratification: Joseph B. Walker, *A History of the New Hampshire Convention for the Investigations, Discussion, and Decision of the Federal Constitution* [Boston: 1888]; and the sesquicentennial, *New Hampshire and the Federal Constitution*, edited by Francis H. Buffum [Concord: 1940].

Jere Daniell referred to several other secondary sources: Lawrence S. Mayo, *John Langdon of New Hampshire* [Concord: 1937]; Walter F. Dodd, "The Constitutional History of New Hampshire, 1775–1792," in *Proceedings of the Bar Association of the State of New Hampshire*, n.s., 2 (1904–1908), 379–400; Chilton Williamson, *Vermont in Quandry, 1737–1825* [Montpelier: 1949]; and two unpublished pieces, Nathaniel J. Eiseman, "The Ratification of the Federal Constitution by the State of New Hampshire" [MA thesis, Columbia University, 1937], and Nancy B. Oliver, "Keystone of the Federal Arch: New Hampshire's Ratification of the United States Constitution" [Ph.D. dissertation, University of California at Santa Barbara, 1972].

Richard F. Upton drew upon additional sources: Lawrence S. Mayo, *John Wentworth, Governor of New Hampshire 1767–1775* [Cambridge, MA: Harvard University Press, 1921]; Elwin L. Page, *George Washington in New Hampshire* [Boston: Houghton Mifflin Co., 1932]; Lynn W. Turner, *William Plumer of New Hampshire, 1759–1850* [Chapel Hill: University of North Carolina Press for the Institute of Early American History and Culture, 1962]; Charles P. Whittemore, *John Sullivan of New Hampshire* [New York: Columbia University Press, 1961]; and Paul W. Wilderson, "John Wentworth's Narrative of the Raids on Fort William and Mary," *Historical New Hampshire*, XXXII (No. 4, Winter 1977), 228–236, and "The Raids on Fort William and Mary: Some New Evidence," *ibid.*, XXX (No. 3, Fall 1975), 178–202.

Karen Bowden cites "The Origins of the New England Village" by Joseph S. Wood (Ph.D. dissertation, Pennsylvania State University, 1978) in addition to the major sources.

John Durel's Portsmouth team culled the Langdon Papers at the New Hampshire Historical Society and the records of both the North and South Parishes. Portsmouth's seacoast location attracted travelers who left written accounts: Marquis de Chastellux, *Travels in North America*, 2 volumes [London, 1787 (reprinted New York: Arno Press, 1968)]; Jacques Pierre Brissot de Warville, *New Travels in the United States of America, 1788*, translated by Mara Soceanu Vamos and Durand Escheverria, edited by Durand Escheverria [Cambridge, MA: Belknap Press of Harvard University Press, 1964]; and Francesco de Miranda, *The New Democracy in America; Travels of Francesco de Miranda in the United States, 1783–84*, translated by Judson P. Wood, edited by John S. Ezell [Norman: University of Oklahoma Press, 1963]. Specific secondary sources include the following: Nathaniel Adams, *Annals of Portsmouth* [Portsmouth, 1825 (reprinted Hampton, New Hampshire: Peter E. Randall, 1971)]; John W. Durel, "From Strawbery Banke to Puddle Dock: the Evolution of a Neighborhood, 1630–1850" [Ph.D. dissertation, University of New Hampshire, 1984]; Howard Tredennick Oedel, "Portsmouth, New Hampshire: The Role of the Provincial Capital in the Development of the Colony, 1700–1775" [Ph.D. dissertation, Boston University Graduate School, 1960]; and David Arthur Oliver, "Captain John Wheelwright of Portsmouth, New Hampshire: Life During the American Revolution" [unpublished report on file at Strawbery Banke, Inc., 1980].

For Exeter, Richard Schubart utilized several histories of the town: Charles Henry Bell, *History of the Town of Exeter, New Hampshire* [Exeter, 1888] and *Phillips Exeter Academy in New Hampshire, a Historical Sketch* [Exeter: W. B. Morrill, 1883]; Donald B. Cole, Exeter, 1947–1970 [Exeter: Phillips Exeter Academy, 1970]; Mary Gordon, *Whitefield and the New Parish* [n.p., 1915]; Nancy C. Merrill, *Exeter, New Hampshire, 1638–1988* [Portsmouth: Peter E. Randall, 1988]; and George Blake Rogers, *The Gilman House* [Exeter: The News-Letter Press, 1906 (reprinted from Phillips Exeter Academy Bulletin, 1 (March 1906), 29–60).

John Resch consulted several Peterborough secondary sources: *Historical Sketches of Peterborough* [Peterborough Historical Society, 1938]; George A. Morison, *History of Peterborough, New Hampshire* [Rindge, NH: Richard R. Smith, Inc., 1954]; Samuel Eliot Morison, *The Proprietors of Peterborough, New Hampshire* [Peterborough New Hampshire Historical Society, 1930]; Albert Smith, *History of the Town of Peterborough* [Boston: George H. Ellis, 1876]; and Edward L. Parker, *The History of Londonderry* [Boston: Perkins and Whipple, 1851].

For Cheshire County, Wilfred Bisson's team reviewed the following secondary sources: Salma Hale, *Annals of the Town of Keene, from its first Settlement, in 1734, to the year 1790; with Corrections, Additions, and a Continuation, from 1790 to 1815* [2nd ed., Keene: J. W. Prentice, 1851]; Stanley A. Johnson, "History of the Rising Sun Lodge of Keene, N.H." [unpublished typescript on file at the Cheshire County Historical Society, 1976]; Oran E. Randall, *History of Chesterfield, New Hampshire* [Brattleboro, Vermont: D. Leonard, 1882]; Martha M. Frizzell, *A History of Walpole, New Hampshire* [Walpole: Walpole Historical Society, 1963]; Westmoreland History Committee, *History of Westmoreland* (Great Meadow), *New Hampshire, 1741–1970* [Westmoreland, 1976]; and Richard Monahon, *Keene Main Street: An Architectural History and Guide* [Peterborough, 1982].

William Taylor researched original materials about the Wolfeboro meetinghouse located by Russell C. Chase. His principal secondary sources were Lawrence S. Mayo's biography of Governor John Wentworth, and Benjamin Franklin Parker, *History of Wolfeboro* (New Hampshire) [Wolfeboro, N. H.: Town of Wolfeboro, 1901].

For Conway Helene-Carol Brown took information from several specific secondary sources: Helene-Carol Brown, "Following the Camp: Campfollowers of the American Revolution" [MA thesis, University of New Hampshire, 1985]; Alvah W. Carver, *Soldiers of the American Revolution of the Town of Conway, New Hampshire* [Conway: Daughters of the American Revolution, Anna Stickney Cahpter, 1977]; and Robert F. Lawrence, *The New Hampshire Churches* [Claremont: 1856].

Stephen Thomas' secondary sources on Joshua Morse were John C. Currier, *History of Newbury, Massachusetts, 1635–1902* [Boston: Darrell and Upham, 1902] and Charles C. Lord, *Life and Times in Hopkinton, New Hampshire* [Concord, N. H.: Republican Press Association, 1890].

Concord's researchers with Frank Mevers drew from Nathaniel Bouton, *The History of Concord, from...1725 to...1853* [Concord: B. W. Sanborn, 1856] and from Concord History Committee, *History of Concord, New Hampshire, from the original grant in seventeen hundred and twenty-five to the opening of the twentieth century,* edited by James O. Lyford, 2 volumes [Concord: Rumford Press, 1903].

John Archer, writing on Toscan, relied principally on newspapers but also used Eiseman's MA thesis at Columbia, Whittemore's biogrpahy of John Sullivan, George Barstow, *A History of New Hampshire* [Concord: 1842], and William F. Witcher, "New Hampshire and the Federal Constitution," *Granite Monthly,* 11 (1888), 206.

Richard Kalkhoff used newspapers and many of the same secondary sources as did the Portsmouth research team and Jonathan Mitchell Sewall, *An Oration Delivered at Portsmouth, New Hampshire, 4 July 1788* [Portsmouth: 1788].

INDEX